P9-CPV-185

WILL TAIWAN BREAK AWAY?

DATE

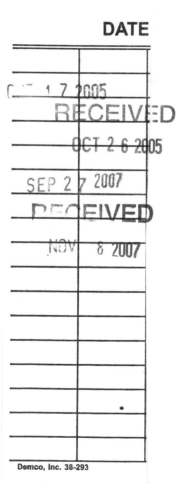

OCT 1 7 2005

RECEIVED

OCT 2 6 2005

SEP 2 7 2007

RECEIVED

NOV 8 2007

Demco, Inc. 38-293

WILL TAIWAN BREAK AWAY?

The Rise of Taiwanese Nationalism

CHING CHEONG

The Straits Times, Hong Kong Bureau

World Scientific
Singapore • New Jersey • London • Hong Kong

DS
799.847
C458
2001

c.1

45945321

7-10-01

Published by

World Scientific Publishing Co. Pte. Ltd.
P O Box 128, Farrer Road, Singapore 912805
USA office: Suite 1B, 1060 Main Street, River Edge, NJ 07661
UK office: 57 Shelton Street, Covent Garden, London WC2H 9HE

British Library Cataloguing-in-Publication Data
A catalogue record for this book is available from the British Library.

WILL TAIWAN BREAK AWAY: THE RISE OF TAIWANESE NATIONALISM

Copyright © 2001 by World Scientific Publishing Co. Pte. Ltd.

All rights reserved. This book, or parts thereof, may not be reproduced in any form or by any means, electronic or mechanical, including photocopying, recording or any information storage and retrieval system now known or to be invented, without written permission from the Publisher.

For photocopying of material in this volume, please pay a copying fee through the Copyright Clearance Center, Inc., 222 Rosewood Drive, Danvers, MA 01923, USA. In this case permission to photocopy is not required from the publisher.

ISBN 981-02-4486-X (pbk)

Printed in Singapore by World Scientific Printers

PREFACE

This book is a collection of selected news reports, analyses and commentaries I wrote in the last two years (1998–2000) on Taiwan when The Straits Times posted me there. It is divided into four sections:

Section A traces the development of cross-strait relations since the March 18, 2000 presidential elections that returned a pro-independence candidate. That marked a turning point in Taiwanese politics as well as in bilateral relations across the strait;

Section B gives a factual account of the election process at different points in time, as well as my interpretation of the result itself;

Section C covers news and analyses on cross-strait relations, especially the unification-independence dispute and the deterioration of cross-strait relations after Taiwanese ex-president Lee Tenghui formulated his 'two-states' theory;

Section D sets cross-strait relations in the broader perspective of the trilateral relationship between Beijing, Taipei and Washington, the latter being a key player in this uneasy co-existence.

No Chinese can be entirely neutral or impartial when faced with the Taiwan issue and neither do I pretend to be so. Readers may notice that I use the term "separatism" instead of "independence" to characterize the breakaway movement. This choice of words indicates my own stance on this issue.

Other than that I try to give an account that is as factual as possible of what happened in the last two critical years and offer my explanations for the developments that led eventually to the change in the political landscape of the island.

ACKNOWLEDGEMENTS

I felt greatly honoured when Dr. Phua of World Scientific Publishing Co. Pte. Ltd. invited me to compile the articles I wrote for The Straits Times on the Taiwan issue and publish them as a separate book.

He lamented the lack of publications in English which reflected the views of non-partisan Chinese over this important issue which even now tends to cause divisions among the Chinese themselves. This remark by such a leading publisher prompted me to accept his invitation.

The book, though published under my name, is the product of much teamwork from members of the East Asia Desk at The Straits Times. I am indebted to Mr. Leslie Fong, Mr. Felix Soh, Mr. Sunny Goh and Ms. Oiken Chin for their leadership and supervision that guided and facilitated my journalistic work in Taiwan. Any shortcomings or deficiencies are solely mine.

I am also grateful for the management of The Straits Times for their kind permission to reprint the articles.

INTRODUCTION

Taiwan: A Tale of Three Centuries

The Taiwan issue is extremely difficult to resolve for it straddles three centuries. Separatism originated in the 19th century, intensified in the 20th century and is likely to explode in the 21st century.

In the 19th century, an upcoming Japan defeated a sapping China in the 1894–5 War and annexed Taiwan. Until its defeat in the Second World War in 1945, it ran Taiwan for half a century and transformed the island to one of the most developed places in East Asia at the time.

Unfortunately the relative supremacy Taiwan inherited from Japan turned out to be the seed of separatism. When Japan surrendered all the territories it annexed from China, including Taiwan, after its defeat, some of the Taiwanese decided that they would not want to rejoin a China that was then more backward in many ways than Taiwan. This is the origin of the Taiwanese independence movement.

The most predominant feature of 20th century politics was the rise of communism and attempts to contain it. The Chinese Civil War (1945–49) itself and the subsequent division of the world into two camps — one capitalist and the other socialist — were products of that time. Both developments foreshadowed the separation of Taiwan from China.

The withdrawal of the nationalist government to Taiwan following its defeat in the civil war served to fortify the rift between China and Taiwan. It prolonged the split between the two that started in 1895 but which was supposed to have come to an end following the defeat of Japan.

Thus in the last 105 years the only time when Taiwan was part of one whole China ruled by one central government was pitifully brief: only four years, from 1945 to 1949. This explains the sentimental detachment Taiwanese feel towards China.

As Taiwan was strategically situated at the tangent of two rival camps, the island formed a crucial link in the US-led "island arc of defence" against communism that stretched from Japan in the north down to the Philippines in the south. During the Cold War, it was dubbed the "unsinkable aircraft carrier" of the US.

As the result of deliberate fortification against mainland China, the state of separatism was intensified. At the same time prolonged separation eventually gave birth to a nascent Taiwanese nationalism, marked by the rise to power of the separatist Democratic Progressive Party (DPP).

In the 21st century, world politics is likely to be dominated by one key issue: how to manage a rising China. This issue has already caused heated debate in the US since the end of the Cold War following the demise of the Soviet Union.

Policy prescriptions so far oscillate between containment and engagement, although there is a tendency to combine the two together to form the so-called "cont-gagement".

As long as the US-led western world is unclear of what to expect from a growing China, the Taiwan card remains the most effective means to slow down its growth or even to thwart it, for it is the most likely way to draw China into a major war and thereby weaken it.

The separatist movement in Taiwan is quick to seize this point by stressing that Taiwan's own security is an essential part of the overall security interests of US, Japan and Asia at large. By linking up its political ideal (to break away from China) with the US global security interest (to weaken China), the DPP greatly complicates the Taiwan issue.

Thus the Taiwan issue straddles three centuries. As such it calls for maximum care and attention to attain a peaceful solution.

If one day Taiwan succeeds in breaking away from China, or should war and bloodshed become inevitable, then who will be to blame?

Certainly one would blame Beijing more. Their failure to run China properly was the underlying factor that turned Taiwan away. After half a century in power the Chinese Communist Party failed to create the necessary economic glamour and cultural charm required to entice the Taiwanese.

In Taiwan there is a 51st Club with the explicit aim of turning Taiwan into the 51st state of America. Although it is treated no more than a joke, it nevertheless drives home one important point: if China is as strong as the US, Taiwan will be more than happy to be part of it. If one could apportion the blame quantitatively, Beijing would have to shoulder at least 50 percent of it on this count alone.

The rest of the blame must be shared between Taipei, for its unwillingness to respect history, and Beijing, for its unwillingness to respect reality.

Despite abundant historical records showing Taiwan as part of China, the separatists deliberately disputed these facts. This infuriates the Chinese.

On the other hand, Beijing's failure to respect the reality that there exists two separate authorities on Chinese territory serves only to alienate the Taiwanese.

Hence a viable peaceful solution would require Beijing to build up China's cultural charm and economic glamour first. It also necessitates a respect for history and reality on the part of Taipei and Beijing respectively.

This process will be a long and trying one. It is a challenge to the talent and innovation of the Chinese people. Whether they can resolve an issue spanning three centuries peacefully will determine whether China can rise to global pre-eminence in this century.

CONTENTS

Section C   Cross-Strait Relations   *111*

Section D China, Taiwan & the US

SECTION

A

Taiwan Nationalism Comes of Age

No One Gains in War Over Taiwan

25 June 2000

Regional Fallout

WHAT if China and Taiwan were to come to blows, will the neighbourhood go up in flames too? The impact on the region will depend on the intensity of the conflict. Broadly speaking, the Chinese strategists have postulated three scenarios.

Blockage: Losers and Winners

AT THE bottom of the scale is a low-intensity conflict, with Beijing using minimal force to bring an increasingly assertive and independence-minded Taiwan to heel. It will mount a blockade on the island with the limited political objective of getting the Taiwanese back to the negotiation table for a peaceful settlement. No missile will be hurled, neither will there be a physical occupation. Since the use of force is limited to enforcing the blockade, loss of life and property will be kept to the minimum. In such a scenario, the United States will not feel compelled to get involved other than to make some form of token protest.

Once that is done and Beijing has made its point, Washington is expected to pile on the pressure on Taiwan to accept the "one China" principle. The negative impact will mainly be borne by the Chinese themselves while other countries in the region might even gain in the short run. Right now, the entire Greater China region is enjoying one of its best moments in history in terms of economic growth. A cross-strait conflict, even at the lowest end of the intensity scale, will suffice to truncate, if not to reverse, the steep GNP growth trends of the past few years.

Other than the quantifiable losses from disrupted trade flows, there is also the longer-term damage to consider. For example, it took Taiwan almost three decades to establish itself as the third largest producer of information technology (IT) products in the world. It is now the island's single largest foreign exchange earner. The Sept 21 earthquake last year demonstrated the risk involved in Taiwan's dependence on the IT industry. A few days of power blackouts disrupted chip-manufacturing operations on the island, which in turn sent the prices of these components soaring worldwide. Not surprisingly, a scramble followed for alternative sources of supply. A blockade lasting three months will devastate the industry in Taiwan.

Similarly, it has taken China more than two decades to establish itself as the second largest recipient of private direct investment. In recent years, such investment has amounted to more than 20 per cent of China's total capital formation. A capital outflow will follow if there is trouble across the strait.

Other than China and Taiwan, Japan's economy is likely to be hurt too if the blockade disrupts its "life-line" — the sea lane through which flows its supplies of oil and other commodities. Though no physical loss will be incurred, the blockade will force up prices across the board as Japan is so dependent on this sea lane.

The Asean region stands to gain in the short run. Those with strong IT industries, like Singapore and Malaysia, will carve a big slice from what was previously Taiwan's share. Similarly, as investment flees China, the Asean countries might be able to intercept this flow and benefit thereby.

Politically, the blockade is likely to provoke Sino-phobia in the region. Japan's rightwing forces will seize this golden opportunity to demand a revision of the post-war Constitution prohibiting its rearmament. Asean countries having territorial disputes with Beijing in the South China Sea will beef up their defence budgets. Ethnic Chinese population in these countries may have to contend with increased suspicion or worse as Sino-phobia rises.

The US stands to gain. So long as its stays on the sidelines, it does not lose the Chinese market. At the same time its defence industry gains as countries in the region start stocking up on arms in anticipation of trouble.

Destroying the Taiwan Military

THE medium intensity scenario postulates a situation in which Beijing wages a war against Taiwan. The objective here is to obliterate its military capability which is seen as underpinning its independence movement.

The outcome: Taiwan is brought to its knees but only after widespread death and destruction have been inflicted on the island and the coastal provinces of China. In this scenario, the US, while feeling obliged to support Taiwan militarily, is not party to a full-scale war with China. Washington's primary concern would be to keep it to a "limited war" to prevent hostilities from spinning out of control. Limited though it may be, the war will set back the economies of China and Taiwan by at least two to three decades.

All the short-term gains enjoyed by the Asean countries in the low-intensity scenario will be nullified as the conflict intensifies. In this medium-intensity scenario, no one gains. Politically, all countries are forced to take sides. This decision is particularly hard to make in those countries having a sizeable ethnic-Chinese population.

The Doomsday Scenario

THE high-intensity scenario postulates a cross-strait war escalating into a full-scale war between the US and China. If Washington were to conclude that splitting China would better serve its national interests, then a full-scale war becomes unavoidable. Conflict on such a scale would embroil other countries far and near and — horror of horrors — raise the possibility of a nuclear war.

Beijing has already told the US and Japan privately that it considers any country providing bases and logistics support to any US forces attacking China as belligerent parties open to its retaliation. In the region, this means South Korea, Japan, the Philippines and, to a lesser extent, Singapore.

If China were to retaliate, east Asia will be set on fire. And the conflagration may not end there as opportunistic powers elsewhere may try to overturn the existing world order. With the US distracted, Russia may seek to redefine Europe's political landscape. The balance of power in the Middle East may be similarly upset by the likes of Iraq.

In south Asia, hostilities between India and Pakistan, each armed with its own nuclear arsenal, could enter a new and dangerous phase.

Will a full-scale Sino-US war lead to a nuclear war?

According to General Matthew Ridgeway, commander of the US Eighth Army which fought against the Chinese in the Korean War, the US had at the time thought of using nuclear weapons against China to save the US from military defeat. In his book The Korean War, a personal account of the military and political aspects of the conflict and its implications on future US foreign policy, Gen Ridgeway said that US was confronted with two choices in Korea — truce or a broadened war, which could have led to the use of nuclear weapons. If the US had to resort to nuclear weaponry to defeat China long before the latter acquired a similar capability, there is little hope of winning a war against China 50 years later, short of using nuclear weapons.

The US estimates that China possesses about 20 nuclear warheads that can destroy major American cities. Beijing also seems prepared to go for the nuclear option. A Chinese military officer disclosed recently that Beijing was considering a review of its "non first use" principle regarding nuclear weapons. Major-General Pan Zhangqiang, president of the military-funded Institute for Strategic Studies, told a gathering at the Woodrow Wilson International Centre for Scholars in Washington that although the government still abided by that principle, there were strong pressures from the military to drop it.

He said military leaders considered the use of nuclear weapons mandatory if the country risked dismemberment as a result of foreign intervention.

Gen Ridgeway said that should that come to pass, we would see the destruction of civilisation. There would be no victors in such a war. While the prospect of a nuclear Armaggedon over Taiwan might seem inconceivable, it cannot be ruled out entirely, for China puts sovereignty above everything else. Gen Ridgeway recalled that the biggest mistake the US made during the Korean War was to assess Chinese actions according to the American way of thinking.

"Just when everyone believed that no sensible commander would march south of the Yalu, the Chinese troops suddenly appeared," he recalled. (The Yalu is the river which borders China and North Korea, and the crossing of the river marked China's entry into the war against the Americans).

"I feel uneasy if now somebody were to tell me that they bet China would not do this or that," he said in a recent interview given to the Chinese press.

Trend Emerging on Chen's Statements

21 June 2000

CHINA has been quick to dismiss any thoughts Taiwan President Chen Shui-bian might have had that his proposal for a cross-strait summit and reaffirmation of the 1992 consensus on "one China" would appease Beijing.

Speaking at a press conference held to mark his first month in office, Mr Chen said he was willing to discuss the issue of a "future one China" on the basis of all past agreement reached, including the 1992 consensus.

He made similar remarks in his inaugural speech a month ago, but did not refer specifically to the 1992 consensus.

Two weeks later, he went so far as to deny the existence of such a consensus. An angry Beijing then ordered its military to be prepared for war.

Essentially, the 1992 consensus harmonised the views of both sides on the nature of political relations across the Taiwan Straits.

In their respective statements, Beijing and Taipei mentioned "one China" and "reunification", leaving only the political definition of China open.

Beijing views adherence or otherwise to this consensus as the litmus test of the new President's political intentions.

Therefore Mr Chen's latest remark could be taken as a slight backdown from his previous stance.

Yet, he still tried to redefine the 1992 consensus as "an agreement to disagree".

While it is true that both sides agree to disagree on the political definition of China, the statement issued by Taipei at the time explicitly upheld "one China" and "reunification".

Clearly, Mr Chen remained half-hearted about the consensus.

Beijing's immediate reaction was to urge him to be more honest.

There was certainly no lack of goodwill in his speech, as evidenced by his invitation to Chinese leader Jiang Zemin to hold a cross-strait summit along the lines of last week's Korean summit.

But Mr Chen seemed to have lost sight of a couple of major differences between the two situations which would make a cross-strait summit highly unlikely.

The first is that, while the people of both Koreas desire reunification, not all Taiwanese want to see the island reunited with the mainland.

The second is that South Korea rejected an invitation to join the United States-led Theatre Missile Defence (TMD) for the sake of achieving reunification. This move contributed immensely towards making the Korean summit a reality.

However, the same could not be said of Taiwan, which was more than eager to join the TMD to protect the island from any Chinese attack.

Compared with a month ago, another positive sign yesterday was Mr Chen's willingness to explore the possibility of a confederation to solve the problem of a "future one China".

This was perhaps the furthest that Mr Chen could go without incurring the wrath of the separatist camp in Taiwan.

Unfortunately, his gesture still fell short of Beijing's minimum demand, which is that Taipei must uphold the "one China" principle.

From the two major speeches Mr Chen has made since he became President, and judging from what he has done in the past month, a clear trend is discernible.

In public statements, he soft-pedals the cross-strait issue, giving Beijing no excuse to mount military pressures and winning international applause and sympathy at the same time.

In practice, however, he tries to push for whatever changes are required to consolidate the island's de facto independence and to wipe out any remnants pertaining to reunification.

For example, on the 76th anniversary of the Chinese Military Academy (CMA) recently, he called for the military to change its strategy from one of "strong defence" at home to one aimed at "winning a decisive battle outside Taiwan".

This was a major departure from previous thinking and could have an important bearing on cross-strait relations because it implied a change from a purely defensive posture to an offensive one.

This was clearly a move to consolidate the island's de facto independence and was done quietly. The official statement did not mention it at all.

At the same event, Mr Chen did not chant the slogan on reunification, which has been the tradition at the CMA since 1949. This was an attempt to remove the symbols of reunification.

A disgruntled military officer put it this way: the rank-and-file, who were brought up in the anti-independence tradition, will find it odd the first time, will get used to it by the second time and will forget all about reunification before long.

Ball's in Chen's Court

18 June 2000

IN 1992, a consensus on "one China" was reached by China and Taiwan through non-government organisations that, in effect, acted as their representatives.

As an important milestone in cross-strait relations that paved the way for the 1993 Singapore meeting between top negotiators from the two bodies — Mr Wang Daohan, chairman of Beijing's Association for Relations Across the Taiwan Strait, and Mr Koo Chen-fu, head of Taipei's Straits Exchange Foundation.

In the absence of official contacts between China and Taiwan, the Wang-Koo meeting was the highest-level contact between the two sides in 50 years.

Rapid growth in cross-strait exchanges followed, giving rise to the need to define more clearly the nature of relations between China and Taiwan, as such exchanges traversed different political and legal jurisdictions.

To characterise bilateral relations, both sides came up with five possible definitions. Each side was to pick the one most acceptable to it.

The resulting choice formed the core of the "one China" consensus.

Beijing's position read: "Both sides of the Taiwan Strait uphold the one China principle and strive to achieve national unification.

"In dealing with practical issues across the strait, no reference will be made to the political implications of one China."

Taipei's position read: "In the process of achieving national unification, both sides uphold the 'one China' principle.

"As to the definition of one China, both sides had different points of views."

It was clear in their respective statements that there were two common points — the concept of one China and eventual unification.

The only difference was the political definition of China.

Taipei's way of treating it was to acknowledge the differences in views regarding the meaning of "one China" while Beijing chose to avoid its political meaning altogether.

By allowing a certain degree of ambiguity, both sides went on to expand bilateral exchanges unencumbered by political sensitivities.

At this point, Taiwan had no difficulty accepting the "one China" principle and eventual unification.

In fact, before the 1992 consensus, then-president Lee Teng-hui initiated a set of "National Unification Guidelines", in which he upheld the "one China" principle unequivocally and charted out a three-stage course towards unification.

Although initiated by the ruling Kuomintang (KMT), the guidelines enjoyed multi-party support.

Founding members of the opposition Democratic Progressive Party (DPP) like Kang Ning-hsiang and Huang Hsin-chieh were even members of the National Unification Council (NUC), a body set up to implement the guidelines.

Until the DPP came to power, there was no serious questioning of the "one China" consensus.

In fact, whenever cross-strait relations hit a rough patch, a reaffirmation of the consensus was seen as a way to smoothen out the kinks.

For example, after former President Lee Teng-hui formulated his controversial "two states theory" last year, he was advised by members of the NUC to return to the "one China" principle.

Similarly, after the pro-independence Chen Shui-bian was elected President in March, giving rise to widespread concern in Taiwan, Dr Su Chi, the former chairman of Mainland Affairs Council, advised him to reaffirm the 1992 formula as a means of averting whatever hostilities that might come from China.

Instances such as these buttress the case that there was a consensus on "one China", and that it was a concept accepted and reaffirmed many times over by Taiwan in the past decade.

The onus is on Mr Chen to explain his recent statement that such a consensus never existed.

Beijing's Back Against the Wall

18 June 2000

Taiwan-China: The Gap Widens
Chinese President Jiang Zemin is pressed for time

He needs time to put a stamp on his legacy — as the man who reunified China, but time is running short as Taiwan shows increasing signs of drifting away.

In the latest signal of its intent, Taiwanese President Chen Shui-bian has denied categorically that there exists a consensus between Taipei and Beijing on the notion of "one China".

It was a provocative statement by the newly-elected leader as it would seem to sweep aside the "one China" principle which Taiwan has adhered to in the past decade, and which has given room for both sides to manoeuvre in problem-prone cross-strait negotiations.

Not unexpectedly, Beijing reacted angrily to Mr Chen's statement by calling on its military forces to step up their preparation for war. If, indeed, the consensus worked out in 1992 is well and truly cast aside, Taipei has effectively forced Beijing into a corner.

China knows that if it were to go to war over Taiwan, the price exacted would be steep.

Aside from the physical toll on life and property, there is also the long-term psychological scar on the national psyche to reckon with.

A case in point is to be found just across the strait. In 1947, the ruling Kuomintang (KMT) crushed an uprising by local Taiwanese. That act of brutal suppression haunted the KMT government for the next 50 years and contributed to its eventual downfall. A similar show of brute force against Taiwan could end up a spectre to haunt the Chinese people for a long time to come.

But if no military action is taken, Beijing's repeated warnings would not be worth a damn.

Given time, which seems to be on Taiwan's side, the separatists would gradually transform de facto independence into a de jure one, which would be in line with the policy of the new government.

If China is in a fix over Taiwan, the same can be said of Mr Jiang.

Internal discussions within the party's central committee have gone as far as to attribute the Democratic Progressive Party's rise to power in Taiwan to the complete failure of his policy towards the island.

Critics say that Mr Jiang's 1994 Eight-Point Programme — the backbone of his Taiwan policy — is so flabby it practically incites separatism.

If even the name, flag and national anthem could be conceded, they argue, what else could not?

One of Mr Jiang's eight points states that under the "one China" principle, anything could be discussed.

The term "anything" has come to be understood as referring to the name, flag and anthem of China.

Mr Jiang has also been criticised by hardliners for relying too much on "great power diplomacy" as a means to achieving unification. Essentially, this strategy calls for building up ties with the United States and other major world powers to create a favourable external environment for resolving the Taiwan issue.

US President Bill Clinton's "Three Nos" declaration in Shanghai in 1998 was seen as an endorsement of this course of action.

In his statement, made as he was winding up his state visit to China, Mr Clinton stated explicitly that Washington would say "no" to Taiwan independence, "no" to two Chinas or "one China, one Taiwan", and "no" to Taiwanese participation in international bodies requiring statehood.

Yet, the failure by Chinese Premier Zhu Rongji to clinch US support for China's entry to the World Trade Organisation last year and the bombing of the Chinese Embassy in Yugoslavia showed up the strategy's shortcomings.

Sceptics say Beijing cannot possibly rely on American goodwill and cooperation to realise its goal of unification, not when the US sees China as its greatest potential challenger and a threat to its global dominance.

Odds of gaining a favourable outcome from such a strategy is as good as "waiting in the woods for fish".

Clearly, Mr Jiang is in an embarrassing predicament.

His patient and flexible approach, while giving rise to strong criticism at home, has been rewarded with the installation of a separatist government in Taiwan.

He has to make a major decision soon on what his next step would be.

But between now and the end of this year, he is forced by circumstance to hold back and wait out the unfolding of certain key events.

The first is the annual stock-taking by the Chinese leadership at its summer retreat at Beidaihe in August.

Then, he has to wait till the US presidential election in November is over and for the new president to make clear his China policy.

So, from now till perhaps early next year, the only policy option available to Mr Jiang is to "wait and see".

Unfortunately, he does not have too much time to wait. The party's 16th Congress will be held in the last quarter of 2002. Going by the rule of thumb that it takes about a year to decide on a new leadership line-up, a new power structure has to take shape by end of next year.

That would mean that Mr Jiang would have to decide by end of 2001 whether he is going to step down from power.

If he is to retire fully, then he has to consider what legacy he will bequeath his people.

"Mao Zedong enabled us to stand up, Deng Xiaoping enabled us to get rich, what will Jiang Zemin enable us?" goes one of the many jingles making the rounds that hint at Mr Jiang's lack of comparable historic contribution.

If he wants to link his name with the unification feat, he would be tempted to stay on for another term to buy time for a solution to the Taiwan problem. In other words, he has just about a year to come up with a major decision on Taiwan.

Annex
China's dilemma

China and its president, Jiang Zemin, face hard choices in dealing with a Taiwan bent on going its own way. Here's why:

Beijing's predicament
— If it goes to war, the cost is overwhelming in terms of lives lost, property destroyed, and damage done to international relations and national psyche.
— If it opts for peaceful means, the Taiwanese will not pay any heed.
— If it adopts a 'wait and see' approach, it loses credibility.

Jiang's plight

— His conciliatory Taiwan policy is seen as a failure by hardliners.
— His "great power diplomacy" is also under fire.
— He wants a unified China as his legacy but has little time to manouevre. Time is running out
— Jiang's response to new developments in Taiwan has to take into account:
  • The August annual meeting of China's top leadership in Beidaihe
  • The outcome of the US presidential election in November
  • The power play preceding the communist party's 16th Congress in 2002, in particular the question of his own tenure in office

Korean Summit Puts Pressure on China, Taiwan

16 June 2000

The historic summit between the South and North Korean leaders has provided momentum for both sides to usher in an age of mutual reconciliation and cooperation, following decades of hostility and confrontation.

In a five-point joint communique signed by South Korean President Kim Dae Jung and North Korean leader Kim Jong Il, national unification was the sole theme.

The first point in the North-South communique specifies reunification as their common objective while the second point prescribes the framework for its achievement.

The remaining three points provide for family reunions, multi-faceted exchanges and a dialogue mechanism, all of which would help reduce tension and create an atmosphere conducive to reunification.

In the communique, both sides envisaged a unification process starting with a loose confederation, working gradually towards a more closely-knit federation and, finally, coming together as a single country.

According to the South Korean side, when all the provisions carried in the 1991 South-North Basic Agreement as well as the July 4 South-North Communique in 1972 are fully implemented, the two sides will become virtually one country.

Though it is premature to hail a unified Korea, the detente process, nevertheless, has an obvious impact on cross-strait relations.

Taiwan is definitely under pressure to negotiate its eventual unification with China. Both the German and Korean unification processes show that for divided countries belonging to the same race to achieve lasting peace, the only way is unification.

The German and Korean examples show that neither political nor economic differences are excuses for perpetuating separation, for both have vastly different political ideologies and institutions, and even wider gaps in per-capita income.

A point worth noting is that in both cases, it is the richer side — in terms of per-capita, not aggregate, income — not the poorer side, that is taking the initiative for unification, knowing full well its financial responsibility in taking care of its poorer brethren.

If both the Germans and Koreans are willing to bury their differences for the greater goal of national unity, there is no reason why the Taiwanese should magnify cross-strait differences as an excuse to split the country.

Taiwan has even less reason to resist unification since the bulk of its foreign-exchange surpluses is derived from trade with China. Taiwanese Economics Minister Lin Hsin-yi testified in the legislature recently that such exchanges benefited Taiwan more than the mainland.

Neither the richer half of Germany nor Korea derived comparable economic benefit from the poorer half.

If the general trend is for divided countries to achieve unification and, through it, a general relaxation of regional tension, Taiwan becomes the odd one out if it continues to resist unification talks.

The latest Korean detente equally creates pressure for China. Before the summit began, the Foreign Ministry spokesman reiterated Beijing's position that neither the German nor Korean model was applicable to solving China's unification problem.

This position is well known, but unfortunately not well explained.

From what has been said previously, Beijing's position seems to be this: the division of both Germany and Korea was the result of international treaties among great powers. Their peoples and the international community at large accept this fact and hence the existence of two sovereign states of the same race.

On the other hand, the division of China is the result of a civil war pending a final settlement. China's sovereignty has never been split, it argues, and the international community accepts only one China.

Since the origin of the division is not the same, both the German and Korean models, which start with two separate sovereign states, are not applicable, it argues.

This logic, though correct, is not tenable.

Whatever causes the division, it is division all the same. Disregarding the historical circumstances leading to the division, one should start with the very fact of reality that there exist two separate authorities — one based in Beijing and the other in Taipei.

If respect for reality could be the starting point, then cross-strait reconciliation might not be that difficult to come by, for Taiwan has indicated that it is prepared to accept a confederation.

During the presidential campaign, Mr Lien Chan of the Kuomintang (KMT) had sounded out the applicability of a confederation system. After his election in March, President Chen Shui-bian said openly that such an option could be considered.

So the Korean model does have its value if Beijing is willing to respect the fact of reality.

Beijing's own model now is peaceful unification under the "one country, two systems" formula. If Taiwan refuses, then non-peaceful means would be considered.

To the Taiwanese, this means a choice of either to die or capitulate. No sensible leader, no matter where his position in the "independence-unification" spectrum lies, could possibly accept the proposal. The last presidential election shows that less than 2 per cent of the total number of voters in Taiwan accept the Chinese unification model.

Now that the Koreans have resolved their longstanding differences via a confederation, Beijing will feel greater pressure to consider the model, or to give stronger reasons for rejecting it.

To non-partisan Chinese, Taipei is to blame for not respecting history — that Taiwan had come under China rule since 800 years ago — while Beijing is to blame for not respecting reality — that there exists two governments over Chinese territory.

Chinese Premier Zhu Rongji said before the Taiwanese presidential election that Beijing was willing to make whatever concessions needed to bring Taiwan back to the fold. Such concessions, no matter how big, were concessions to fellow Chinese, he said.

Following this line of argument, there is still much room for Beijing to concede. Taiwan has indicated its willingness to accept the Korean model starting with a confederation. Is Beijing willing to concede on that point?

Return of the Native

11 June 2000

TAIWAN'S new President was crafty indeed.

In word, Mr Chen Shui-bian made sure there was nothing in his May 20 inauguration speech that could goad Beijing into taking immediate military action against the island. There were sighs of relief all round.

In deed, however, he made it clear to all who were watching him that the island was as good as independent, which does nothing to ease tensions across the Taiwan Strait.

His pro-independence Democratic Progressive Party (DPP), which ousted the ruling Kuomintang, paid great attention to every detail of the inauguration ceremony so that this message was not missed.

The ceremony kicked off with the overture, Harbinger Of Victory, a warrior song of the island's aborigines.

It ended with God Bless Our Land Formosa, the lyrics of which call explicitly for the creation of a Republic of Taiwan. THE title of Mr Chen's address — Taiwan Stands Up — was also significant. He would reiterate these words three times in the speech.

By borrowing from Chinese communist leader Mao Zedong's 1949 declaration that "The Chinese people have stood up", he was signalling to Beijing that what he did on May 20 was similar to what Mao did half a century ago: proclaim the birth of a new nation.

Indeed, the inauguration ritual itself showed that there was a major change in the order of the day.

The new President took his oath not only before the portrait of Dr Sun Yat-sen, revered as the "father of modern China", as all his predecessors had done, but also before the people.

"He wanted to tell the people that his power was bestowed upon him by the local Taiwanese and not by some obscure source rooted in the Chinese tradition," explained a member of the organising committee.

Officiating at the transfer of executive power to the new Cabinet was Mr Peng Ming-min, called the "father of Taiwan's independence movement" as far back as the late 1960s. He was outlawed for his beliefs and went into exile for most of his life.

His presence spoke volumes of the change in the political order.

The native Taiwanese motif was in full display in the entertainment segment of the celebrations. Only songs and dances of local origin were performed and by local troupes only.

The island's anthem was sung by popular singer A-Mei, who is an aborigine. Even the state banquet featured local cuisine.

Thus, every opportunity to show off a separate Taiwanese identity was not missed.

An analysis of the inauguration speech revealed an interesting pattern.

For example, he referred to "Taiwan" 35 times, "Republic of China" nine times and "Formosa" twice. Some people joked that perhaps he felt more at home without "China".

He was careful to avoid calling the Taiwanese, Chinese. At the end of his speech, he declared "Long live the people of Taiwan".

Even his predecessor, Mr Lee Teng-hui, did not go this far at his inauguration — and he had even more reason to do so.

He was the first native-born Taiwanese to be elected President in the island's first popular vote in 1996. Yet he merely held a big rally to thank the people for their support.

To many observers, therefore, May 20 was not just a presidential inauguration.

"It was a celebration of independence," said Mr Yan Xuetong, senior researcher at the Institute of International Relations in Beijing.

Ritual aside, the substance of Mr Chen's speech made the inauguration ceremony seem more like a declaration of independence.

He started with history when he touched on the cross-strait issue.

Taiwan's history, he said, was only about 400 years old, beginning with the Dutch discovery of Formosa in 1604.

"Formosa" was the pet name separatists used to refer to Taiwan. For example, Mr Chen's private foundation was named the Formosa Foundation.

To this group of people, the term inspires an almost religious devotion. Yet the very name reminds the Chinese of the humiliation they had suffered in the past.

The argument that Taiwan's history was only 400 years old was typical of the historical conception of the separatist movement.

This is clearly debatable for antique records showed that the island was brought under Chinese influence for at least twice that long.

For example, a rudimentary census conducted in the Southern Sung dynasty (1127–1279) contained population figures of the island, while the Yuan dynasty (1271–1368) first created a local government to supervise the island, showing that it was under China's effective administration. Mr Chen also described the history of Taiwan and China as two separate but similar ones, whereas Beijing considered the history of Taiwan as part and parcel of the history of China.

In fact, it was the defeat suffered by China in the 1894-95 Sino-Japanese War that forced it to cede Taiwan, thereby separating the island from the mainland.

"By establishing two separate historical developments, Mr Chen craftily made a case for Taiwan to claim a separate statehood," said Mr Yan.

Moreover, he shied away from the crucial "one China" principle even though Beijing has been toning down its demand in order to bridge the gap.

Just before the inauguration, Beijing even indicated to Mr Chen that it was ready to accept him if only he would admit that he was a Chinese.

For the separatists, it is anathema to call themselves Chinese. For the first time, calling Taiwanese Chinese became a real problem.

The new chairman of the Mainland Affairs Council (MAC), Ms Tsai Ing-wen, one of the masterminds behind ex-President Lee's controversial "two states" theory, defined her own identity in a three-part statement: I am Taiwanese, with a Chinese origin, holding an ROC nationality.

Ms Tsai was applauded for this characterisation and it soon became the model answer for the Taiwanese when asked about their identity.

Noted Mr Yan: "This is tantamount to saying goodbye to China."

Professor Wang Gangwu, director of the East Asia Institute in Singapore and an expert in overseas Chinese affairs, confirmed that this was how most overseas Chinese in various countries identified themselves.

In the Chinese language, the term "Chinese" could be rendered as either *zhong guo ren* (people of China) or *hua ren* (people of Chinese origin). The Taiwanese were willing to call themselves Chinese only if it meant the latter.

Clearly, a new Taiwanese nationalism has emerged, which has led some Taiwanese to repudiate their "Chinese-ness". This new-found identity was the result of a decade-long de-sinofication started by Mr Lee.

His efforts bore fruit. In 1990, a MAC survey showed that 85 per cent of the people saw themselves as both Taiwanese and Chinese. Today, this figure has dropped to below 35 per cent.

Ten years ago, 65 per cent would call themselves Chinese if they were given an "either-or" choice. Now, only 15 per cent would do so.

Demographic changes is one factor in this shift in the Taiwanese sense of identity. More than half of the 22 million-strong population were born in Taiwan after 1949, so they would have few connections with the mainland. Then there is the deliberate policy to split the island from the mainland, with former President Lee casting himself in the role of the Moses of Taiwan leading his people away from China.

Beijing's questionable approach to Taiwan is also to blame.

Its Taiwan policy could be summarised as a stark choice between war and "one country, two systems", both of which are unacceptable to the Taiwanese.

The outlook for reunification is therefore bleak.

With or without a war, it will be hard to have a one China now, given the vibrant growth of Taiwanese nationalism.

The only chance Beijing has of assimilating Taiwan is if China grows rich with strong cultural charm.

Short of this, forget about reunification.

Annex
China Tones Down Demand on 'one China'
Pre-1992 Definition of 'one China'

Beijing used to define the principle in a three-part statement: There is only one China in the world. Taiwan is part of China. The People's Republic of China (PRC) is the sole legal representative of China.

In dealing with Taipei, it changed the last part to: "The sovereignty and territorial integrity of China is inviolable."

1992 Consensus

In 1992, both sides reached a consensus on how they should handle the "one China" principle.

Beijing maintains that "both sides of the Taiwan Strait uphold the 'one China' principle and strive to achieve national unification. In dealing with practical issues across the strait, no reference will be made to the political implications of 'one China' ".

Taipei maintains that "in the process of achieving national unification, both sides should uphold the 'one China' principle. As to the definition of 'one China', both sides have different point of views".

In other words, Beijing does not insist that "one China" should mean the People's Republic of China (PRC).

1998

To make "one China" easier for Taiwan to accept, Mr Wang Daohan, Beijing's top negotiator on cross-strait issues, defined it in 86 characters.

In essence: China does not refer to the PRC nor the Republic of China (Taiwan's official name), but a future unified China to be brought about by both sides.

Part 2 Next Sunday looks at the Chinese Predicament as it Presses Ahead with Reunification.

Lee Teng-hui Perpetuates His Legacy

24 May 2000

MR LEE Teng-hui shocked many when, in his last week in office, he said he would support a Democratic Progressive Party (DPP) member against his own party's incumbent Taipei mayor Ma Ying-jeou in the next race still two years away.

If the feisty leader appears confident of his ability to exert influence even after he has vacated the presidency, he has good reasons to believe so.

This is not only because the new President, Mr Chen Shui-bian of the pro-independence DPP, is said to be his choice successor, but also because some of his key aides have been appointed to major positions in the new government.

Central to Mr Lee's line is the assertion of Taiwan's position as an independent sovereign state separated from China. All other policies revolve around this theme.

For example, he formulated the "two states" theory to provide a theoretical framework for his line.

He banned the "three direct links" to prevent excessive people-to-people exchanges with the mainland. He devised the "no haste, be patient" policy to avoid excessive economic dependence on China.

At the same time, he came up with "pragmatic diplomacy" to expand the island's international space.

He advocated a strong defence for Taiwan, making the island the world's top arms importer, in anticipation of military pressure from Beijing.

So it is interesting that the key figures who had a hand in the formulation of the above policies have now taken up important posts in Mr Chen's Cabinet.

There is former Defence Minister Tang Fei, who is now the Premier.

He sees eye to eye with Mr Lee on the need for Taiwan to have a strong defence, which includes having Taipei join the US-led theatre missile defence (TMD) system.

The Taiwanese press said that Mr Tang was picked by Mr Lee. Though this is hard to confirm, Mr Lee's active lobbying of the Kuomintang (KMT) not to bar its members from serving a DPP-run government lent support to such reports.

With Mr Tang as Premier, Mr Lee helped Mr Chen solve the most difficult problem of securing the loyalty of the military, which had long been exposed to anti-separatism political education.

Legal expert Tsai Ying-wen, the architect of the "two states" theory, chairs the Mainland Affairs Council, the highest authority handling cross-strait relations.

Few people would have believed that this rather shy woman helped formulate the highly controversial theory that almost plunged Taiwan into a war with China.

She has since pledged that Taiwan would stop referring to it, adding that its substance and spirit would remain nevertheless.

In other words, she will still stick to the theory without mentioning it.

As an expert on Taiwan's negotiation to get into the World Trade Organisation (WTO), she had been working behind closed doors on how Taiwan could bypass WTO stipulations so as to preserve its restrictive economic policies towards the mainland.

Dr Chen Po-chih, a professor of economics at the National Taiwan University, is the chairman of the Council for Economic Planning and Development, a body that maps the future course of development for Taiwan.

He is known for his long-standing association with the independence movement and has written copiously on the means to achieve it. He is said to be the theoretician behind the "no haste, be patient" policy.

When he accepted the appointment, the academic defended the same policy, saying that national security should always prevail over economic interests.

He cited as an example China's warning to Taiwanese investors against supporting Taiwan independence in the run-up to the presidential elections.

While he said he would "adjust the policy slightly", he also stressed that there was nothing inherently wrong with the policy itself because it was necessary to preserve the best resources in the island.

He also saw no contradiction between the policy and the popular demand to open up the three "direct links".

The new Foreign Minister is Professor Tien Hung-mao of the Centre of National Policy Studies.

THE centre, which is funded by the Evergreen Group of shipping tycoon Chang Jung-fa, one of the heavyweights who supported Mr Chen in the March elections, is known to be close to Mr Lee.

It has even been called his "institute for research on independence".

Mr Tien's close ties with Mr Lee are beyond doubt.

A year before the presidential election, he began to tell people that it was not unconstitutional for Mr Lee, who had been in office since 1988, to seek another term.

Many regarded this as Mr Lee's way of sounding out public opinion towards him extending his presidential term.

Since he took up directorship of the centre in the early 1990s, Mr Tien had been helping Mr Lee to formulate his "pragmatic diplomacy".

He questioned the value of traditional diplomacy in which both Taipei and Beijing are engaged in a zero-sum game vying for diplomatic recognition.

Instead, he suggested creating a situation that is conducive to "dual recognition" by other countries.

As official links with other countries are impossible, he suggested opening up unofficial channels.

For this he is recognised for introducing the so-called "track two diplomacy".

He also proposed a flexible approach, for the sake of participation, towards issues regarding Taiwan's name, its flag and anthem in international organisations and events.

To get around the difficult diplomatic situation, he suggested the full-scale mobilisation of non-governmental organisations, scholars and retired government officials to help raise Taiwan's international visibility.

All these moves tallied with Mr Lee's own view.

This shows that in the crucial issue of upholding the sovereignty of Taiwan, as well as the means towards this end, Mr Chen inherits — lock, stock and barrel — not only his predecessor's concepts, but also those of his team.

These are strong enough reasons to believe that Mr Lee's influence will not wane soon — not in the next two years, at least.

Cloud of War Remains Despite Progress in Sino-Taiwan Ties

22 May 2000

MOST Taiwanese are glad that their new President, Mr Chen Shui-bian of the pro-independence Democratic Progressive Party (DPP), avoided an immediate head-on collision with China while still being able to preserve the island's identity and dignity.

Opinion polls showed that more than 50 per cent of the public endorse the position adopted by Mr Chen on cross-strait relations.

Pro-DPP scholar, Dr Lo Chih-cheng of the Political Science Department of the Soochow University, claimed that Mr Chen had made considerable concessions in his statement and Beijing should take note of this fact.

"Most people measure Mr Chen's speech using Beijing's yardstick, that is, to what extent he returns to the 'one China' principle," he said.

"Yet if one uses a different yardstick and measures the extent Mr Chen has departed from his original position, one would be able to appreciate his concessions," he added.

He noted several significant changes.

First, Mr Chen vowed not to declare independence unless being attacked.

Second, he did not rule out unification if it was the choice of the people.

Third, he mentioned his willingness to work towards a future "one China".

It is a big step for the Taiwan leader, once a staunch supporter of independence, to make these concessions, he maintained.

Dr Lo also said that one thing good of Mr Chen was that although he made such big concessions, no one in Taiwan would call him "traitor". This showed that he was a worthy negotiator that Beijing could deal with.

The essence of his speech was to create a consensus among the Taiwanese themselves regarding cross-strait policy, according to Mr Yen Wan-ching, Director of DPP's Department of Chinese Affairs.

Only the extremists at both ends of the unification-independence spectrum demonstrated against the speech — the majority agreed that it was a good presentation of Taiwanese position.

"The ability of Mr Chen to formulate a consensus over a very important issue at the inception stage of the new government is extremely important. It makes for political stability," Mr Yen said.

"Similarly, it also creates a consensus among major powers in the region. The essence of his policy is a respect of the status quo. By upholding it, nobody's interests are damaged. By stating clearly this policy, the international community will know that if there is someone who tries to change the status quo, it is definitely not Taiwan," he added.

Another innovation was the strategic ambiguity regarding future development. "Taiwan can head towards independence or unification, depending on how Beijing treats us. Thus instead of China blaming us for making troubles, the onus lies now with Beijing."

Most praised Mr Chen for his ability to manage the crisis and avoided an imminent war.

Although Beijing issued a sternly-worded statement, observers however interpreted it in quite a positive light.

According to Dr Gerard Chow, Director of the Institute of Mainland China Studies at the National Sun Yat-sen University, the fact that Beijing responded so quickly showed that it also wanted to end the current phase of high tension that has developed since Taiwan's presidential elections on March 18.

Obviously the speech did not meet even the threshold requirement of Beijing, which was upholding the 'one China' principle, yet Beijing seemed to understand now that this was too much of a demand for a pro-independence president newly in power.

"So it was willing to accept temporarily the reality as given and end the threat of war first", he said. "There are lots of goodwill in from Beijing's statement," according to Dr Peter Lin, also from the National Sun Yat-sen University.

"Although the pressure is still there, there is no mention of the use of force, this is a subtle departure from similar statements issued before and after March 18," he noted.

"This shows that Beijing knows such intimidation no longer works," he added.

He also noted the call to return to the talks between Beijing's Association for Relations Across the Taiwan Strait (Arats) and Taipei's Straits Exchange Foundation (SEF). Both were charged by their respective governments to handle cross-strait relations in an unofficial capacity.

He said that it took almost 24 months for the contact between Arats and SEF to resume after the missile testing during the 1996 presidential election.

Yet this time, Beijing was so quick to promise a re-opening of talks between the two, indicating that Beijing, although unhappy with Mr Chen's speech, would have to take it as given.

Dr Lin also noted in the statement that Arats was willing to discuss with any properly authorised organisations or individuals. This showed that it did not rule out discussing with Nobel laureate, Dr Lee Yuen-tseh, although it was extremely upset that he provided the final impetus to send the separatist Chen to the presidential palace.

Dr Lin found an area of potential consensus in Beijing's statement.

It stressed strongly that cross-strait dialogue could be re-opened if Taiwan returned to the 1992 consensus.

Judging from the messages coming out of Taiwan's Mainland Affairs Council and from Dr Koo Chun-fu of SEF, this seems to be the position of Taipei as well.

Therefore, Beijing's statement, stern as it is, has shown that the door for negotiation was still wide open.

However, almost all scholars interviewed agreed that although Mr Chen avoided narrowly a war, the cloud of war remained and there was not too much time for him.

Dr Lo said that both sides were stuck with the same sovereign issue.

China considered sovereignty a principle and not an issue.

So did the Taiwanese.

No president could go to the negotiating table if the outcome was to turn Taiwan into a part of China.

With nationalism high on the Chinese side and patriotism intense on the Taiwanese side, there was little ground for long-term optimism, he concluded.

'Enough to Avert War but Not Enough for Peace'

21 May 2000

Taiwan's new President Chen Shui-bian yesterday avoided a political — and perhaps even a military — confrontation with China by removing an immediate excuse for Beijing to use force, but the outlook for bilateral relations in the years ahead is unclear.

In his inaugural speech, Mr Chen reaffirmed his oft-repeated "Four Nos" — no declaration of independence, no change of the island's name, no constitutional amendment to give legal effect to the "two states" theory, and no referendum to change the status quo.

He also pledged adherence to the National Unification Guidelines which, adopted in 1991, stipulate that Taiwan adheres to the "one China" policy, but that there are now two separate "political entities".

Showing its displeasure, Beijing issued a sternly worded statement criticising his "evasive" and "insincere" attitude towards the "one China" principle.

In a bid to alleviate Taiwan's fear that the negotiation would be held on unequal footing, it even invented a new jargon — "one China, across-Straits negotiations" — to describe such discussions.

Commenting on Mr Chen's speech, Dr Lu Jianhua at the Institute of Politics of the Chinese Academy of Social Sciences said:

"It is good enough just to avoid an outbreak of war in the near term, but it falls far short of what is required to establish durable peace across the strait."

The academic saw both substantial and symbolic issues in the speech that disturbed Beijing.

The most crucial one was his unwillingness to uphold the "one China" principle.

In his speech, "one China" is still an issue, not a principle.

Except for the "no change" pledge regarding the National Unification Guidelines, there was nothing pro-active in his speech that showed his commitment to "one China" nor "unification", not even the 1992 consensus in which both Beijing and Taipei pledged adherence to the principle.

Mr Chen also said he would continue expanding Taiwan's international space, which showed that he would stick to ex-president Lee Teng-hui's line.

A number of symbolic gestures also reflected his pro-independence mentality.

The inaugural ceremony started with a song glorifying Mount Jade, the highest mountain in Taiwan, a song that pledges to build an independent Taiwan.

Likewise, it ended with another song: God Bless Our Land, Formosa.

The term Formosa, a pet name which the independence advocates loved to call their island, was used several times in the speech. This had never been the case previously on similar occasions.

While he chanted "long live the people of Taiwan", he did not do so for the Republic of China (ROC) — which is Taiwan's official name — a ritual formality of all previous presidents.

It was against the wish of independence-minded Taiwanese to see a long-living ROC.

His reference to Taiwan's history, which, according to him was only 400 years old when it was called Formosa, was the typical interpretation of pro-independence historians.

Thrice he urged the Taiwanese to stand up and "overcome intimidation with hope, conquer fear with faith, and transcend fear, threats and oppression".

"By thus agitating the people, Chen is pointing an accusing finger at Beijing. Yet it was Chen's and his associates' attempt to break away from China that precipitated cross-strait tension," Dr Lu said.

"This is grossly unfair to people in the mainland," he added.

He admitted that it is difficult for Beijing to wage war on the basis of Mr Chen's speech, and there is little Beijing could do at this moment except to watch carefully for further developments.

"From Chen's speech, it is clear that he tries to drag on the issue indefinitely, by using democratisation as a pretext, and by internationalising the Taiwanese issue as a shield," he said.

"Under this circumstance, although it is difficult for China to use force, Beijing would draw a loosely defined timetable for its eventual solution.

"There is no way Chen could avoid returning to the 'one China' principle," he predicted.

Without One-China Principle, Chen's Policy Unlikely to Work

20 May 2000

ONE of the foremost tasks of Taiwan's new President Chen Shui-bian is to develop a policy towards China that reconciles the ideology of the new ruling Democratic Progressive Party (DPP) — which is strongly pro-independence — with the practical political and legal reality of cross-strait relations.

Failure to do so implies instability affecting not only the Chinese on both sides of the strait but also the entire East Asian region.

Now that the DPP assumes ruling position with its implied responsibility not only to the Taiwanese but also to the international community, Mr Chen has to consider seriously the extent to which his platform could be put into practice.

So far, he has done two things. He keeps on sending out goodwill messages to Beijing and tries to be as non-provocative as possible — not a small change from his pre-election image as an uncompromising advocate of independence.

He also tones down his rather stern and inflexible policy which he announced during the election campaign. If his original position papers — on cross-strait relations, defence and foreign policies — remain intact, the outlook is bleak.

This change in posture and flexibility takes many people by surprise; even the US government comments favourably that Mr Chen demonstrates a degree of maturity and responsibility required of a statesman.

It raises hope that the new President will be less dogmatic when he comes to grips with reality.

Yet the conflict inherent in an emerging Taiwanese nationalism against a restrictive political and legal reality remains unchanged. Unless he is able to resolve this basic contradiction, the days ahead for him will not be smooth.

According to one of his mainland-policy advisers, Professor Julian Kuo, a known moderate within the DPP, there is little hope for him to implement the party's ideology intact.

The political reality precludes an over-assertion of Taiwanese nationalistic aspirations. Attempts to do so, as represented by outgoing President Lee Teng-hui's "two-states theory", meant upsetting the delicate trilateral balance between Beijing, Washington and Taipei, with serious implications for the island.

The legal reality prescribed by the Constitution and its derivative laws also reduces the room for the implementation of the DPP ideology. These documents define clearly Taiwan as part of China.

"Unless the Constitution is itself amended, which Chen has promised not to do, all Taiwanese are legally Chinese, whether they like it or not", explains Prof Kuo. He describes the predicament as "Taiwanese heart encaged by Chinese laws".

Prof Kuo has long been advocating a transformation of the party to rid itself of the ideological intricacies developed out of past ethnic conflicts. His book, The Pains Of DPP's Transformation, is an authority on this issue.

Yet, he is not optimistic. "In past years, the DPP has conducted several major rounds of intra-party debate on its independence programme, but none succeeds in deleting this very word from the party charter," he notes.

Now that the DPP wins ruling power, it is even less convincing to tell the die hard fundamentalists that the independence charter is a hindrance to the growth of the party.

After today, a new factor will complicate the picture. In all previous cabinets, the majority was made up of non-Taiwanese. In Mr Chen's new government, for the first time, this provincial composition is changed drastically.

There are only five non-Taiwanese in the 40-member Cabinet, making it the lowest ratio that the minority (the mainlanders) is represented. Even under the authoritarian rule of General Chiang Kai-shek and his son Chiang Ching-kuo, the percentage of the minority (then the Taiwanese) was still much higher than in this Cabinet.

At the same time, people from southern Taiwan — traditionally the stronghold of the independence movement — make up a disproportionately large share in the Cabinet. If one takes Taichung City in central Taiwan as the line of demarcation, only four members (or one-tenth) are from northern Taiwan, the rest are from the south.

This ethnic and geographical bias shows that, although Mr Chen is trying hard to lean towards a more centrist position, his choice of team members shows that he is still dominated — willingly or subconsciously — by his natural inclination towards independence.

With a Cabinet composed of people listing heavily towards independence, it is hard to anticipate any major breakthrough in cross-strait relations.

While people are hopeful that, with the end of President Lee's reign, the ban on the "three direct links", as well as the "no haste, be patient" policy, could be scrapped.

Yet, some members of the new Cabinet are quick to reiterate that they would continue Mr Lee's line.

For example, new Transport Minister Yeh Chu-lan makes it clear that she is opposed to the direct links.

"Other people might consider it good, not me", she says bluntly.

On the notorious "no haste, be patient" policy, the new chairman of the Council for Economic Planning and Development, Dr Chen Po-chih, defends the need to continue with it and says that it can, at best, be "slightly adjusted".

The vice-governor of the Central Bank, Mr Chen Shih-meng, said that should the policy be repealed, then a "national-security due" should be levied on Taiwanese investment in the mainland to prevent excessive investment from going there.

Yet the root cause still rests with the President. Half a month before the inauguration, he had issued a six-point policy brief to Taiwan's overseas diplomatic missions, in which he defines Taiwan as an independent sovereign state called the Republic of China under its existing Constitution.

He promised that there will be no declaration of independence, no change of the name of the country, no plebiscite to determine unification or independence and no amendment of the Constitution to legalise the "two-states theory", unless China uses force.

He said that he is prepared to discuss any issue with China, including the "one China" issue as long as it is "an issue" and not "a principle".

He proposed setting up a formalised channel for dialogue and visits, creating confidence-building measures to reduce military risks and expanding economic and trade links with China under the framework of the World Trade Organisation.

He said he is willing to enter into a peace treaty or a basic law with China as an interim arrangement governing bilateral relations on the basis of equality and in accordance with the UN dispute-resolution mechanism.

The final outcome of any such arrangement should be open-ended.

From Mr Chen's point of view, this is a great concession from the position papers he published during the election campaign, yet it still falls far short of China's demands.

"There is no lack of goodwill from Chen, yet there is still no sight of the key element, namely the one-China principle," said Director Fan Xi-zhou of the Taiwan Institute at Xiamen University.

"As long as he is evasive on this very crucial principle, all his so-called goodwill becomes a camouflage to cover up his separatist moves," he adds.

With China still uncompromising on this very basic principle, there is little chance that Mr Chen's policy will work.

What Is He Going to Say?

14 May 2000

ALL EYES will be watching Mr Chen Shui-bian on Saturday, and Beijing, in particular, expects him to watch what he says as Taiwan's new President if he does not want a cross-strait conflict.

Just two days ago, he assured the people that his May 20 speech would represent a change for the better in the island's currently tense relations with China.

He compared himself to the late American President Richard Nixon, the staunchly anti-communist leader who opened links with China and made a landmark visit to Beijing in 1972.

By likening himself to Mr Nixon, Mr Chen has raised expectations that something dramatic — like a breakthrough in cross-strait ties — was forthcoming.

Despite the positive prospect he held out, it is difficult to see how he can defuse the crisis with China without meeting Beijing's demands.

His mainland-policy advisers have identified three key Chinese demands. Beijing's fundamental demand is for him to uphold the "one China" principle. It also expects from both sides a commitment towards reunification in the long run.

However, for operational purposes, both sides should return to the 1992 consensus regarding that principle.

"There is no room for mistakes," said Mr Chiu I-jen, the new deputy secretary-general of the National Security Council, who heads a group of writers drafting Mr Chen's speech.

But he made it clear that it would be almost impossible for Mr Chen to say explicitly that he upholds the "one China" principle, as demanded by Beijing.

THE reason, he said, is that he was already getting a lot of flak from pro-independence fundamentalists in his Democratic Progressive Party (DPP) for being too soft towards Beijing.

DPP chairman Lin Yi-hsiung has warned Cabinet members — many of whom do not belong to the party — against implementing policies that favour reunification.

According to Mr Chiu, the DPP has had three major debates in the past 10 years to decide if it should drop its independence platform to make the party more acceptable to voters. The platform remained intact each time.

"This shows the strength of support for independence within the party," he said. "An open endorsement of the 'one China' principle, therefore, is tantamount to political suicide."

Mr Chen's advisers thus have the hard task of finding an indirect way to best address China's demand.

According to Mr Julian Kuo, an adviser and a moderate in the pro-independence camp, the speech will stress that, as the 10th President of the Republic of China (ROC), he will uphold the ROC Constitution.

Article 4 states that "the territory of the ROC, according to its existing national boundaries, shall not be altered except by resolution of the National Assembly".

Mr Kuo pointed out that the current constitution applies to the whole of China. So, by saying he will uphold the charter, Mr Chen is, in fact, telling Beijing, implicitly, that he will adhere to the "one China" principle.

He also noted a May 3 editorial in the Wen Wei Po, a pro-Beijing newspaper in Hongkong, which said that Taiwan's existing constitution "embodies the 'one China' principle".

As for China's demand for eventual reunification, he will stress that any future development should be kept open-ended. "This represents the greatest possible concession that an ardent supporter of independence could make," Mr Kuo added.

At the operational level, China has said that cross-strait dialogue could resume once Taiwan returned to the 1992 consensus.

But the current dispute between the two sides was over what consensus was reached in 1992.

"We understand it as 'one China, but differently defined', yet Beijing seems to have a different understanding," he said.

A senior Chinese official on cross-strait affairs said recently that "one China, but differently defined" had never been the consensus.

According to Mr Tang Shubei, the 1992 consensus allowed both sides to address the "one China" principle differently.

Beijing maintains that "both sides of the Taiwan Strait should uphold the 'one China' principle and strive to achieve national unification. In dealing with practical issues across the strait, no reference will be made to the political implications of 'one China' ".

As for Taipei, it pledges that "in the process of achieving national unification, both sides should uphold the 'one China' principle. As to the definition of 'one China', both sides had different points of view".

Different treatment of the "one China" principle is not the same as "one China, but differently defined", argued Mr Tang, vice-president of the Association for Relations Across the Taiwan Strait (Arats), which handles cross-strait affairs unofficially.

Said Mr Kuo: "Without a consensus on what consensus had been reached, it would be difficult for Mr Chen to uphold it."

YET he admitted that there was also strong domestic pressure for Mr Chen to return to the 1992 consensus.

The pressure came from cross-strait heavyweights such as Mr Koo Chen-fu of the Straits Exchange Foundation (SEF), Arats' counterpart, who stressed recently the need to do so.

Hence, Mr Chen probably would try to meet Beijing's demand indirectly by saying that he did not object to — or was willing to honour — all agreements reached between Arats and the SEF.

The only affirmative statements from him would be a reiteration of what he had already said before, namely, the "four no's" — no to independence, no to changing the name of the country, no to constitutional amendment to legalise the "two states" theory, and no to holding a plebiscite to determine Taiwan's future.

To appease the pro-independence camp, he would stress that Taiwan was already a sovereign state.

Dragon Lady, A Leader in Her Own Right

7 May 2000

SENIOR members of Taiwan's Democratic Progressive Party have expressed their worries openly about Ms Annette Lu, the fiery woman who is to become the island's Vice-President.

They fear she may cause trouble for the new President, Mr Chen Shui-bian, and aggravate cross-strait tensions.

Indeed the joke among rank-and-file party members is that should Mr Chen be assassinated, his bodyguards should shoot her as well because her taking over the presidency might mean more trouble for Taiwan.

Concern over Ms Lu surfaced long before the Taiwanese went to the polls on March 18. Yet no one expected problems to crop up so soon — even before the inauguration on May 20.

While the President-elect demonstrated a measure of self-restraint in addressing cross-strait issues, his deputy agitated Beijing by declaring that "Taiwan is not part of the People's Republic of China" and that she was not "Chinese" if that was taken to mean a national of the People's Republic of China.

She defined Taiwan as a "distant relative" and "close neighbour" of China instead of belonging to the same family. Her remarks drew very strong reactions from Beijing.

At home, she has allowed the rift between herself and Mr Chen to surface in an important team-building phase. She complained openly that she was being sidelined on all major decisions, including the appointment of the new Premier and the formation of the new Cabinet.

She demanded that Mr Chen return to his election platform calling for a "co-rule by both sexes", or she would initiate a constitutional amendment to scrap the vice-presidency altogether.

Although Mr Chen played down talk of a rift initially, he admitted in public finally that she had not been his first choice as Vice-President.

Few expected Ms Lu, pugnacious as she is, to bring trouble and embarrassment to Mr Chen and the party so soon.

When he picked her as his running mate, the four major factions within the party, including his own, objected strongly. A decision had to be deferred for several months pending intra-party mediation.

Ms Lu is known as a fervent feminist and a staunch supporter of the independence cause. She is also egotistical, once declaring that those who did not vote for her were traitors.

So the question is: Why did Mr Chen pick her? There are at least two theories.

Soon after he announced his choice, New Party convener Lee Ching-hwa postulated that she was President Lee Teng-hui's preferred candidate because she was both strongly pro-independence as well as pro-Japan.

Since President Lee began his annual bid for Taiwan's membership in the United Nations in 1993, she has been his strong supporter. Each year, when the United Nations is in session, she would be in New York mobilising support from the non-government organisations to make Taiwan's voice heard in the world body.

In 1995, when Japan celebrated the 100th anniversary of its victory over China in the Sino-Japanese War that forced China to cede Taiwan to Japan, Ms Lu attended the celebrations, thanking the Japanese for defeating China.

"If not for the war, Taiwan would still be controlled by China," she said at the time.

According to the New Party's Mr Lee, while most Chinese were outraged at what she said, the Taiwanese President praised her for daring to speak her mind.

In choosing Ms Lu, the argument goes, Mr Chen struck a tacit bargain that calls for President Lee to abandon his own party's presidential candidate, Mr Lien Chan.

The other theory has to do with Mr Chen's need to win the backing of pro-independence voters.

Within the pro-independence camp, the so-called fundamentalists regard both the Democratic Progressive Party and Mr Chen as traitors to the sacred cause of founding a new and independent Taiwan.

They were seen to have betrayed their mission by soft-pedalling on the demand for outright independence for the sake of removing the biggest stumbling block in the party's quest for power.

Die-hard supporters of independence were a force not to be dismissed given the intense competition faced by Mr Chen in the presidential race.

There were 150,000 co-signatures in support of the Taiwan Independence Party's run for the presidency, and using the rule of thumb that each signature would bring in two actual votes, the fundamentalist bloc offered a harvest of 300,000 votes.

To ensure that he did not betray their cause, the independence camp insisted that Ms Lu be made Vice-President in return for its full support.

As it turned out, in the final reckoning, Mr Chen won by a slim margin of about 300,000 votes.

There is one fact common to both theories: Ms Lu is the standard-bearer of the battle for Taiwan's independence, instead of Mr Chen.

With her as his No. 2, the independence advocates felt more at ease.

This background perhaps explains why she has dared to challenge Mr Chen — she knows full well that he owed his victory partly to her role in attracting the pro-independence votes.

It also explains her uncompromising attitude towards Beijing.

She has vowed that she will not be a silent Vice-President, and has shown herself true to her words very quickly.

How well the new Taiwan government manages fragile cross-strait relations in the days ahead will depend on many factors, not the least of which will be the ability of Mr Chen to tame his own vice-president.

Chen-Lee to Co-Rule Taiwan?

31 March 2000

Taiwan's President Lee Teng-hui met President-elect Chen Shui-bian yesterday amid an extremely cordial atmosphere in which the outgoing leader passed on important statecraft to his successor.

This was the first time they met after Mr Chen was elected in the presidential polls on March 18.

After the meeting, the President-elect pledged to uphold Mr Lee's principles regarding cross-strait relations, stressing parity and democracy.

He also upheld the incumbent President's view to take greater initiatives to enhance Taiwan's international profile.

These were the most controversial parts of Mr Lee's legacy that had on many occasions plunged Taiwan into a near-war situation with China. Yet, Mr Chen pledged adherence to them.

Obviously, Mr Lee found in him a much loyal follower.

The outgoing President also passed on his experience on a variety of touchy issues.

Mr Chen told the press that he wanted Mr Lee to become Taiwan's peace and human rights envoy. This meant that he would facilitate the outgoing President's overseas visits, in defiance of Beijing's objection.

Right now, Mr Lee can hardly go beyond Taiwan because any such trip would be regarded by Beijing as calculated moves to assert a separate statehood.

Television footage showed Mr Lee going out of his door to wait for Mr Chen a few minutes before the latter's arrival and greeting him heartily on arrival.

He also instructed his steward to make necessary alterations in the doorway so that Mrs Chen, on a wheelchair, could have easier access. This body language showed the intimacy of relations between the two men.

In fact, political observers had indicated before the election that if Mr Chen got elected, Mr Lee would become his coach.

Now that Mr Lee has been dumped by his own party, many believe that a tacit "Chen-Lee" co-rule arrangement was more likely now than a coalition between Mr Chen's Democratic Progressive Party (DPP) and Mr Lee's Kuomintang (KMT).

The appointment of Defence Minister Tang Fei as Premier seemed to confirm this view.

According to the pro-unification United Daily News, President Lee recommended Mr Tang to Mr Chen should his No. 1 choice, Nobel laureate Lee Yuan-tseh, decline the offer of the premiership.

Mr Tang confirmed that before he agreed to take up the offer, he cleared it first with President Lee and obtained the latter's approval.

The pro-independence Taiwan Daily also reported that the whole issue of appointing Mr Tang was "well within President Lee's grip". According to the report, it was only after Mr Lee had been assured that his personnel arrangement would be carried out that he felt comfortable stepping down as KMT Chairman.

Mr Lee also helped clear the way for Mr Tang. As a career soldier loyal to his own party, Mr Tang said that he would take up the offer only if the KMT agreed.

After losing the presidential election battle, the only way for the KMT to exercise power was through the legislature, where it still enjoyed a majority. It could veto the Premier if it wanted to.

Therefore, the KMT wanted to force the DPP to agree to a coalition government. It said that it disallowed members sitting on the new Cabinet unless the DPP reached an overall agreement with the KMT on a coalition government. It blamed the DPP for splitting the KMT by approaching its members on a private and individual basis.

From KMT's point of view, this was not unreasonable. Yet Mr Chen disagreed, for it amounted to sharing power with the KMT.

The KMT was therefore reluctant to approve Mr Tang's appointment. Taipei Mayor Ma Ying-jeou even proposed to mete out penalties to KMT members taking up offers from the DPP without KMT's prior consent.

At this point, President Lee stepped in. He said that the KMT should have the interests of Taiwan, not the party, at heart. Although forced to step down by his own members, he still wielded considerable influence and his remark cleared the way for Mr Tang.

With him as Premier, several of Mr Lee's top confidants, especially those from the National Security Council and National Security Bureau, would also serve the new government.

Thus Mr Lee was providing not just advice but also the necessary talents to help staff Mr Chen's new Cabinet.

Honoured by the President-elect as the "titular head of state" while exercising real control over key personnel, local observers said that an era of "Chen-Lee co-rule" had probably begun.

Chen's Choice of Tang Fei as Premier a Smart Move

30 March 2000

President-elect Chen Shui-bian's appointment of Defence Minister Tang Fei as premier is a smart move in view of the overriding need currently to stabilise Taiwan's military, according to analysts.

The election results have left the military in a dilemma — it is obliged by the constitution to swear allegiance to the president, who is the supreme commander of the army, navy and air force, yet all relevant laws also obliged it to defend the island against both communism and Taiwan independence.

Twelve general-rank military officials had indicated their intention to resign because they "cannot swear loyalty to a president who advocates independence".

Defence Ministry spokesman Kung Fan-ting had also stated that anti-independence education remained a key element in the political work of the military.

Against this background, the appointment of the Defence Minister as Premier would go a long way to quell the strong anti-Chen mood in the military.

Mr Chen could also stabilise the various units directly linked with national security. These included the National Security Council, the Defence Ministry, the National Security Bureau, the National Police Administration, the Investigation Bureau and the Coast Guard.

With a military man as Premier, these units could feel more at ease because there could be smoother transition of classified materials from one party to the other, without fear of creating a security vacuum.

Mr Chen also indicated that he had potential cross-strait crisis in mind.

Given Mr Tang's mainland background and strong anti-independence inclination — typical of the military — Mr Chen hoped that the general could alleviate Beijing's fear that the new government is heading towards independence.

Mr Chen's decision yesterday surprised many people because he was known to be opposed to a government headed by a military man.

When President Lee Teng-hui appointed ex-Defence Minister Hau Pei-tsun as premier in 1990, he waged a strong campaign against the move.

The appointment of Mr Hau was meant to dispel suspicion against Mr Lee in the military. The President came to power in 1988 when the late president Chiang Ching-kuo died. As he was not well entrenched then, he had to rely on Mr Hau to help stabilise the domestic situation.

In the absence of pressure from the outgoing Kuomintang for Mr Tang to reject the offer, the new ruling party remains optimistic. The Director of Organisation of the Democratic Progressive Party (DPP), Mr Kok Chun-min, said that as Defence Minister, Mr Tang had initiated thorough reform within the establishment to make it politically neutral and non-partisan. The DPP therefore had high respect for him.

It's 'One China' Principle or Nothing

29 March 2000

THE secret envoys of Taiwan's President-elect Chen Shui-bian failed to open Beijing's door due to Mr Chen's unwillingness to uphold the "one China" principle.

Sources in Beijing said that as long as Mr Chen refused to acknowledge that Taiwan is part of China, there would be no cross-strait dialogues, whether openly or covertly.

Yet on this crucial point, Mr Chen tried to play semantics.

While Beijing called "one China" a principle, Mr Chen called it an issue, saying that as long as "one China" was an issue but not a principle, he was willing to discuss it.

Vice-president-elect Annette Lu said that as long as "one China" meant cultural China and not political China, she could accept it.

In fact, Beijing even doubted if the pro-independence Democratic Progressive Party president had any sincerity at all in his recent goodwill gestures because he was never willing to call himself a Chinese nor his country China.

They noted that in his 4,000-word statement made after the March 18 election, the name Taiwan was used more than 20 times while its official name, the Republic of China (ROC), was mentioned only once — in connection with his official title, the 10th President of the ROC.

As long as he was evasive on this crucial issue, Beijing would not pay any attention to his goodwill gestures, including the envoys, which Taiwan's right-wing New Party legislator Feng Hu-hsiang claimed were dispatched secretly to the mainland to try to contact or hold discussions with the Beijing authorities.

From official statements issued thus far, as well as the elaboration by ranking officials, Beijing had in fact softened its stance regarding its bottomline.

First, it was prepared to return to the 1992 consensus reached in Hong Kong of "'One China' but defined differently".

When Taiwan President Lee Teng-hui promulgated the "two states theory" last July, China abandoned the consensus.

A willingness to return to the consensus meant that Beijing was willing to allow some flexibility.

Second, in all its statements, emphasis was placed on the prevention of independence rather than the promotion of "unification".

Although this did not mean that it had abandoned the unification ideal, but the more pressing issue now was to prevent independence.

In other words, as long as Taiwan ceased to promote separatism, Beijing was willing to leave the final outcome open-ended.

These two concessions represented Beijing's readjustment to accommodate the new reality following the elections.

Mr Chen announced his own "three no" policies soon after getting elected — no declaration of independence, no constitutional amendment to redefine Taiwan's status and no plebiscite to determine the island's future.

But what Beijing wanted from him was an unequivocal declaration of his adherence to the "one China" principle. Failing this, any envoy would be turned away.

Meanwhile Beijing held a National Conference on Taiwan last week to take stock of the new situation in the island.

On the bright side, according to sources close to the conference, Beijing concluded that three basic elements affecting its Taiwan policy had not changed.

They were the international recognition of the "one China" principle, Beijing's commitment to a peaceful solution, and the majority of Taiwanese still opposed separatism.

Hence there was still room for optimism.

Yet there were also causes for concern.

The separatist policy initiated by President Lee would be succeeded by Mr Chen, who was likely to foster the growth of indigenous Taiwanese nationalism.

The rise to power of the minority DPP would increase political uncertainty and the entire political landscape of Taiwan had been completely changed as a result of the elections.

These dark spots called for greater attention, the conference concluded.

The conference concluded that Mr Chen would try to perpetuate the current state in which there was neither unification nor independence.

This would allow time for the independence movement to gradually erase the cultural and sentimental ties between mainland China and Taiwan, so as to reduce domestic resistance against separatism at home.

Right now, a solid 60 per cent of voters opposed independence.

The tactics of sending envoys to knock at China's door was merely a way to defer unification indefinitely.

However, in so-doing, the island would have to depend heavily on foreign arms supply as well as strong American support.

The key therefore was the US attitude. Sources close to the conference said that China had a good discussion of the likelihood of American intervention in the event of a military solution.

Basically the Chinese would try its best to avoid a direct military confrontation with the US by all means.

However if the US intervened and war against the US became inevitable, China would do all it could to win.

Finally, China was prepared to sacrifice the entire eastern half in order to wage a holy war defending sovereignty and territorial integrity.

The conference noticed that the US was aware of the gravity of the situation and tried to conduct preventive diplomacy by sending envoys to both capitals to calm things down.

This was proof that the US realised its lack of legitimacy to intervene in the event of a war across the strait.

The conclusion following this stock-taking exercise was that China would give peace a chance by waiting for Mr Chen to uphold the "one China" principle, although it did not hold much hope on him.

Should he fail to do so during his inaugural speech, China would unilaterally announce a certain time frame during which political negotiation under the "one China" principle should be conducted.

Beijing will not hold any meetings with him or his representatives before his official swearing-in on May 20, Mr Chen Yunlin, Director of the Taiwan Affairs Office of the State Council, reportedly said.

Meanwhile, preparation for military action would step up.

"For the first time, we are seriously contemplating the use of force," said a ranking official at the national conference.

'New' Chen Offers Ray of Hope for Cross-Strait Ties

22 March 2000

A THIN ray of optimism seems to have appeared over the Taiwan Strait after Taiwan's presidential election chose Mr Chen Shui-bian of the pro-independence Democratic Progressive Party (DPP) as its new President.

Mr Chen, who once chanted "Long live Taiwan's independence" at a campaign rally, seems to be revising his own stand now to make himself less objectionable to China.

For example, the DPP said it would revise its constitution to take out terms such as "Republic of Taiwan" and references to plebiscites.

To dissociate himself from a body that advocates independence, Mr Chen said he would give up all his party posts.

A changeable Chen has now said he was willing to discuss the "one China" problem as long as it was as an issue and not a principle nor a precondition to talks.

As a gesture of his sincerity, he offered to visit China and invited Chinese leaders to see Taiwan.

At the same time, Parliament yesterday agreed to let the islands of Kinmen, Matsu and Penghu conduct direct trade with Fujian.

This means lifting a 50-year-long ban on direct links in trade, transportation and postal communication between the two sides, starting with the small islands.

Beijing has long urged opening up the three direct links to facilitate exchanges.

The Taiwanese also welcome such a move as it reduced greatly the cost of moving people and goods across the strait.

So much for the olive branch. The ball is now clearly in Beijing's court.

Disappointed as it is with the election result, Beijing has greeted the outcome with calm and restraint.

According to sources close to the Chinese authorities, after a thorough study of the situation, Beijing has drawn two conclusions from the election result.

On the bright side, 60 per cent of voters still oppose separatism and the more extreme ones took to the streets demanding the ousting of the chairman of the Kuomintang (KMT), President Lee Teng-hui.

Judging from what they shouted during the demonstrations — "defending the KMT and the Republic of China" — the people are clearly angry with Mr Lee, who tried to terminate both.

This shows that, even after 12 years of rule by a separatist president, the majority in Taiwan still favours unification. To Beijing, this is a consolation.

Another bright spot is that all five candidates urged closer ties with China, including the scrapping of two of Mr Lee's notorious policies, namely the ban on "three direct links" and the "be patience and no haste" policy restricting investments in China.

"This proves a total bankruptcy of the separatist President's policy, which the Taiwanese are reluctant to follow," said Deputy Director Zhou Zhi-huai of the Taiwan Institute, Chinese Academy of Social Science.

Thus, with the President coming from the pro-independence minority, any agreement reached with Beijing regarding "one China" could be accepted easily by the majority which is prounification, he added.

The "Nixon surprise", in which the door of communist China was opened by a United States president who was ardently anti-communist, might be repeated.

If Mr Chen, given his strong pro-independence stance, repeated the same surprise, nobody in Taiwan could accuse him of selling out the interests of Taiwan.

That explained why Beijing was willing to permit Mr Chen a "wait-and-see" grace period. However, this period will not last long.

Its decision will be based on an analysis of Mr Chen's policy statements during the election campaign and how he acts now.

First, Beijing believes the separatist policy will be pursued in an obscure way. Even though the DPP claimed that it was willing to revise its independence programme, Beijing does not believe it is sincere.

"Instead of an outright declaration of independence, Mr Chen's tactics are to toy with semantics so as to blur the focus," Mr Zhou said.

For example, China had said that under the "one China" principle, anything could be discussed. Mr Chen turned it into "if 'one China' is an issue, it could be discussed".

This is said to show his great reluctance to return to the crucial principle underlying cross-strait relations.

Second, Mr Chen would follow Mr Lee's line in pushing forward the so-called "pragmatic diplomacy". He would continue to seek membership of the UN and other international bodies requiring statehood.

Third, on cross-strait ties, he would try to perpetuate the current split because he said openly, after election, that he would seek the legitimisation of the status quo.

Fourth, on bilateral economic relations, he would relax restrictions on trade and investment and take active steps to open up the "three direct links".

Fifth, he would continue to buy arms and seek to forge de facto military alliances with the US and Japan, via the Theatre Missile Defence mechanism.

Although he said he wanted to have a confidence-building mechanism with China and to establish a hotline, he still considers China his main threat and will speed up an arms race.

These suggest that cross-strait relations will enter a period of great uncertainty.

Mr Fang Haiquan, deputy director of the Taiwan Research Centre in southern China's Guangdong province, said China had waited for 20 years and yet it had been rewarded with a pro-independence president.

It would not wait for another 20 years. Most likely, it would wait while making military preparations.

Whether the thin light of optimism will continue to shine on the Taiwan Strait is anyone's guess now.

SECTION

The 2000 Elections

Changing Aspirations of Taiwanese Signal Watershed

30 March 2000

WHETHER outgoing President Lee Teng-hui's resignation as chairman of Kuomintang (KMT) is the sorry outcome of a humiliating election defeat or a watershed in Taiwan politics depends on the perspective from which it is viewed.

As 60 per cent of Taiwanese see it, he is forced to end his political career prematurely after plunging the island into a near-war situation with China and disintegrating his own party.

In the March 18 presidential elections, the KMT suffered a stunning defeat, losing its 51-year hold on power to the pro-independence Democratic Progressive Party (DPP). Disgruntled members demanded that he quit immediately to bear responsibility for the debacle.

However, the other 40 per cent of Taiwanese see him as a national hero who, for the first time in 400 years, has given a separate identity to the Taiwanese and helped transfer top political power from alien sources to indigenous ones.

These diametrically-opposed assessments of Mr Lee reflect a major development in Taiwan: The birth of a new local nationalism out of Chinese soil.

It is the emergence of this new phenomenon, with its full vigour and vitality, that explains the surprise rise to power of the former opposition DPP.

Before the election, most people had thought that it was premature for the pro-independence party to assume power.

The rapid growth of the so-called "Taiwanese nationalism" owes a lot to the democratisation process propelled full steam ahead during President Lee's 12-year-rule.

First, he lifted all the relevant laws banning pro-independence activities in the name of promoting greater freedom of speech and association.

Then, he initiated direct elections at all levels of government so that political power transferred naturally from the mainlanders, who are numerically smaller, to the locals.

Finally, he introduced changes in cultural and educational fields to help foster the local character. The changes made to school textbooks, in particular, helped fade out the island's historical, cultural and geographic ties with China.

While Beijing regarded all these measures suspiciously as being separatist in nature, the Taiwanese considered them as policy adjustments to reflect accurately the changes taking place within Taiwan.

The population has changed. Fifty per cent of the voters in the March 18 election were below 40, born in Taiwan and with little connection with China. The traditional bonds between the two sides are bound to be loose.

Their lot has changed. With a per capita income 10 times that of their counterparts in the Chinese mainland, there is little incentive for Taiwan to merge with China.

Their aspirations have changed. Taiwanese feel that after half a century's hard work, they have finally come of age. They expect the world to accord them the same respect and dignity that all other nations enjoy and yet this legitimate demand is denied them because of China's inflexibility.

It is, therefore, not surprising to find that some of the world's best-known figures who originated from Taiwan have a natural inclination towards independence.

Nobel laureate Lee Yuan-tseh is a typical example. Despite his very cordial relations with Beijing, he expressed his full support for the pro-independence DPP candidate, President-elect Chen Shui bian.

Similarly, Mr Stanley Shih, chairman of the Acer Group, one of the world's largest producers of personal computers and laptops, also expressed open support for Mr Chen although most of his computers are manufactured in China.

Indeed, there is a long list of indigenous Taiwanese, apart from Dr Lee and Mr Shih, who have risen to world-class fame.

However, the rapid rise in world status of Taiwanese individuals is not matched by a similar rise in the island's international profile. Most times, Taipei is shut out of the world's important forums because of Beijing.

This incongruity contributes to a growing aspiration to claim separate statehood. As greater numbers of Taiwanese reach out to the world, the stronger is this aspiration.

These demographic, socio-economic and psychological changes in Taiwan that have taken place since the late 1970s prepared the fertile ground for the growth of the new fervour.

With or without President Lee, the indigenous sense of pride will grow, but the President catalysed it. In 1991, an overwhelming 80 per cent of people called themselves Chinese. By last year, the figure had dropped to 57 per cent. In the same period, those who called themselves Taiwanese increased from 16 per cent to 38 per cent.

This sharp change in the people's self-perception could not have been achieved within a decade if not for Mr Lee's catalytic role.

Beijing's insensitivity to the emerging aspiration of the Taiwanese, as well as its intimidation, serves to fan this nascent sense of pride.

It is the rise of this Taiwanese fervour that sent the DPP to the presidential palace, much earlier than expected. In turn, the DPP victory will give further momentum to its growth.

The more hawkish Vice-President-elect, Ms Annette Lu, gave an address in English proclaiming the birth of "a new nation", defying American warnings against provocation. This high-flying mood is typical of newly-emerging states in the initial days of the nation-building process.

The potential implication is serious. Unlike in the past, it is no longer a handful of foreign-backed separatists questioning Chinese legitimacy to claim Taiwan, but a new nation-building spirit growing out of local soil and with widespread support asking for separate statehood.

In short, it is "Taiwanese nationalism" pitted against Chinese nationalism, an issue that clearly calls for sensitive handling.

The attempt by the DPP, now in power, to try to abrogate its independence programme is certainly a move more than welcome. In this respect, Beijing's willingness to allow time for the DPP to disentangle itself from the independence clause will certainly help.

Why Teng-hui Destroyed the KMT Party

28 March 2000

MOST Western media interpret Taiwan's presidential elections, won by the pro-independence Democratic Progressive Party (DPP), as either the victory of democracy or the victory of David (the courageous Taiwanese) against the mammoth Goliath (the intimidation of mainland China).

These views, however, tend to ignore two key facts.

First, the level of support for the DPP has not gone up.

Second, it is the split within the Kuomintang (KMT), rather than the success of the DPP, that contributes to the latter's victory.

Taiwan's election history shows that in all island-wide elections — including those for president, governor, legislators and national assembly delegates — the DPP has had an insurmountable barrier limiting its votes to below 40 per cent.

It clinched its best result during the March 18 presidential polls, winning 39.3 per cent. But this was an improvement of only 0.6 percentage point over the 38.7 per cent it obtained in the provincial governor election six years ago.

Thus it is simply too superficial to hail DPP's victory either as a "David versus Goliath" type victory, or that of democracy.

The DPP's insurmountable barrier is its own independence programme.

Fully aware of its crippling effect, the party's candidate Chen Shui-bian pacified his own people and the international community immediately on being elected President, saying he is not going to declare independence.

His own manifesto, together with the fact that 60 per cent of the population voted against independence, shows that the "David-Goliath" analogy was fallacious.

Neither do the mainstream views ask a crucial question: Why should the losing KMT abandon a sure-win ticket lining up Vice-President Lien Chan with former Governor James Soong, as demanded by its rank-and-file members.

The two men together obtained 59.9 per cent of total votes, way ahead of Mr Chen. Thus if the KMT was not split, it was almost a certainty that the DPP would not have won.

This in turn begs a more pertinent question: Why should President Lee Teng-hui, also chairman of the KMT, go against the wishes of his own members by rejecting a Lien-Soong ticket.

Of course, no one knows the exact reason.

Yet, by piecing together bits of well-known facts, a fairly reasonable picture emerges.

First, Mr Lee is a man of vision and his vision is Taiwanese independence. This explains why he once likened himself to the biblical Moses who took the Jews out of Egypt.

His own vision makes him more akin ideologically to the DPP than the KMT. It also explains why he adopted many of the proposals put forward by the DPP. Political gossip has it that Mr Lee is KMT chairman during the day and DPP chairman at night.

Furthermore, he does not have any affection for the party of which he is chairman.

He once called it disdainfully "an alien authority" that came to rule Taiwan. A century-old party was, in his eyes, only "two or three years old".

In contrast, he contributed to the growth of the DPP by various means, including monetary, in the name of promoting party politics. The DPP, on its part, never denies that it "feeds on KMT milk".

This sentimental attachment to the DPP instead of the KMT also explains a curious psyche of President Lee.

In elections, he would rather sacrifice his party's candidate in favour of a DPP candidate if the KMT man is relatively weak and if both of them are facing a common challenge from less-independence-minded candidates.

This, in Taiwanese politics, is called qi-bao (abandon-save) strategic voting, a form of political manoeuvring unique to Taiwan and started by Mr Lee.

He first used it in the 1994 Taipei mayoral race and again in the 2000 presidential elections. In both instances, Mr Chen was the beneficiary.

In a 1995 overseas visit, Mr Lee said one of his dreams was to effect a peaceful transfer of power before he died. Its exact meaning had long been a riddle in Taiwanese politics. The KMT interpreted this as a peaceful transfer of power from the older to the younger generation. The DPP said it meant a peaceful transfer of power from the KMT to the DPP.

Now, five years later, the answer is finally revealed. After Mr Chen's win at the presidential polls, Mr Lee congratulated the DPP and hailed the successful transfer of power as a hallmark of democracy.

In DPP's road to power, the biggest stumbling block had been Mr James Soong who is known to be pro-unification. As a mainlander, he enjoys a support level close to, if not exceeding, that of President Lee himself.

For example, Mr Soong received 56 per cent of votes in the 1994 provincial elections while Mr Lee got 54 per cent in the 1996 presidential elections. As the constituencies for both elections were largely the same, it means he was as strong, if not stronger, than Mr Lee.

The just-ended presidential elections proves this point.

Without any party support, Mr Soong still managed to get 36.8 per cent, against DPP's 39.3 and KMT's 22.1 per cent.

If Mr Soong were to pair up with Mr Lien, there would have been little chance for a peaceful transfer of power during Mr Lee's lifetime from the KMT to the DPP.

In fact, this was exactly DPP's worry before the election. The party's campaign advertisement had appealed for votes, saying it took decades to groom a man the calibre of Mr Chen. Should he fail this time, it would take the DPP at least another decade to bring up another candidate like him, it reasoned.

Now 77, President Lee might not have been able to realise his dream before he dies. This was probably why he tried to remove the obstacle on the DPP's behalf.

Initially, he and Mr Soong were on good terms. He even said once that there were two persons he liked most — his granddaughter and Mr Soong.

But, according to a Soong confidant, their relations soured as soon as Mr Lee found that both of them had basic differences, which surfaced over the Diaoyutai dispute in the early 1990s.

Mr Soong reportedly said Taiwan could perhaps tie up with China against Japan in solving the Diaoyutai dispute.

Given the anti-mainland and strongly pro-Japan mentality of the president, this casual remark sounded a warning note that the honeymoon between them was to end soon.

When the election results showed that Mr Soong was as popular as himself, they hardened Mr Lee's determination to remove him.

Without Mr Soong's prior knowledge, the president reached a consensus with the DPP to scrap the provincial structure, cutting the ground from under the then governor's feet. This hopelessly humiliating move led to Mr Soong leaving the KMT eventually.

Thus Mr Lee helped the DPP to remove the largest obstacle to power.

Though chairman of the KMT, he chose to collude with the DPP in pursuit of his vision of an independent Taiwan and wrecked his own party towards that end.

It was after losing the election that many KMT members woke up to the dire fact that they had been cheated by their own chairman. This explained the furious 120-hour demonstration held spontaneously by the rank and file demanding that Mr Lee stepped down.

Mission accomplished, the former KMT chairman is only too happy to let someone else take over the party's helm.

Teng-hui's Legacy — Good and Bad

25 March 2000

TAIWAN President Lee Teng-hui stepped down as Kuomintang's chairman yesterday, leaving a legacy of democratisation, a proliferation of "black-gold politics" and erroneous cross-strait policies.

It is hard to size up the President as Taiwanese society is divided sharply along the unification-independence rift, and anything he does necessarily draws support and criticism from different sectors.

Nevertheless, one can still identify several areas over which there is no dispute.

Taiwan's society is basically democratised. Thanks to Mr Lee's strong determination and unrelenting efforts, it has become one of the most democratised societies in the world. The people enjoy freedom of words and deeds unparalleled in any other Chinese community.

The government is transparent and the flow of information is uninhibited. The vibrant press performs an effective role of check and balance on the government.

Most important of all, the people enjoy their full right to choose top leaders via truly free elections.

Observers from law-abiding societies would be stunned to find highly-placed politicians making libellous and irresponsible allegations against political foes.

Another undisputed, but unenviable, legacy of Mr Lee's is the proliferation of "black-gold politics", or political corruption.

His predecessors, the late Presidents Chiang Kai-shek and son Chiang Ching-kuo, learnt from hard experience in the Chinese mainland that corruption could lead to the demise of an empire.

During the Chiangs' rule, they were very strict in preventing a coalition of politics, money and the underworld. People with gangland connections were forbidden to render public services.

Under Mr Lee's rule, however, this vigilance dissipated. He personally has to take responsibility for this.

During his time, the two most popular ministers of justice resigned in protest against top-level interventions to stop investigations into major syndicates.

According to official statistics, 11 per cent of national assembly delegates, legislators as well as county councillors have underworld links. Yet, whenever this problem was brought up to his attention, the President was impatient.

He once said: "If one talks about an issue for many years without being able to resolve it, why can't we change our mindset and accept it as part of our culture?

"Take vote bribery as an example. Can't we view it from another angle? Just as we give offerings to God several times a year, can't we treat vote bribery as dedication to our voters once every several years?"

This permissive attitude of the President's explains why "black gold" is so rampant in Taiwan.

In the just-ended presidential election, "black gold" was the single most important domestic issue addressed by all candidates.

A third undisputed fact was that Mr Lee's cross-strait policy is basically wrong.

No matter how the independence-minded sector reveres him as the greater defender of Taiwan's separate identity and sovereignty, the fact is that all his cross-strait policies are abandoned.

None of his successors, be it Kuomintang's Lien Chan or opposition Democratic Progressive Party's (DPP) Chen Shui-bian, dared to uphold his "two states" theory during their election campaigns. The theory almost plunged the island into a war situation.

Instead, the two men pledged a return to the 1992 consensus reached between governments on both sides of the strait regarding the "one China" principle, but defined it differently.

In other words, Taiwan is back to square one after several years of meaningless effort to depart from that consensus.

They also openly scrapped his "no haste, be patient" policy restricting Taiwanese investment in China, as well as his policies banning direct links in trade, transportation and postal communications.

Towards the end of his 12-year rule, the legislature enacted a law, against the Cabinet's wish, legalising the three direct links on a smaller scale benefiting several frontal islands.

This is good evidence that people are fed up with Mr Lee's unrealistic policy and it heralds a full-scale opening up after the President's departure.

Public opinions over other policy areas are more divided. For example, a popular criticism coming from Mr Lee's own party is that although he brought about full democracy to his people, he was in fact extremely dictatorial within the party.

Roughly a third of the standing body of the central committee, KTM's decision-making organ, is appointed by him. Another third is recommended by him, leaving the rest to be truly elected. In such an instance, hardly any check and balance on the President can be exercised.

The fatal failure of the recent presidential elections is the direct result of this dictatorship. Although many rank-and-file members wanted Vice-President Lien Chan to pair with former governor James Soong, which they considered a sure-win ticket, the President refused, due to personal grievances against the latter.

The election result proved the point. Together, Mr Lien and Mr Soong obtained 60 per cent of total votes, way ahead of Mr Chen.

If the President had not been so high-handed, the party would not have lost its ruling position and he would not have to step down.

His dictatorial style also extends to other areas of public life.

During his reign, he revised the Constitution six times, each increasing his own power but reducing others' ability to exercise any check and balance on him.

After all these amendments, the President is virtually above everyone else.

He appoints or has influence over the choice of the No. 1 man of all the branches of government, as well as the Speaker of the National Assembly.

In short, the President gives his people power, and he amasses even more power in his own hands.

Now that his party has abandoned him, he feels more relaxed in supporting the independence movement. A source close to him told the press that he could now speak his mind and do whatever he likes. This is taken to mean that he would work more openly for independence.

Yet it is dubious if he could still exert any influence at all because even the DPP would consider him a liability as far as cross-strait relations is concerned.

Lee's Jekyll-and-Hyde Moves Fracture KMT

23 March 2000

OUTSIDE the headquarters of Taiwan's former ruling Kuomintang (KMT) yesterday, angry party members gathered for the fifth consecutive day to demand that their chairman, President Lee Teng-hui, step down.

The reason: Mr Lee sold the KMT out to the opposition Democratic Progressive Party (DPP) and rank-and-file members have a bitter sense of being cheated by their own leader.

In contrast, at an American Chamber of Commerce gathering, an elated Julian Kok, policy adviser to DPP candidate and President-elect Chen Shui-bian, told a perplexed group of US businessmen that the party had indeed the KMT chairman to thank for its victory at last Saturday's presidential polls.

The reason: "Have you not heard a political joke that the KMT chairman is at the same time moonlighting for the DPP?" Dr Kok asked the US group which did not seem to understand why the DPP gained power so soon.

Dr Kok's frank reply confirmed a popular saying that Mr Lee was "KMT chairman during the day and DPP chairman at night" and thus explained the fury of the protesting KMT members.

In a book by British novelist R. L. Stevenson (1854–1890), The Strange Case Of Dr Jekyll And Mr Hyde, a man behaved diametrically different in different circumstances. President Lee is a real-life example.

As President of the Republic of China (ROC), the name Taiwan calls itself, his job should be to uphold the ROC Constitution and name China. Yet, during Mr Lee's 12-year rule, he repealed all the relevant laws barring independence and as a result, separatism became a very vibrant movement.

As the initiator of the Guidelines for National Unification, he should be staffing his team with like-minded people. Yet important posts in his National Unification Committee and National Policy Advisers were given to prominent advocates of independence.

As KMT chairman, his job should be to strengthen the party's ruling position. Yet he gave active financial support to the DPP in its natal stage. The latter did not deny that it "feeds on KMT milk".

Mr Lee even said openly that one of his dreams was to see a peaceful transfer of power (from the KMT to the DPP) before he died.

Five years ago, then-DPP chairman Shih Ming-teh said that perhaps Mr Lee's most important contribution to Taiwanese democracy was to bring about a disintegration of the KMT.

Indeed, during the President's 12 years in power, he conducted several rounds of purges that drastically weakened and split the KMT.

The last and most fatal of all was the purge of former KMT general secretary James Soong who, despite his mainland origin, enjoyed great support from local Taiwanese. For this reason, the DPP eyed him as the most formidable stumbling block to power.

To serve the DPP's interests, Mr Lee rejected the Lien-Soong ticket against the majority will of party members.

The result was as expected: a heavily-split KMT enabled the DPP to win the election by an extremely narrow margin of only 3 per cent.

Mr Lee's mission, and the DPP's target, was accomplished but, with it, the KMT also crumbled to pieces.

After the elections, the KMT was split into four factions. Those members from the military and those with mainland backgrounds strongly demanded that Mr Lee step down immediately.

Among them were 12 general-grade military men who said openly that they would resign because, as long-time defenders of the ROC, they could not swear loyalty to an independent-minded president.

They wanted Mr Soong to return to the KMT and to help fuse the party together. Although the independent candidate had openly declined such a possibility, they did not give up this hope.

Many of them also expressed their determination to join Mr Soong's party if one was formed.

Another faction was made up mostly of those who had fought the hard election battle for Vice-President Lien Chan. They too wanted to see Mr Lee stepping down immediately and replaced by Mr Lien.

Most of them represented the younger generation of KMT members who wanted reform and less provocative cross-strait policies.

For example, Taipei Mayor Ma Ying-jeou proposed a four-point programme, the first of which was the immediate resignation of the standing committee, including Mr Lee.

The third faction is more supportive of the President and thought that, despite losing the election battle, he should be allowed to step down in honour and at a time he deemed fit because there should be a smooth transfer of power.

They supported Mr Lee's proposal to set up, under his direction, a "Party Restructuring Committee" to see how it could be revamped.

This proposal was rejected by the other two factions as impractical. "One simply cannot have the patient performing an operation on himself," said pro-Lien KMT member Chen Shue-shing.

The last faction belonged to the diehard Lee supporters.

They took out full-page advertisements in newspapers detailing Mr Lee's contribution in the past years and blaming Mr Soong for causing the party to end up in such a miserable state.

This last group of people is most likely to defect to the DPP if Mr Lee steps down in a humiliating way.

Although the KMT has pledged to reform itself and make a come-back four years later, most of its members are pessimistic right now.

Uppermost is the lack of leadership at the top. A KMT member joked that there are only four KMT members at national level: President Lee, Vice-President Lien, former Governor Soong and Mayor Ma. In other words, there is a dearth of political stars that could help unite the party.

Then there is the ideological split as to whether the KMT should preserve its China identity or be fully localised.

The two factions supporting Mr Soong and Mr Lien are more inclined to have a KMT with a China flavour while the other two prefer a much more localised KMT. Unless this split is settled, there will be no clear direction for future reform.

Right now, scrambling for the huge party assets rather than revamping the party seems to be of more immediate concern as each faction wants to get the lion's share.

Until these problems are resolved, reform is still nowhere in sight.

The End of KMT's Half-Century Rule

20 March 2000

COME May 20, President Lee Teng-hui will end his 12-year rule of Taiwan, and with it, his own party's grip on power for the last half a century.

In last Saturday's presidential elections, the ruling Kuomintang (KMT) suffered a disastrous and humiliating rout at the hands of the opposition Democratic Progressive Party (DPP).

The KMT obtained only a dismal 23.1 per cent of the total vote, way below the historical average of about 60 per cent. The DPP grabbed 39.3 per cent, while former KMT heavyweight and former provincial governor James Soong garnered 36.8 per cent.

Angry rank-and-file party members gathered outside KMT headquarters and the presidential residence for almost 24 hours demanding that Mr Lee step down as party chairman immediately to take responsibility for the debacle. The President will resign from his powerful position in September.

The protesters insisted that they would respect the election outcome, but that they held President Lee personally responsible for the rout.

They blamed him for ignoring widespread calls from the rank and file earlier on for a "Lien-Soong" ticket in the presidential elections and instead doing all he could to stop such a team-up from materialising.

When Mr Soong defied party orders to run as an independent candidate, Mr Lee mounted a massive attack against him.

The most damaging was the so-called slush-funds scandal, which led to a sharp drop in support for Mr Soong, who had been a clear frontrunner until then.

So even though he survived the mudslinging campaign, he never managed to regain the lead he had enjoyed.

After failing to knock Mr Soong out of the race, Mr Lee turned to the qi-bao strategy to prevent him from getting elected.

This is an election tactic in which one sacrifices (qi) one's preferred candidate in order to save (bao) a lesser one.

Had it not been for these election tricks, Mr Soong would surely have won the election, losing as he did to Mr Chen by only a narrow three percentage points.

KMT members, furious to see the party's power transferred to a pro-independence DPP, accused Mr Lee of double-dealing. They insisted that he had been supporting the DPP's Mr Chen Shui-bian all along while paying lip service to supporting KMT candidate Lien Chan.

Mr Chen's election victory only seemed to confirm this long-standing suspicion many people harboured against Mr Lee.

For one thing, they doubt that he has any affection for the party of which he is chairman.

In an interview with the late Japanese writer Ryotaro Shiba in 1993, he had called the KMT an alien authority that came to rule Taiwan.

He also regarded the party, which has been in existence for a century, as being only several years old (counting only the period after he became party chairman).

In 1994, he said that one of his dreams was to effect a peaceful transfer of power before he died.

People read his remarks as meaning the transfer of power from the KMT to the DPP, or from a party representing reunification to one standing for independence.

Hence, the people's rage when the DPP knocked the KMT off its ruling perch on Saturday.

The president has not hidden his close relationship with Mr Chen, the DPP's rising star who had been found drunk in the president's residence on one occasion.

In a frank admission to another Japanese writer Katsuhiko Eguchi in 1997, he revealed that his ideal successor was Mr Chen.

During the 1994 Taipei mayoral election, Mr Lee dumped the KMT's weak candidate in favour of Mr Chen so as to deny victory to the candidate of the New Party.

KMT members said that the same thing happened for the presidential elections.

Seeing that the KMT's Mr Lien had a slim chance of winning while Mr Soong was still a very strong contender despite the slush-funds scandal, Mr Lee orchestrated a similar move by sacrificing the KMT's own candidate.

The signal to switch votes came a week before ballot day.

Mr Hsu Wen-lung, a close friend of the President and a pro-independence entrepreneur, called a press conference to say that Mr Chen, and not Mr Lien, was best placed to implement the President's policy. This caused die-hard Lee supporters to vote for Mr Chen.

The pro-independence Taiwan Daily published an article in which it hailed a "peaceful transfer of power" and expressed the hope that with Moses at the helm, Joshua would be able to implement his line.

Mr Lee has likened himself to the biblical Moses who led the Jews out of Egypt. He has also asked Mr Chen to study the works of Joshua, Moses' successor.

A mainstream newspaper, the Industrial and Commercial Times, said that while the KMT suffered a disastrous defeat, Mr Lee had realised his own dream.

It was this deliberate move to let the pro-independence DPP gain power that caused the uproar among the KMT's rank-and-file members.

Thus the massive demonstration outside the KMT headquarters and the presidential residence could be seen as a majority vote against separatism.

Endorsement, Threat Swung Votes

19 March 2000

THE hardy opposition Democratic Progressive Party (DPP) probably has both Nobel laureate Lee Yuan-tseh and Chinese Premier Zhu Rongji to thank for Mr Chen Shui-bian's come-from-behind victory.

Mr Chiu I-ren, the former DPP general secretary, believes Dr Lee brought the party an extra 5 per cent of the votes while Premier Zhu, with his verbal threat, contributed another 3 per cent.

Now the party's campaign manager, he was referring to Dr Lee's sacrifice — the latter had abandoned his academic neutrality and sided politically with Mr Chen.

The open endorsement by the renowned academic tipped the balance in Mr Chen's favour.

Mr Zhu's warning also helped because it backfired. Mr Chiu believes that by intimidating the Taiwanese, the Chinese leader drew an antagonistic response from the public.

"Mr Zhu forced a siege mentality upon us. If we succumb this time, we shall have to accept the 'one country, two systems' formula next time," he argued.

"To be sure, there are some supporters who were intimidated and we lost their votes but, at the same time, some undecided votes flowed in our direction.

"On balance, we gained more votes than would otherwise be the case."

Professor You Ying-kun, another Chen campaign manager, attributed the success to the party's wise tactical deployment.

"We know perfectly well that unless the ruling Kuomintang splits, we shall have no chance at all because all past records showed that the DPP could never muster more than 40 per cent of votes in any national-level elections", he said.

Prof You felt that since Mr Soong was splitting the KMT vote, the DPP strategy was to prevent neither of the pan-KMT candidates, the other being Vice-President Lien Chan, from being knocked out prematurely.

"This explains why we did not hit Soong hard over his slush fund scandal," Prof You revealed.

The finely-balanced tripartite relationship was maintained till the very last week, when the DPP delivered its deadly blow by unveiling Dr Lee as its cross-strait adviser.

Mr Chiu also listed reasons why the DPP's victory is significant:

It is the first time that power has been transferred from an alien source to a local authority.

"For the first time in 400 years, Taiwan has a government of its own," he declared.

The DPP victory, he noted, also signified the maturity of Taiwan's democratic development, which emphasised a peaceful transfer of the country's top political power based on the mandate of the people.

Jubilant as its members are feeling right now, the DPP will prove to the Taiwanese as well as the international community that it is a responsible party.

Now that the DPP is in power, both Beijing as well as mainlanders residing in the island will feel "quite uncomfortable".

"If the DPP fails to alleviate their worries, it will make life for everybody rather difficult," he said.

The party's immediate concern is to line up a credible Cabinet.

It is no secret that the DPP lacks expertise in administration at the national level.

The party will therefore rely heavily on the reputation of Dr Lee to help it recruit the necessary talent.

Though the task is unenviable, the DPP is extremely upbeat in facing the challenges ahead.

China's Warning ... Still Room for Peace

18 March 2000

CHINESE Premier Zhu Rongji's stern warning against Taiwanese independence, regarded by many analysts as a move before making a formal war declaration, has caused widespread concern in Taiwan and in the region.

Taipei responded by upgrading the state of military alertness. In Washington, a cautious US government summoned the Chinese ambassador to express its concern.

Japan studied the potential implications under the Joint US-Japan Defence Guidelines, while the Asean countries were concerned whether the next target after Taiwan would be the South Sea.

Yet a closer look at Mr Zhu's statement, and the elaboration by Mr Tang Shuibei of China's Association for Relations Across the Taiwan Strait (Arats) showed that there was still room for conciliation. Arats is a semi-official organisation set up to handle cross-strait relations.

Dr Wei Yung, professor of political science at the National Chiao Tung University, said that people should be cool-headed and study China's last offer for peace carefully.

According to him, several important facts emerged from the White Paper, Mr Zhu's remarks and Mr Tang's elaboration.

First, the bottomline is that there shall be no separation. All forms of Taiwanese independence, whether in explicit or implicit forms, will not be tolerated.

Second, under the "one China" principle, nothing could not be negotiated. This included the definition of "one China" and Beijing's reunification formula of "one country, two systems". Dr Wei considered these as major concessions on Beijing's part.

Third, the so-called reunification time-table could be extremely flexible so long as Taiwan is not heading towards independence.

"Reunification takes time, but to wage a war against separatism takes only 24 hours," Mr Tang has said.

Dr Wei concluded that despite using harsh words, Beijing still left the door wide open for a peaceful solution.

"From Beijing's point of view, it was not exacting unacceptable terms," he said. "It was merely asking for the same set of values which Taiwan previously adhered to."

When Taiwanese President Lee Teng-hui came to power, he promulgated the 1992 Guidelines for National Unification in which the "one China" principle was upheld and eventual unification was a clearly stated objective.

Furthermore, both sides reached in 1992 a consensus to uphold the "one China" principle, leaving its definition open to interpretation.

It was Mr Lee's departure from his own guidelines and the consensus by formulating the "two states" theory last July that caused the current tension.

Thus, Dr Wei concluded that any new president who returned to the guidelines and consensus stood a good chance of avoiding war.

He pointed out that even the pro-independence Democratic Progress Party (DPP) was aware of this last chance for peace.

Mr Chen Shui-bian, the opposition party's presidential candidate, had indicated to the foreign press that he was willing to accept "one China" and "reunification".

Unfortunately, his remarks seemed only for foreign consumption. As the DPP has not openly announced this new flexibility at home, what Mr Chen said was no better than any other election gimmick.

Since war was not inevitable, Dr Wei suggested that all parties concerned be extremely sober in facing the volatile situation.

First, the Taiwanese voters should choose their president carefully, by asking themselves what they wanted exactly.

Then the president-elect should be serious about addressing China's concern.

Finally, Taiwan's important allies, including the US and Japan, should recognise that there was an obvious chance for peaceful solution and should influence the course of development in the right direction.

Dr Wei predicted that even if Mr Chen got elected today, Beijing would not use force immediately but would state two obvious conditions for peace.

First, there should be an open and unequivocal pledge by Mr Chen to return to the "one China" principle, leaving no room for the DPP to toy with jargon.

Second, it would set a certain time-frame to start political negotiation.

Chen May Benefit From Zhu's Warning

17 March 2000

CHINESE Premier Zhu Rongji's strongly-worded warning against any attempt at independence by Taiwan may not be totally unfavourable to pro-independence presidential candidate Chen Shui-bian in the island's polls tomorrow.

What appears to be detrimental to the Democratic Progressive Party's (DPP) Chen at first view is now expected to work for him.

The fearsome style with which Mr Zhu delivered the warning alienated almost all Taiwanese, who might now express their anger by picking the one Beijing dislikes the most.

The DPP is clearly turning this widespread outrage into support for itself, while continuing to stress its readiness to compromise on its sacred goal of independence, so as to be even more sure of victory.

Taiwanese Vice-President Lien Chan of the ruling Kuomintang (KMT) has made use of China's threat to prove his point that electing Mr Chen means choosing war with China.

However, he does not dare to carry this tactic too far lest he elicits an outpouring of disgust, which might be translated into further support for the DPP.

Independent candidate James Soong has stressed that neither Mr Lien nor Mr Chen can eliminate the threat from China as Mr Chen advocates independence, while Mr Lien supports the "two states theory", which China loathes.

Unfortunately, Mr Soong's mainland origin has become a distinct liability at a time when public opinion is dead set against Beijing.

Most commentaries in the Taiwanese press agree that Beijing is trying to reverse the momentum that Mr Chen now enjoys following the open support given to him by highly-regarded Nobel laureate Dr Lee Yuan-tseh last Friday.

The different camps estimate that Dr Lee's move will add at least three to five percentage points to Mr Chen's original support level, giving the DPP candidate sufficient votes to clinch a victory.

Mr Hsu Wan loong of Chi Mei Enterprise, known for his close ties to President Lee Teng-hui, has said openly that Mr Chen is the most able person to implement the line of the president.

His remark confirms for the first time what is known as the "Moses-Joshua relationship" in Taiwanese politics.

President Lee had likened himself to the biblical Moses who led the Israelites out of Egypt. When Mr Chen was defeated in the 1998 Taipei mayoral race, Mr Lee told him to study the works of Joshua, Moses' successor, who eventually helped build the Jewish nation.

Mr Hsu's statement proves that a long-suspected tactic called *qi bao* (to abandon in order to support) has been in play.

Believing that Mr Chen is Mr Lee's preferred successor, voters might now be persuaded to abandon Mr Lien and support Mr Chen.

This explains why Premier Zhu had deemed the Taiwanese President a manipulator.

For the first time, people think Mr Chen might win the election. The local stock market has responded with a precipitous plunge.

The turn of events has alarmed Beijing, and it was obliged to make a strong statement through Mr Zhu.

Although it is impossible to ascertain the impact of Mr Zhu's warning on the election result, some things can be predicted.

Firstly, whoever is elected has to abandon independence as a political goal, although the way he goes about it must be acceptable at home. He must at least pay lip service to the notion of "one China".

The winner also has to enter into political negotiations with Beijing, which entails not just discussion over practical issues, but also a speeding up of the whole process.

He also cannot remain evasive on the issue of unification. Until now, all the three major candidates had refrained from talking about the possibility of unification as their ultimate goal.

It is hard for these delaying tactics to be used further.

Beijing will watch out for these three elements in the inaugural speech of the new president to decide if there will be peace or war.

The Undecided Will Rule

12 March 2000

WITH a week to go before Taiwanese voters go to the polls on Saturday, the essentially three-cornered presidential race remains a tight one, with none of the leading candidates able to muster a convincing lead.

The most recent opinion polls, which have ceased since Wednesday, under a law banning them 10 days before the presidential election, showed that each of the big three would draw about a quarter of the total votes.

So it would be a really close call for the ruling Kuomintang's Lien Chan, independent candidate James Soong and the Democratic Progressive Party's Chen Shui-bian.

Two other candidates — the New Party's Li Ao and independent candidate Hsu Hsin-liang — have been languishing in the opinion polls and are unlikely to produce an upset.

While the polls, conducted by various newspapers and bodies, provided no clues at all as to who the eventual winner will be, they nevertheless elicited some interesting trends.

For example, they showed that the alleged slush fund scandal did hurt Mr Soong, who saw support for his candidacy plunge from a high of 38 per cent in the middle of last year to about 26 per cent.

Although an official investigation conducted after the allegations surfaced did not uncover anything improper, the damage done to the former Taiwan governor's erstwhile clean image had already been done.

But what makes Mr Soong such a formidable contender is that despite the scandal and strong attacks from both the ruling Kuomintang (KMT) and the opposition Democratic Progressive Party (DPP), he has managed to keep his support level in the region of 25 to 28 per cent. Such is the popularity of the former KMT stalwart.

His track record during his tenure as the island's provincial governor is the basis for his strong showing.

Widespread public dissatisfaction with the ruling KMT and the DPP's pro-independence stance gained him more supporters.

By comparison, KMT candidate and current Vice-President Lien Chan has come across as bland.

Yet, he has made an impressive comeback in recent months. Polls showed support for him climbing steadily from below 15 per cent just six months ago to an all-time high of 27 per cent recently.

This spectacular rise was thanks largely to the KMT's grassroots mobilisation machinery, the tough disciplinary measures taken against expelled pro-Soong party members, as well as to President Lee Teng-hui, who has campaigned on Mr Lien's behalf on many occasions.

To be sure, Mr Lien lacks the charisma of his rivals, Mr Soong and Mr Chen.

But through some clever packaging, this "weakness" has been turned into positive attributes — steadiness and thoughtfulness.

Such qualities appeal greatly to those Taiwanese who do not want to rock the boat or who believe that the KMT remains the best party able to ensure the island's peace and prosperity.

The DPP's Mr Chen has been ranked mostly second in popularity polls, surpassing Mr Soong only on one or two occasions.

There is a limit to the support that the DPP can garner. Since the introduction of free elections in Taiwan, the DPP has made impressive gains in local elections, but has yet been able to muster more than 35 per cent of total votes at the national level.

This is because national-level elections are more likely to be dominated by cross-strait issues and the opposition party is handicapped by its pro-independence stance.

Given the deadlock even at this late stage of the election campaign, there is an election strategy that is likely to weigh on the minds of the candidates over the next few days — the so-called *qi-bao* (dump-save) effect.

In the 1994 Taipei mayoral race, pro-KMT voters were told to dump the party's weak candidate and cast their votes instead for the DPP's Mr Chen, who defeated the rival candidate from the New Party.

Four years later, the New Party abandoned its own candidate in favour of the KMT's Ma Ying-jeou, who then ousted incumbent mayor Mr Chen.

Since it is a deadly tactic, each candidate tries his utmost to prevent himself from getting "dumped".

Given the bad blood between Mr Soong and President Lee, the most talked-about scenario in recent days is one in which Mr Lee will sacrifice both the KMT candidate and party interests in order to help Mr Chen win, thus denying Mr Soong victory on Saturday.

Such a drastic measure seems irrational as it will cause the KMT to lose its ruling position for the first time in five decades and has been dismissed vehemently by the pro-Lien camp.

Yet no serious political observer can rule out such a possibility entirely, given the precedent was set in the 1994 Taipei mayoral race.

The DPP is banking on a repeat of this strategy. This perhaps explains why it has put on a massive advertising campaign in recent days questioning Mr Lien's loyalty to Mr Lee.

By driving a wedge between the two men, the DPP hopes that Mr Lee will get infuriated enough to "abandon Lien" and help Mr Chen.

The likelihood of such a tacit corroboration between the KMT and the DPP will be Mr Soong's nightmare.

He has tried to counter this by appealing to KMT members who oppose Taiwan independence to abandon Mr Lien and support him instead. He put out a big advertisement equating Mr Lien with Mr Chen and hence with war.

With no more than 5 percentage points separating the leading and third-placed candidates in the last polls taken, the votes of uncommitted Taiwanese will prove decisive.

Come Saturday, it will be these undecided voters who will determine who becomes Taiwan's next President.

In the next few days, all eyes will be on this "silent quarter" and the three candidates' efforts to clinch their votes.

China's White Paper May Fan Taiwanese Nationalism

26 February 2000

China's White Paper on Taiwan has added a new element of uncertainty on the outcome of the island's forthcoming presidential elections.

The first big unknown is whether it will fan the growth of "Taiwanese nationalism".

In calling the island's regime "a local authority in one part of China", the document relegated Taipei to a position of inferiority vis-a-vis Beijing.

Though stating the obvious, it was too insensitive to the feelings of the Taiwanese, who long for a status of equality in dealings with mainland China.

By adding a new condition justifying the use of force, the White Paper served as an ultimatum forcing Taipei into negotiations at gunpoint.

Beijing's new positions were likely to produce an "antagonistic mentality" on the part of the Taiwanese, who might use their votes to express their indignation.

Such a situation is not impossible.

After ruling Taiwan for 12 years, President Lee Teng-hui has successfully created a new identity for the island's 21 million-strong population, the so-called "New Taiwanese".

Until now, this local nationalism has only been in an embryonic stage, but it could develop rapidly if the Taiwanese perceived a common external threat, such as the subservience and coercion embodied in the document.

Should this local nationalism rear its ugly head, the result could be very similar to what happened four years ago when Beijing conducted missile tests and military exercises to influence the outcome of the presidential elections.

Instead of taking Taiwanese votes away from Mr Lee, whom Beijing disliked intensely, the Chinese action had the unintended effect of ensuring his victory.

The White Paper also showed that all the three major candidates in next month's elections — namely, the ruling Kuomintang (KMT) candidate Lien Chan, Mr Chen Shui-bian of the main opposition Democratic Progressive Party (DPP) and Mr James Soong, an independent — have failed to meet the criteria set by Beijing.

Before the paper was released on Monday, all three men were extremely careful in managing President Lee's "two states" theory, which calls for a separate statehood for Taiwan.

To neutralise the effect of his formulation, the candidates seized on two hitherto taboo policies.

They called for the scrapping of the restrictive "go slow, be patient" policy that curtails Taiwanese investment in China and for the implementing of the three direct links in trade, post and transportation with the mainland.

Yet, they fell short of repudiating the crux of the "two states" theory.

The White Paper would appear to hurt Mr Chen most.

But if he manages to turn the general resentment against Chinese intimidation into votes for him, he stands to gain.

Mr Soong would equally feel the heat for one of his strengths lie in the popular belief that he could better handle cross-strait relations.

Neither was Mr Lien spared as one of the KMT's selling points was its ability to defuse the crisis and maintain stable cross-strait ties.

The White Paper nullified all such claims.

Beijing Imposing Position Before Things Go Out of Control

23 February 2000

CHINA issued its second White Paper on Taiwan on Monday to make sure that the island's presidential election campaign does not deviate from the "one China" framework which Beijing insists is the basis for cross-strait talks.

The fact that none of the three leading presidential candidates had mentioned "one China" in their respective programmes disturbed Beijing. Neither was the term "unification" mentioned.

More worrying was the fact that all the three men seemed to uphold, in one way or the other, President Lee Teng-hui's "two states theory".

Mr Lien Chan of the ruling Kuomintang (KMT) stressed that the "two states" theory was an accurate description of the status quo, and hence it formed one of his four principles governing cross-strait relations.

Mr Chen Shui-bian of the opposition Democratic Progressive Party (DPP) re-worded it as "special relations between two separate states". He has vowed to amend the Constitution to give legal effect to the theory if elected.

Although he criticised the President severely for formulating the theory, Mr James Soong, an independent candidate, nevertheless defined cross-strait relations as "quasi-international" relations.

Only Mr Li Ao, who is the candidate of the pro-unification New Party (NP), came close to Beijing's position. Independent candidate Hsu Hsin-liang acquiesced.

Yet the two men combined mustered less than 5 per cent of support among the Taiwanese, according to polls.

Faced with this, Beijing deemed it necessary to state its own position before things got out of control.

The most striking feature of Monday's White Paper was the addition of a new condition justifying the use of force: if Taiwan tried to delay unification indefinitely.

The previous document set only two conditions: if foreign forces invaded the island and if it declared independence.

The new condition showed that Beijing was worried that Taiwan would pursue a de facto independence policy without saying so.

For example, all the three major candidates defined Taiwan in much the same way as "a state with independent sovereignty" and as such there was no need to declare it "independent".

If such is their understanding, then the negotiations that each man has pledged to start with Beijing could hardly lead to unification.

From China's point of view, this was exactly the tactic Mr Lee employed.

Beijing and Taipei reached a series of agreements through their top negotiators Wang Daohan and Koo Chen-fu respectively in 1993, among which was an important tacit understanding allowing both sides to define the "one China" principle differently.

In other words, Beijing was not dictating its definition to Taipei. This was considered a major achievement as it had the effect of freezing cross-strait differences.

But soon after the understanding was reached, the Taiwan President redefined cross-strait relations as "one China with two governments, or with two equal entities".

He tried to give substance to this redefinition by making a visit to the United States in 1995 and by making a bid to get Taiwan into the United Nations. His efforts culminated in the "two states theory" promulgated last July.

To stop this tactic of delaying the unification process indefinitely, Beijing felt compelled to add a further justification for the use of force.

Thus, the second White Paper conveyed a much more serious message than the first.

While President Lee was not named at all in the first document, he was labelled "the overall representative of separatism", "the culprit of instability in the Taiwan Strait", "the biggest stumbling block in Sino-American relations" and "the trouble-maker that threatens peace and stability in the Asia-Pacific region" this time round.

While the sensitive issue of the Taiwan government's legal status was avoided in the last document, the new White Paper defined it unequivocally as a local government in one part of Chinese territory. In other words, Taiwan's room for manoeuvre has been shrunk further.

While the first White Paper, issued after the 1993 Wang-Koo talks, conveyed a note of optimism on the future development of cross-strait relations, the second admitted frankly that there existed a grave crisis in the Taiwan Strait.

Taiwan's New Optimism

12 February 2000

TAIPEI — China has visibly stepped up its "carrot and stick" policy towards Taiwan in recent times in a bid to hasten political dialogue across the Taiwan Strait.

A national conference on Taiwan, held last December, mapped out a two-pronged approach towards the runaway island.

The "stick" treatment meant greater war-preparedness against separatist tendencies there.

Sources said that the conference decided to set up a special military committee, whose job was to design different security scenarios aimed at winning a high-intensity limited war against both external military intervention and separatist forces.

The "carrot" treatment, on the other hand, meant greater flexibility for Taiwan within the framework of "one country, two systems", although Taiwan had rejected altogether unification based on this model.

While it was always necessary to brandish "the stick", the conference decided that henceforth, greater emphasis should be placed on "the carrot".

This represented a basic change in the assessment of the situation. Following Taiwan President Lee Teng-hui's promulgation of the "two states" theory, there was great pessimism in Beijing that war was unavoidable. Sources said that after careful stock-taking of the international and domestic situation in Taiwan, the conference concluded that the three fundamental elements governing cross-strait relations had not changed.

They are — the international consensus that Taiwan belonged to China, Beijing's policy of peaceful unification under the "one country, two systems" model, and Mr Jiang's eight-point programme promoting cross-strait dialogue.

That was the basis for China's new-found optimism. Reflecting this mood, Mr Jiang dropped the reference to the use of force in his New Year address.

The usual two-part statement said that China strived for a peaceful solution but would not commit itself to the non-use of force.

Sources stressed that the deliberate omission did not indicate that China gave up the non-peaceful option, but it helped to ameliorate the tense situation.

The conference also assessed the presidential election situation in Taiwan and devised different strategies in response to different candidates getting elected.

Sources summed these up in three terms: "la", "guan" and "ya".

"La" meant to win over and it applied to Vice-President Lien Chan of the ruling Kuomintang (KMT) if he got elected.

China preferred to deal with the KMT because it provided an appropriate platform for political negotiation. Beijing insisted that any such negotiations be held between parties, not governments or states.

"Guan" meant to observe, or to wait and see, and it applied to independent candidate James Soong if he got elected.

"Ya" meant to pressure and it applied to candidate Chen Shui-bian of the Democratic Progressive Party (DPP). Beijing would pressure the DPP to prevent any moves towards independence.

Whatever the case, Beijing should re-open dialogue with Taiwan once Mr Lee stepped down, the conference concluded.

Signalling this stance, Mr Jiang reiterated the "two hopes". His New Year statement said that Beijing placed hopes on both the Taiwanese people and the authority.

Sources close to Beijing explained that the standard policy statement used to place hopes for unification on both the people and the authority.

But, after Mr Lee made his US trip in 1995, Beijing mentioned only the people and not the authority. It was the first time in several years that "the authority" element surfaced again.

The significance was obvious — now that Mr Lee was nearing the end of his term, with a new president going to take over soon, Beijing left room for dialogue with the new authority.

The conference also concluded that post-unification Taiwan would be able to enjoy far greater flexibility under the "one country, two systems" model than either Hongkong or Macau.

This message was made public both by Mr Jiang, at his New Year address, and by Vice-Premier Qian Qichen, at a meeting marking the 5th anniversary of the proclamation of Mr Jiang's eight-point programme.

Mr Jiang said that any solution based on the "one country, two systems" model would take into consideration the vastly different characteristics between Taiwan, Hongkong and Macau.

By stressing their differences, he wanted to assure the Taiwanese that, as long as they agreed to unification, the system for Taiwan could be extremely flexible.

A Chinese scholar close to the authority said what the leadership had in mind was so flexible that the formula could have been termed "one country, three systems".

Mr Qian echoed Mr Jiang's point by analysing the similarities and differences between Taiwan, Hongkong and Macau and said that, based on these differences, Taiwan should enjoy far greater autonomy and flexibility.

He also stressed that after China's entry into the World Trade Organisation, he would be glad to see Taiwan also admitted.

He was also optimistic that the "three direct links" could materialise when both were members.

The stage seems set for another spell of optimism across the Taiwan Strait.

Bid to Dissolve KMT Inc.

16 January 2000

IN A DESPERATE bid to defend its position in the upcoming presidential elections, Taiwan's ruling Kuomintang (KMT) has agreed to cut its ties with lucrative business operations.

Vice-President Lien Chan announced on Jan 2 that he was prepared to place all KMT assets in trust should he be elected president on March 18.

Mr Lien, with Premier Vincent Siew as his running mate, are vying for the top posts as the KMT's candidates.

The announcement sent shock waves across the island because the plan amounted to dissolving what could be potentially the largest business conglomerate in Taiwan.

The KMT owns, through seven major holding companies, aggregate assets of over NT$176 billion (S$8.8 billion) and raked in a net profit of NT$12 billion in 1998.

This made the KMT, as a group, the third-largest enterprise in asset terms in Taiwan after Chinese Petroleum Corporation (assets: NT$508.6 billion) and China Steel Corporation (assets: NT$185 billion).

In net profit terms, it was one of the five major companies that managed to earn a pre-tax net profit exceeding NT$10 billion.

The assets exclude the huge amount of land and property held directly by the party and its offshoots such as the China Youth Corps (CYC).

The real estate holdings are staggering. For example, the building housing the party's headquarters and the prime site on which it sits, opposite the Presidential Palace, are valued at more than NT$15 billion.

The CYC owns a string of tourist resort properties spread across the island.

"If these properties are included in the count, the KMT as a group could easily become the largest business conglomerate in Taiwan," said Professor Chang Ching-hsih of the Economics Department at the National Taiwan University, a scholar known for his long-standing research into the ruling party's businesses.

KMT party enterprises have long been a target of attack.

Firstly, the rather obscure origins of their assets lead many people to believe that they were accumulated illegally by turning state assets into party assets.

This is hardly surprising given that Taiwan has been under one-party rule for almost 50 years and the distinction between party and state has never been clear.

According to Prof. Chang, this amounted to a misappropriation of state property, which should rightfully be returned to its legal owner, in this case, the state.

Secondly, the KMT has often been accused of adopting policies that favour its own businesses.

Prof. Chang pointed out that many sectors were opened up slowly in order to preserve a near monopolistic operating environment for party enterprises.

He found a positive correlation between the pace of market opening and the degree of involvement of party business in the finance, petrochemical and media industries.

Or else the party business could have obtained inside information ahead of the market.

Critics have questioned how the party businesses still managed to make handsome profits during the 1997-8 Asian financial crisis when many Taiwanese firms suffered great losses.

"The reason we have to stop any ruling party from running its own business is that there is no other way of preventing unfair practices," Prof. Chang said.

Finally, the opposition Democratic Progressive Party (DPP) has accused the KMT of unfair political competition because having a lucrative business arm allows it to mobilise huge resources to buy or influence votes.

Such resources, the DPP claims, arose from the monopolistic nature of the businesses but instead of accruing to the state treasury, they went into the KMT coffers.

In other words, the KMT made use of public resources to bolster its own rule.

From the ordinary people's viewpoint, the most serious charge against party businesses is the symbiosis between power and money.

The interlocking relationship between the two means that the interests of small investors are neglected.

Prof. Chang identified 13 major financial scandals between November 1998 and October 1999 which brought great losses to small investors in the share market.

All of these cases involved Mr Liu Tai-ying, who heads the KMT Business Management Committee, the party's investment arm.

"Why should the KMT enterprises be involved in all these scandals?" Prof. Chang asked. "Isn't it true to say that the party businesses are black?"

He pointed out that during the past two years when firms hard hit by the Asian financial crisis turned to the KMT for help, the main factor in deciding whether they got help was their political allegiance and loyalty to the ruling party.

In return for such help, they had to make political contributions to the KMT during elections.

He concluded that this was the root cause of political corruption in Taiwan.

Hence ridding the KMT of its business operations has long been a call from the public but such calls had fallen on deaf ears in the past.

Within the party, it has been taboo to talk about it. It is said that only two people know the exact size and location of party businesses: Mr Lee, who is chairman of KMT, and Mr Liu.

Former KMT vice-chairman and ex-premier Hau Pei-tsun admitted that even people of his seniority were denied access to details.

So Mr Lien's bid to place party business under trust means a great commitment to revamp the party and clean up Taiwan's political environment.

But most people view this as an election gimmick to boost his popularity, which is trailing that of independent candidate James Soong and the DPP's Chen Shui-bian.

This was the case even after the KMT launched a massive mudslinging campaign against Mr Soong over a slush fund scandal.

In that campaign, all the state organs, like the tax authority, the criminal investigation bureau, as well as the watch-dog Control Yuan, cross-examined Mr Soong, creating tremendous pressure on his supporters.

Yet to the disappointment of the KMT, the candidate who gained the most from the scandal was not its man, but Mr Chen, whose popularity outstripped Mr Soong's for the first time.

So the KMT had to change its strategy by projecting Mr Lien as a reformer instead and the most attention-grabbing move was to tackle the party business.

"This is the KMT's sore point. To tackle the sore point squarely proves Mr Lien's determination," a KMT insider said.

Many people, however, doubt Mr Lien's sincerity and ability.

To put the assets of a huge business empire — the third largest, if not potentially the largest, in Taiwan — in trust would require years of legal and accountancy preparatory work.

With the presidential elections less than two months away, not even the barest minimum of these tasks could be accomplished to prove Mr Lien's unequivocal commitment.

Neither is the opposition satisfied or convinced.

It views putting party assets in trust as being tantamount to money-laundering, if the assets were obtained illegally in the first place. It wants the KMT to allow an independent commission to probe into the nature of ownership of each asset.

Any asset without clean proof of KMT's original ownership should be turned over to the state and not kept in trust.

Prof. Chang estimated that if such measures were taken, the KMT could be easily stripped of three quarters of its assets.

Opposition was also strong within the KMT because of strong vested interests.

Although President Lee has thrown his full support behind Mr Lien, the "shopkeeper" — as Mr Liu is nicknamed — showed his displeasure openly.

Without denying the accusations made by the opposition, he defended stoutly the role of party businesses in Taiwan's economic development and financial stability.

He argued that during the early years of high-technology development, KMT enterprises performed the role of venture capital, providing funds for Taiwan's entrepreneurs when there was no other source of risk capital.

As for financial stability, he cited the case of missile testing by China during the last presidential elections in 1996. Along with others, the KMT enterprises threw their full resources into stabilising the financial sector.

They did the same last year when cross-strait tension was heightened following the President's espousal of his "two states" theory.

Again during the Asian financial crisis, KMT enterprises bailed out a number of large businesses in Taiwan, thus effectively thwarting the penetration of the financial virus into the Taiwanese economy.

Mr Liu also argued that party businesses were an important instrument in furthering the government's foreign policy objectives.

The go-south policy, a programme to encourage the diversification of Taiwanese investments into South-east Asia, for example, was spearheaded by party enterprises.

Taiwan's diplomatic relations with some countries were achieved following painstaking ground-laying work in the form of investment by party enterprises, the latest example being Palau.

Investment there by KMT enterprises several years ago paved the way eventually for the establishment of official relations.

"There were times when some work had to be done in a non-official manner," Mr Liu stressed.

"This was dictated by Taiwan's unique circumstances. Without formal diplomatic relations, the party enterprises in many cases had to take up government functions," he explained.

Reluctant to accept all of Mr Lien's proposals, Mr Liu tried to confine the impact to those enterprises in which the KMT had more than 50 per cent ownership.

"If the KMT had only a minority interest in an enterprise, what right does the KMT have to place that under trust?" he asked.

By this definition, the total number of enterprises in which the KMT has investments would be reduced sharply from more than 300 to only about 20.

For example, the China Development Corporation (CDC), the acknowledged flagship of KMT enterprises in which Mr Liu is chairman of the board of directors, would be exempted because legally the KMT owns only 2 per cent of its shares.

Many KMT party functionaries also fear that Mr Lien's plan could backfire.

Although a welcome move, the power-money symbiosis that he is attempting to break is so well entrenched that its dissolution might cost the KMT its right to rule Taiwan.

"He either swims or sinks," was how one of them put it.

Prof. Chang agreed.

Lien-Siew Ticket Could Destroy the KMT

11 September 1999

Taiwan's ruling Kuomintang (KMT) could be in for another major split following President Lee Teng-hui's decision to pair up Vice-President Lien Chan and Premier Vincent Siew for next year's presidential elections.

The majority of the party's rank and file and senior business leaders wanted Mr Lien's running mate to be former Taiwan governor James Soong.

Not that they have anything against Mr Lien. A steady and humble man with a proven administrative track record, he is much respected within the party. But coming from a well-to-do family, he lacks the grassroots affinity to garner votes.

Opinion polls have shown him falling consistently short of the threshold — about 30 per cent of total votes — required to win the presidency.

Hence the preference for Mr Soong, who enjoys popular support.

The former governor's reform-oriented image would have helped to compensate for Mr Lien's rather conservative one.

The Lien-Soong ticket was once described as the KMT's "sure-win dream combination", but Mr Lee chose to ignore it.

This prompted Mr Soong to join the race as an independent candidate, thus precipitating a split in the party, which became obvious at the recent KMT national congress held to endorse the Lien-Siew ticket.

Several KMT heavyweights unhappy with the pairing did not attend it, and some party legislators petitioned Mr Siew to relieve himself temporarily of the premiership for the sake of fairness to all candidates.

Former Justice Minister Liao Cheng-hao lashed out at the premier, saying he had been forced to conduct illegal eavesdropping "by his superior". He also hinted at an obscure connection between Mr Siew and the underworld.

Although the former minister declined to provide concrete evidence, his reputation as someone who waged a relentless battle against gangland activities lent credence to the accusation.

Many people saw this "anti-Siew" movement as an expression of some party members' disapproval of the Lien-Siew ticket forged by Mr Lee. So, unless the President succeeds in reversing this mood — and unless the KMT wins the election — the party is likely to split.

He had, from the very beginning, rejected the Lien-Soong combination.

After downsizing the provincial structure, which cost Mr Soong the governorship, he offered the former governor an overseas appointment and told him — quoting a Buddhist saying — that "a truly free man is one without any position".

Mr Lee was wary of being over-shadowed by Mr Soong.

Mr Soong had received 56 per cent of all the votes in the 1994 provincial elections, while Mr Lee captured only 54 per cent in the 1996 presidential elections.

Since the constituencies involved in both elections overlapped each other to a great extent, many people saw Mr Soong as having received a stronger mandate than Mr Lee.

Complicating things further were their ideological differences over the reunification-independence issue. Mr Soong is definitely against Taiwan's independence from China.

These events help explain why Mr Lee went all out to sideline Mr Soong.

Most observers also agree that the President wanted to continue to exert influence as KMT chairman even after he steps down from the presidency next March.

They say he is a man of vision who also has a deep sense of history. He has set for himself a mission to place Taiwan firmly on the path to independence because he believes it is good for the people.

Before he relinquishes the presidency, he has tried to define clearly the political line, as expressed in his "two states" theory, and to put in place the people he wants to implement it.

To ensure that future leaders do not stray from his chosen course, he wants to continue to exert influence in his capacity as KMT chairman. This would be possible only if he gets to hand-pick his successors and if they are relatively weak.

The Lien-Siew ticket meets these criteria.

On the other hand, if Mr Soong were nominated for vice-president, Mr Lee's influence would cease the moment he stepped down from the presidency.

Mr Lien himself could have favoured Mr Soong as his running mate. For example, two days before the vice-presidential candidate was announced formally, he wrote a personal letter to Mr Soong in a last-ditch effort to rescue the Lien-Soong match.

Failing to do so, he next tried to persuade the highly-respected Nobel laureate Lee Yuan-tseh to run with him. Obviously, Mr Siew was not his choice, but Mr Lee's.

By rejecting a combination that would have enjoyed the greatest support within the party, Mr Lee placed not only the KMT's ruling position at risk, but also its unity.

Observers said that during his 12 years in power, the ruling party had already suffered one major split, and this second one could be more damaging.

The first split came when Mr Lee's pro-independence line began to rear its head.

Following the 1991 and 1992 constitutional amendments, many KMT members sensed that Mr Lee was heading towards independence and this led to a mass exodus of grassroots members.

Some of those who left the party founded the New Party (NP), the second largest opposition party in Taiwan.

The next split will be even more damaging because it will involve senior party members and because the KMT's ruling position will be threatened seriously.

Some observers are saying that Mr Lee could well be the leader who destroys the ruling party.

KMT Rule May Be at Stake With Lien

8 September 2000

TAIWAN'S ruling Kuomintang (KMT) has formally adopted Vice-President Lien Chan and Premier Vincent Siew as its team to run in next year's presidential elections.

In picking this pair of candidates who lack popular appeal, its hope in preserving its ruling status would become even more reliant on the Lee Teng-hui factor, among others.

The choice of Mr Siew came as no surprise after a last-ditch effort to team Mr Lien with popular ex-governor James Soong failed.

Most observers agree that the Lien-Siew ticket means that President Lee's policy line, as well as the party's assets, would remain largely intact after he steps down next year.

It also means that for the first time, the KMT is faced with a real threat of losing its 50-year-old ruling status.

The fatal weakness of the Lien-Siew ticket is its singular lack of popular appeal. Opinions surveyed by polling organisations of all political shades returned surprisingly consistent results, showing that voters' preferences were former governor James Soong (31 to 33 per cent), who is running as an independent, former Taipei mayor Chen Shui-bian of the opposition Democratic Progressive Party (DPP), (21 to 25 per cent), and Mr Lien (15 to 18 per cent).

If opinion polls are any guide, it is highly likely that the KMT would lose its ruling position as its candidate is way behind even the minimum threshold required to capture the presidential seat, estimated to be at least 30 per cent of total votes. Thus, the election battle ahead of Mr Lien would be extremely difficult.

To be fair, he does not deserve this low rating. Having graduated from an Ivy League university, he worked his way up the hierarchy and was one of the rare ones in Taiwan who had a complete range of experiences, stretching from economics to politics, and from domestic to foreign issues. Many people who knew him agree that his unassuming personality makes him a good leader. He has a mild temperament and is therefore not likely to let his decision-making be affected by mood swings.

He is ready to shoulder responsibility and never pushes the blame to his subordinates if things go awry.

Though he comes from a well-to-do family, he is conspicuously humble and has, throughout his public service career, maintained an extremely low profile, to the extent that he often allowed his subordinates to steal the limelight from him.

His lack of ego could result in his being unwilling to defend stoutly the power that is legitimately his.

One of the recent complaints against him was that during his premiership, he had allowed the President to encroach upon the power of the Premier bit by bit such that the President now wields substantial extra-constitutional authority.

The strength of Mr Lien is also his weakness when it comes to winning votes from the people, something he is not quite accustomed to or comfortable with, especially when it means boosting himself and slinging mud at others.

Compared with either Mr Soong or Mr Chen, most voters see Mr Lien as a dull and unexciting man, lacking both originality and the guts to initiate reforms.

He definitely lacks the charisma and streetwise wit, often associated with politicians in Taiwan. Unlike Messrs Soong and Chen, Mr Lien is seen by many as belonging to the aristocratic class and lacking affinity with people at the grassroots.

Picking Premier Siew as his running mate did not improve his overall image. In fact, the moment the Lien-Siew ticket was formally adopted at the party's national congress, Mr Lien's popularity index dropped.

The nomination of Mr Siew intensified the gutless, non-innovative and dreary image. WITH a pair of candidates that lack popular appeal, the KMT's hope in preserving its ruling status will now be dependent on three other factors.

First and foremost is the Lee Teng-hui factor. The Lien-Siew ticket means that President Lee's position as initiator of policies will continue unabated.

To the extent that Mr Lee, after 12 years in office, still enjoys more than 50 per cent support in Taiwan.

Political analysts found that about 10 to 15 per cent of voters would follow Mr Lee's choice blindly.

This is termed the "Lee Teng-hui complex". He was obviously trying to translate this complex into concrete support for the Lien-

Siew ticket when he told a mass gathering recently: "Go home and tell your parents and neighbours that it is Lee Teng-hui's choice".

If the transfer of support from Mr Lee to Mr Lien materialises, it will be a decisive factor in compensating for the latter's low popularity.

Another major factor is the huge financial support, both direct and indirect, that can be mobilised in his favour.

Thanks to the party's own investment arm, which recently announced that it made a profit of more than NT$10 billion (S$504 million), the KMT is prepared to wage an expensive election war.

There was press speculation suggesting that the KMT central planned to spend about NT$10 billion on the elections, not including those spent by local party organisations.

Although party spokesman Huang Hwei-jen denied the reports, analysts said that even during the 1996 presidential elections, when President Lee was the most obvious winner, the KMT had to spend between NT$6 billion and NT$7 billion to get him elected.

This time round, with a much weaker Mr Lien, it was just reasonable to assume a much higher figure.

There are indirect means too. A NT$150 billion fund, that belonged formerly to the Taiwan provincial government but placed under the control of the Executive Yuan when the provincial structure was scrapped, could become a formidable resource in terms of "buying" local votes.

Before the province was scrapped, the money was earmarked for local small-scale development projects. During election times, projects could be swapped for votes. With Mr Siew in command of this fund, it will become a distinct advantage.

Perhaps this explains why when the Lien-Siew ticket was formally adopted, there was a huge anti-Siew movement in the legislature — out of fear that the fund, which many legislators have been eyeing, would be used to bolster the weak Lien-Siew ticket.

Political inertia might also help this unexciting pair. Some studies show that at times of heightened political tension, voters might opt for a leadership structure with a higher degree of predictability and conformity.

Although most Taiwanese were fed up with KMT rule, they become extremely cautious in elections in which highly controversial issues could affect the result.

But there is no such thing as a sure thing in elections. Thus, for Mr Lien and the KMT, the battle has only just begun.

Ex-Taiwan Governor's Polls Move Adds to Jitters

17 July 1999

On a day already rife with reports that Chinese troops had been put on combat alert, former Taiwan governor James Soong added to the jitters in Taiwan when he announced his decision to run as a non-party candidate in next year's presidential elections.

He also made a veiled attack against President Lee Teng-hui's "two states" principle, the cause of the latest tension with China.

Mr Soong's announcement came after a meeting with Mr John Chang, the secretary-general of the ruling Kuomintang (KMT), who tried to persuade him to partner Mr Lien Chan as the Vice-President's running mate.

Mr Chang initiated the meeting to prevent a split in the KMT should Mr Soong decide to run for President without the party's endorsement.

In a speech announcing his decision, Mr Soong said that Mr Lee's declaration — that Taiwan was a sovereign state — was "rash, careless and impetuous".

Without mentioning the President, who is KMT chairman, by name, he criticised the senior party leadership for side-stepping the normal decision-making mechanism, resulting in "rash decisions" being made.

The majority of the party's grassroots members, he said, were fed up with such a dictatorial style of leadership.

"The people have lost confidence in the government and they are yearning for changes. They demand more reforms and greater democracy...and I am always with them," he said.

He added: "Prospects for the Lien-Soong ticket were destroyed long time ago by the top KMT leadership."

Mr Lee and Mr Soong fell out over the President's decision to downsize the Taiwan provincial administration, which took effect late last year.

Although the majority of party members prefer Mr Soong, and numerous opinion polls are showing that he is leading Mr Lien by a wide margin, President Lee has remained unmoved, for obvious reasons.

If Mr Lien is installed as the next President, Mr Lee can still call the shots behind the scenes, something he cannot do with Mr Soong. However, polls showed Mr Soong enjoying 35 per cent of popular support, followed by the opposition Democratic Progressive Party's presidential candidate Chen Shui-bian with 26 per cent support and Mr Lien 14 per cent.

The President had no choice but to bow to party pressure to retain Mr Soong. Hence the Soong-Chang meeting yesterday.

Mr Soong's "go it alone" announcement did not surprise anyone, but his chances of winning the election have been somewhat diminished by Mr Lee's "two states" declaration, which is bound to affect the outcome of the presidential race.

Most observers felt that the theory puts Mr Soong, who is against independence for Taiwan, in an awkward position.

To support the theory would be against his own beliefs, but to oppose it could cost him the votes of local Taiwanese. That was why DPP's Mr Chen dared him to clarify his position.

Yesterday, Mr Soong stressed that "security and prosperity are the people's most fundamental demand".

The desire to safeguard this demand, and to change an undemocratic leadership style, had prompted him to take up the presidential race, he added.

How the DPP can benefit from the "two states" theory remains unclear.

Some people think that it could boost the party's status as it was the first to propose it.

The opposition party was quick to seize an opportunity by saying that Mr Lee was borrowing the idea from the DPP.

Others, however, are worried that the tense cross-strait situation would invoke the people's deep-rooted fear that pro-independence would plunge Taiwan into the abyss of instability and insecurity.

The past has shown that whenever cross-strait relations are tense, people tend to vote conservatively.

Mr Soong's move to run as an independent is certain to split the party — and votes.

This split would be further intensified by the "two states" theory, which many KMT members, especially those who came to Taiwan in 1949, cannot accept.

Moreover, the fact that a decision that affects 22 million Taiwanese was taken in such an undemocratic manner infuriated many KMT members.

Yet the KMT can count on one significant factor: the charisma of Mr Lee.

In Taiwan, his theory is portrayed as a means to give its people international dignity, which is cherished by most Taiwanese.

Opinion polls showed that although many questioned his decision-making style and were worried about the adverse effects of his remarks, more than half of those polled were highly supportive of him, thinking that he was the only man who dared to challenge "Chinese hegemony over Taiwan".

This populist support for a strong leader, coupled with the fact that people treasured internal stability when faced with an external threat, could win for the KMT sufficient votes to retain the presidential seat.

DPP's Chen to Run for Taiwan's Top Post

11 July 1999

Taiwan's largest opposition Democratic Progressive Party (DPP) yesterday formally nominated former Taipei mayor Chen Shui-bian as its presidential candidate.

"All the 391 representatives voted unanimously for Mr Chen," DPP chairman Lin Yi-hsiung announced at the party's special congress.

Mr Chen was the only candidate seeking endorsement from the party and the special congress was held merely to formalise the ipso facto candidate.

The DPP changed its rules in May to override what was known as the "four-year clause". Under this clause, any party member would be banned from participating in elections twice in four years.

Mr Chen, who lost the Taipei mayor's post to Mr Ma Ying-jeou of the ruling Kuomintang (KMT) last year, would not be eligible for next year's presidential race if not for the changes.

In his acceptance speech, Mr Chen outlined six major policy thrusts he was committed to; top among them was Taiwan's security.

He was keen to win the trust of Washington, Tokyo and Beijing.

Pledging to contribute to peace, stability and prosperity in the Taiwan Strait, he commended President Lee Teng-hui's latest formulation on Taiwan's status, expounded in his talks with a German press delegation.

Mr Lee had said there existed two Chinas on both sides of the strait and that the relation between Beijing and Taipei should be regarded as that of between two sovereign states.

Mr Chen said he would pursue this issue further when he gets elected as President.

The DPP's major rallying call in the election would be party rotation to stop power corruption, he said.

The KMT had been running Taiwan uninterrupted for half a century. Without the checks and balance provided by party rotation, there was bound to be rampant corruption, he added.

To Rule Taiwan, DPP Needs Revamp

20 May 1999

TAIWAN'S main opposition Democratic Progressive Party (DPP) held its national congress recently to get itself ready for next year's presidential elections amid a major ideological split that forced its former chairman Hsu Hsin-liang to quit,

The two-day congress saw the party adopt the "Resolution on Taiwan's Future" to water down its independence stance.

While the party programme has said that it would strive for an independent Republic of Taiwan, the resolution now says that Taiwan is already independent and that its current name is the "Republic of China".

The programme has also called for a referendum to declare independence. The resolution makes clear that any change to the status quo would be decided by a referendum.

In other words, the party has changed the purpose of a plebiscite from one seeking independence actively to one preventing reunification passively.

The resolution is a major compromise on DPP's position on independence, though its original programme was left intact.

Another major document which the DPP congress adopted was the "Nomination Procedure for Presidential Candidate". Many people saw that as being tailor-made for ex-Taipei mayor Chen Shui-bian's candidacy.

The party has well-defined regulations on the nomination of candidates to public office, including that of president and vice-president. But none of them has been adhered to.

For example, one of the regulations bars a member from seeking nomination to more than one public office within a four-year period. This was meant to prevent the concentration of power in one man. If followed strictly, Mr Chen would not have been eligible for nomination as the party's presidential candidate as he had just run in last year's Taipei mayoral race, won by Kuomintang's Ma Ying-jeou.

Given that no DPP man is as popular with the people as Mr Chen, it is easy to see why the party decided to use the new nomination procedure to override existing regulations.

After the two resolutions were adopted, DPP chairman Lin Yi-hsiung declared jubilantly that the party was "ready for 2000".

The party may be ready for the elections, but is it ready for power?

Many people are less optimistic.

Merely giving the party's independence programme a cosmetic dressing, instead of scrapping it, would not win it more votes. If anything, it made the party look hypocritical.

The DPP had until now failed to realise that its very goal of independence was the single most important source of danger to Taiwan because China would never accept an independent Taiwan. Refusal to recognise that the party itself could be a threat to Taiwan's security ruled out any hope of the DPP becoming the ruling party.

Similarly, changing the party's rules and regulations to suit one member showed that the DPP was not as democratic as it purported to be. It demonstrated only the parochial nature of the party: to get votes, principles and political visions could be sacrificed.

Ironically, it was Mr Chen himself who formulated the independence programme and devised the "four-year clause".

Obviously, he owes the Taiwanese public an explanation for the about-turn.

Did the party water down its independence platform for the sake of getting more votes, or did the move represent a serious reconsideration of its feasibility? If it was the latter, then why was the independence programme not scrapped altogether?

Similarly, he should explain why he should be exempt from the "four-year clause", which he designed to prevent party members from amassing too much power.

For that matter, the DPP, too, owes the people an answer.

If a party chooses to cover up its shortcomings instead of correcting them, and to change its rules so readily for the sake of expediency, how can the public trust it?

The rise of the DPP has provided a welcome alternative to the ruling KMT because it has thus far been able to project a democratic and clean image. This perhaps explains why the 160,000-strong party was able to grab top positions in lower-level governments from the KMT within a short 10 years.

However, when it comes to power at the national level, voters are unsure about the DPP's trustworthiness. Many believe the party is still immature. The two resolutions can only confirm this impression.

The problem with the DPP is that the party has stagnated after its rather meteoric rise.

Mr Hsu said in his farewell speech to the party he helped to found: "Taiwan is now facing a new turning point in history. Because those beside me fail to go forward, I must go forth alone."

In his view, the DPP remains a populist grouping that has failed to address the big challenges of the times. When he called for a review of the independence programme, he was attacked fiercely by fundamentalists in the party.

The DPP's anti-business stance has also threatened the continued growth of Taiwan. The so-called Bayer affair was a good example. The chemical producer was forced to cancel its investment plan because of anti-business sentiment in a DPP-ruled county where the investment was to be located.

Though much has been done since then to improve the party's relations with the business world, the mainstream thinking within the party remains disquieting to big business.

The party's inability to transform itself from a populist group to a responsible party has prompted the departure of one of its co-founders. If the DPP's vision is to become Taiwan's ruling party, it had better undergo a major revamp first.

SECTION

C

Cross-Strait Relations

Pressure on Taiwan Grows With Macau's Return to China

21 December 1999

WITH Macau now under Beijing's control again, together with Hongkong, Taiwan knows full well that China will work on bringing the nationalist island — its last separated territory — back into the mainland's fold.

In Beijing's view, Taiwan's days as a separated province of China are numbered.

After all, the "one country, two systems" formula — under which Hongkong and Macau are governed — was originally conceived for the purpose of persuading Taiwan to agree to reunification with the mainland.

Its application in Hongkong, which was returned to China in July 1997, and now Macau, serves well as a trial run.

The international community's reaction to the "one country, two systems" concept has so far been generally positive.

For its part, Beijing has taken pains to avoid meddling in Hongkong's local affairs so as to prove to the world the feasibility of its reunification model.

Growing international acceptance has been a big headache for Taiwan. There was pressure, too, from the US.

Annoyed by Taiwanese President Lee Teng-hui's "two states theory" — which upset the delicate tripartite equilibrium between Washington, Beijing and Taipei — US President Bill Clinton made an oblique reference to Hongkong, which Taipei read as a subtle endorsement of China's reunification model by the US leader.

The difficult task for Taiwanese officials lies in telling the world that the model is not working as well as it appears, according to an official of Taiwan's Mainland Affairs Council (MAC) who declined to be identified.

"People far away tend to see things in broad strokes. No one is paying attention to the details," he said. "The 'one country two systems' formula in Hongkong is not encouraging at all if one were to scrutinise it in detail."

Taiwan is not happy that post-1997 Hongkong has appeared to abandon its neutral position regarding relations between Taipei and Beijing.

The official identified four problem areas:

First, whenever there is a difference of opinion between the central government and Hongkong, "one country" always takes precedence over "two systems".

Second, the principle of "a high degree of autonomy" applies only to non-political matters. The Hongkong government has to second-guess Beijing's wishes when dealing with political affairs.

Third, Hongkong's liberty, human rights, democracy and rule of law are being eroded gradually.

"So if a system is eroding gradually instead of collapsing suddenly, no one would be able to discern the change," the official said.

"Finally, Hongkong no longer can maintain its position of neutrality as it did under British rule, either in cross-strait relations or in situations involving confrontation between China and the Western world."

The MAC drew this conclusion after documenting 58 major incidents since the handover in 1997, the official said.

The most recent one involved Taiwan's top representative in Hongkong, Mr Cheng An-kuo.

Mr Cheng apparently offended Beijing when he spoke on government-funded RTHK radio about President Lee's so-called "two-states" theory, which called for relations between the two sides to be on a "special state-to-state" basis.

As a result, his visa was not renewed and he had to leave the territory on Dec 10.

At the same time, RTHK chief Cheung Man Yee was packed off to head the Hongkong trade office in Tokyo.

"We hope the future Macau government will not follow the footstep of Hongkong and try to corner us," the MAC official said.

He was referring to Hongkong's refusal to sign a bilateral trade treaty as part of Taiwan's bid to join the World Trade Organisation.

A country's WTO accession process required it to conclude bilateral-trade treaties with its main trading partners.

Though negotiations between Hongkong and Taiwan were completed long ago, the territory has yet to sign the treaty as it wants to wait until China gets into the WTO first.

Taiwan concludes that Hongkong has become China's pawn to further its foreign policy objectives.

"Given the two-year experience in Hongkong, we do not hold out much hope for Macau, which is even more submissive to Beijing," said the official.

Macau's insistence that Taiwan changes the name of its representative office was seen as a move to corner Taiwan.

"But whether the 'one country, two systems' formula works well or otherwise does not really bother us. Even if it works out jolly good there, we shall not accept it," the official said emphatically.

According to the official, the model presumes an inequality of relations between two governments, one central and the other local.

Both Hongkong and Macau do not challenge this position, but Taiwan views its relationship with Beijing as one between two equal entities.

Besides, the model also presumes that conflicting values can co-exist within a system.

The fact that there is a tendency to place "one country" above "two systems" is a strong indication that Hongkong has had to compromise its own interests and views.

Finally, the model is a unilateral approach which China dictated to Britain and Portugal. Historical circumstances and geopolitical reality meant that the latter two had no choice but to accept it.

However, Taiwan has its own view on how reunification should be achieved and hence is unlikely to swallow what is meted out to it. Thus the validity of the model to solve the reunification problem remains dubious.

When it was first advanced two decades ago, the majority of people in Taiwan still considered themselves Chinese. Now the majority regard themselves as Taiwanese.

A major weakness of the model is its inability to cope with this changing sense of identity.

Unless this is addressed or redressed, it is very likely that Macau will be the last place where the "one country, two systems" model is applied.

Next: Taiwan

21 December 1999

AFTER Macau's return to China, Taiwan will be next.

This message was spelt out clearly in Chinese President Jiang Zemin's speeches at ceremonies marking the handover of Macau and the establishment of the Special Administrative Region (SAR).

At the handover ceremony, Mr Jiang said that "the implementation of the concept of 'one country, two systems' in Hongkong and Macau has played and will continue to play an important exemplary role for our eventual settlement of the Taiwan question".

"The Chinese government and people are confident and capable of an early settlement of the Taiwan question and a complete national reunification," he added.

He reiterated the same theme a few hours later at a ceremony marking the formation of the new Macau SAR government.

On both occasions, he stressed the words "early settlement", which was not the case previously.

Observers noted that now that Macau has returned to Chinese rule, the time had come for the settlement of the Taiwan issue.

Speaking at a nationally televised rally held in Beijing last night, the Chinese leader urged the Taiwanese authorities not to "go against the tide of history, erect obstacles to the development of the cross-strait ties or act against the fundamental interests of Taiwan compatriots and the entire Chinese nation".

"The Chinese government and people will never tolerate any attempt to split China," he warned.

In his speech in Macau, Mr Jiang also explained at great length how the "one country, two systems" model could best be implemented in Macau.

He stressed the great degree of freedom granted to Macau in handling its external relations.

There are indications that Beijing is willing to allow greater flexibility in Macau-Taipei relations than in Hongkong-Taipei relations.

On the eve of the handover, Macau's Xinhua director Wang Qiren, Beijing's representative in the enclave, confirmed that if Taiwan agreed to change the name of its representative office to make it look unofficial, Beijing would not object to official links between Macau and Taiwan.

This showed more flexibility compared to Hongkong-Taipei relations where the two governments were not supposed to have official contacts.

That is why the Macau SAR government has no plans to create a post similar to that held by Mr Paul Yip, special adviser to Chief Executive Tung Chee Hwa.

The post was created to take care of bilateral relations between Hongkong and Taipei in an unofficial capacity.

Similarly, Beijing has allowed de facto direct air links across the Taiwan Strait via Macau, but not Hongkong.

Taiwanese passengers can fly on Air Macau, making a stopover there, between two destinations on both sides of the Taiwan Strait without changing planes.

This greatly reduces the hazards of cross-strait travel.

Recently, its agreement to allow Eva Air, a Taiwanese carrier, to acquire 5 per cent of the shares of Air Macau was considered a step forward in giving Macau a greater role to play in cross-strait exchanges.

Mr Wang also stressed that the present system of granting visas to Taiwanese travellers on arrival would remain unchanged.

This means that Taiwanese can enter the territory virtually visa-free, whereas they cannot do so when entering Hongkong.

Obviously Beijing hopes that the more flexible approach, a Portuguese legacy, can be further expanded so that Macau can help foster closer links between the mainland and Taiwan.

Re-Writing the History of Taiwan

9 October 1999

TO MANY schoolchildren, history and geography are boring subjects. To politicians such as Taiwanese President Lee Teng-hui, history and geography are powerful tools they can use to shape a young person's mind.

The island's first Taiwan-born President and one set on independence, Mr Lee knows unless he changes the way the two subjects are taught in schools, his mission to take Taiwan out of China may never succeed.

The mission was stated explicitly in an interview with the late Japanese writer Ryotaro Shiba in 1993.

Likening himself to Moses who led the Israelites out of Egypt, the President, a Christian, had said: "Alas, we have already started off. A bright future awaits Moses and his men. Yes, we have begun our journey...whenever I think of the Feb 28 incident, exodus is the right conclusion."

On Feb 28, 1947, an uprising by the locals against the high-handed rule of the Kuomintang (KMT) was suppressed by force. Many died and others were given life imprisonment.

In line with his mission, Mr Lee began to forge a new Taiwanese identity, starting with changes in the primary and lower secondary school curriculum.

Reacting to Mr Shiba's remark that it was a waste of time for Taiwanese children to memorise ancient Chinese dynasties' names, he showed his abhorrence for the two subjects' curriculum.

"It is absurd that our curriculum in history and geography is full of stuff about China," he had said. "I shall ask our schools to replace them with those of Taiwan."

In 1998, the Ministry of Education came up with a plan on curriculum reform to be implemented in 2001.

The plan was for history and geography not to be taught as separate subjects but to be combined, together with civics, into a new subject called the humanities.

The content would also focus more on Taiwan's culture and history. Less attention would be devoted to Chinese history.

One of the guidelines of the Education Reform Committee said that the new humanities course should deal with things "nearer home" first, then extend outward.

Based on this guideline, educationist Peng Ming-hui, a member of the working group on the humanities subject, described its approach in terms of five concentric circles.

The innermost one is the student and the interactive effects of school, family and community, followed by counties and cities, Taiwan, Asia, and finally the world.

Clearly then, China is either to be left out or treated only as part of Asia.

Even more controversial is the attempt to re-interpret history.

While most of the existing textbooks tell students that Taiwan is part of China with a history than spans over 3,000 years, the new guidelines separate the island's history from that of China and suggest that it is only about 400 years old.

According to the new guidelines, the history of Taiwan has seven phases:

- Prehistoric era
- The Dutch-Spanish occupation
- The Ming Dynasty occupation
- The Qing Dynasty occupation
- The era of increasing international pressures
- The Japanese occupation
- The period under the Republic of China

According to pro-unification legislator Fung Hu-hsiang, this re-interpretation of history has serious long-term political repercussions.

Presented this way, Taiwan's relationship with China is no different from its relationship with its previous colonial overlords Holland, Spain and Japan.

The kinship or the "flesh and blood relations" between Taiwan and the mainland is therefore much diluted, if not completely wiped out.

Moreover, by emphasising Taiwan as a place occupied by others every now and then, it undermines China's claim that Taiwan is, historically, part of China.

Dr Fung pointed out that this interpretation of history coincided with Mr Lee's own historical view, manifested in his remark to author Shiba that "all those who ruled Taiwan were foreign powers... even the KMT is but another alien authority that came to rule Taiwan".

Dr Fung said to annihilate a nation, the first thing to do would be to wipe out its history. Similarly, to sever ties between Taiwan and the mainland, Taiwan's history had to be rewritten.

The curriculum reform would serve this purpose, he said. "Two to three generations down the road, the basis for reunification would be undermined completely."

Democracy a la Taiwan: Uproar over term extension

21 September 1999

TAIWAN'S National Assembly played "dirty politics" recently when its members voted to extend their current term by another two years, which translates into an extra NT$6 million (S$300,000) in each pocket.

Not unexpectedly, this created an uproar, with both politicians and the public condemning the deputies for advancing their self-interest under the guise of reforming the national body.

Under the Constitution, Taiwan has five administrative tiers: a central government, two metropolitan cities, two provinces, 23 counties and cities, and numerous villages. Each tier consists of a government and a body of representatives.

At the central level, there is an additional body, the National Assembly, which selects the President and Vice-President, and drafts or amends the Constitution.

Since all the government heads and representatives are now elected, each with different terms, it means that there is an island-wide election biennially — a waste of resources.

Overhauling the Constitution became important. The first to go was the province, scrapped last year.

Then came the National Assembly, redundant as the President is elected. Its remaining task — constitutional revision — could be vested in the legislature.

Assembly deputies, naturally, were unwilling to amend the Constitution to wipe themselves out.

After repeated bargaining, they finally agreed to phase out the National Assembly in stages. In exchange, they extended their own terms for another two years.

There are many benefits from this move. For one, it will guarantee that they stay on the public payroll for another two years and receive about NT$6 million each.

As the amendment passed also did away with Assembly elections — which would have been held next March when their current term expires — deputies stood to save between NT$30 million and NT$40 million in election expenses. This was a clear case of benefiting oneself at the public's expense.

The deputies' move drew flak as people argued it was unconstitutional. Since they were given a four-year mandate, they should step down when their time was up.

Given the people's strong opposition, both the ruling KMT and the opposition Democratic Progressive Party (DPP) did not dare support the amendment. Instead, they vowed to penalise members who voted for it.

The deputies, working closely with Speaker Su Nan-cheng, rushed the Bill through the three readings in one single sitting, leaving no room for public discussion. Mr Su also approved putting the Bill to a secret ballot so that deputies who voted for the amendment would not be identified.

This shows that the deputies knew that the amendment's substance and procedure were problematic. It also highlighted the breakdown of the party system as both the KMT and DPP were helpless in stopping their members in the National Assembly from going ahead.

When pressure on the Speaker to resign grew, he said the extension was not self-aggrandisement but to give the President ample time to draft a "basic law" to replace the existing Constitution.

He said that the Assembly would freeze the present Constitution until the day China is reunified. Meanwhile, a "basic law" was needed to reflect the present political reality.

When President Lee Teng-hui first announced his "two states theory" in July, the presidential office hinted that there would be a major constitutional amendment to codify the theory. The undertaking, according to a spokesman, would be the biggest since the scrapping of the provincial structure.

China reacted strongly and threatened to use force should Mr Lee's theory become law. As a result, Taiwan was forced to deny such a plan in public. But Mr Lee was considering replacing the Constitution with another piece of legal document.

Disclosing Mr Lee's highly sensitive ulterior motive greatly embarrassed the President. His spokesman denied flatly that he had any prior knowledge of the "basic law."

To prove the President's innocence, the KMT expelled Mr Su from the party, which means that he loses the Speaker's post, his membership in the party's Central Standing Committee and his representation as a KMT Assembly member.

Made a scapegoat, a defiant Mr Su revealed that the motion — to extend the term of the delegates — was drafted by three KMT delegates close to the President, who therefore was fully aware. He also disclosed that the three had decided that the motion be proposed by the DPP deputy Liu Yi-teh to avoid embarrassing the ruling party.

The puzzle is now solved.

A separatist President collaborated with the like-minded opposition in an attempt to replace the existing Constitution with a "basic law," to give effect to the "two states" theory with regard to ties with China.

To ensure that the deputies supported the "basic law," the President agreed to reward them by giving tacit approval to extending their tenure.

When the plan generated strong opposition at home and from China, the President denied any prior knowledge and made a scapegoat of the Assembly speaker.

This, then, is "democracy" a la Taiwan.

Taipei Plans to Suspend Charter

7 September 1999

TAIWAN'S National Assembly Speaker said yesterday that the island planned to "suspend" the present Constitution and instead draft a "basic law" to reflect its current constitutional reality.

The Speaker, Mr Su Nan-cheng, used the term "suspension" twice and "temporarily frozen" once when referring to constitutional amendments at a press conference held to explain why delegates to the National Assembly should vote to extend their four-year term by another 25 months. The term of the current session expires in May next year.

The extension proposal has caused a major uproar in Taiwan with many people seeing it as a self-aggrandisement of the delegates.

Many members of the public want the assembly to be scrapped because they do not see it as playing a useful role.

According to Mr Su, the extension was necessary "to provide sufficient time and space for a major constitutional revision".

Observers pointed out that soon after President Lee Teng-hui proposed his "two states theory", the presidential office had hinted that a major constitutional and legal amendment effort would be undertaken to give effect to the new theory.

China reacted by saying that any such moves would be deemed a declaration of independence and would mean war.

To avoid strong reactions from Beijing, the ruling Kuomintang (KMT) backed down and said it would not revise the Constitution, but the opposition pro-independence Democratic Progressive Party (DPP) proposed "freezing" the current Constitution and replacing it with a "basic law" or a "special law".

It was meant to be similar to the "basic law" of West Germany before unification.

When asked by The Straits Times to clarify the terms "suspending" and "freezing" the present Constitution, Mr Su deliberately avoided all these terms but stressed that "the Republic of China Constitution will still be there but it will not be implemented until there is a unified China".

"Before unification, we need to have appropriate laws to reflect our current constitutional reality," he said.

"Whether it be called the amendment of specific articles or the drafting of a basic law does not matter," he explained. "The important thing is to have the current constitutional reality adequately reflected."

When asked if this was meant to give effect to Mr Lee's "two states" theory, he said this was beyond his power to decide and would be discussed by a team of experts.

He said a 60-strong team would be formed to look into how the constitutional reality could be best expressed. The team would discuss the island's status, political structure, relations between its central and local governments and the rights and obligations of its people.

Delegates would meet behind closed doors and come up with a draft. Consultations would then be held island-wide to solicit the people's views.

Mr Su said the experts selected were those acceptable to both the ruling and opposition parties. They would have to agree to two basic pre-conditions before they were invited.

They had to agree to respect the Republic of China Constitution and use it as the framework on which amendments would be based. They also had to agree to consider "the situation before unification".

Mr Su said he had to set these two pre-conditions because he had to take the island's stability, especially the reaction of Beijing against constitutional amendment, into consideration.

Mainland Policy Stays, says Teng-hui

3 September 1999

TAIWAN President Lee Teng-hui said yesterday that his mainland policy is still governed by the National Unification Guidelines (NUG), which envisages a three-phase approach towards eventual unification with China.

This was the first time he reiterated the guidelines since he formulated his "two states" theory almost two months ago, saying that Taiwan-China relations were those between two states.

In his statement commemorating Armed Forces Day, he said: "In view of the drastic development in the cross-strait situation, our mainland policy remains unchanged and we continue to abide by the National Unification Guidelines.

"Under the principles of peace, rationality, equality and mutual benefit, and based on economic development and democratic construction, we continue to push for exchanges, dialogue and consultation so as to play a more positive role in China's modernisation process."

According to sources close to the presidential office, to give effect to his "two states" theory, Mr Lee had originally planned for a major law revision exercise that included the Constitution and the NUG.

But China has vowed to use force should there be any constitutional amendment to give effect to the "two states" theory. Beijing saw such a move as a declaration of independence.

Since the United States also frowned upon his move, Mr Lee was forced to shelve his original plan, and said he still honoured the NUG.

Failing to amend the Constitution and laws, he nevertheless managed to get his "two states" theory adopted as the resolution of the ruling Kuomintang (KMT) in the party's national congress last Saturday.

The opposition Democratic Progressive Party (DPP) yesterday tried to push through a Bill asking for amendment of more than 33 laws and regulations to give effect to the "two states" theory.

Sponsoring the Bill, DPP legislators Lin Chuo-shui and Shen Fu-hsiung said more than 300 clauses and provisions in these 33 laws needed to be amended.

While the substance of the laws remains unchanged, they sought to substitute the term "mainland area" wherever it appeared with "the People's Republic of China" (PRC) and "Taiwan area" with "the Republic of China" (ROC), the island's official name.

At the same time, the term "Chinese" would be specified to mean either PRC or ROC nationals depending on the specific case.

Similarly, wherever the law mentions relations between Taiwan and the mainland, it was proposed that this be changed to relations between the ROC and the PRC.

Furthermore, phrases like "before unification" should be rewritten to say "before the relations between the ROC and the PRC are defined".

The DPP wanted to make this Bill their priority when the legislature resumes session after the summer break but the KMT said it did not support the Bill.

Since the KMT enjoys a clear majority in the legislature, the Bill will not be passed if it keep its word about not supporting the proposal.

More Taipei money for missile defence

28 August 1999

TAIWAN will increase its defence budget for the installation of the theatre missile defence (TMD) system against alleged threats from China, Defence Minister Tang Fei told a legislative hearing yesterday morning.

Without giving a specific figure, he said that he would ask for an increase of defence budget from its current ratio of 2.6 per cent of gross domestic product (GDP) to 3.5 per cent to generate the necessary resources for the TMD system. The defence budget for the fiscal year of 1999 is US$7.8 billion (S$13.2 billion).

Taiwan's defence budget as a ratio of GDP was among the lowest of all industrial nations.

Compared with other countries facing a similar threat, the island's was disproportionately low, he said, citing South Korea's 6 per cent and Israel's 8 per cent as examples.

To ensure that the research and development of the TMD system did not crowd out other defence priorities, an increase of budgetary appropriation was needed, he stressed.

He estimated that the total cost involved in TMD installation would be as high as NT$300 billion (S$15.5 billion) spread over the next eight years.

This was based on the calculation that each unit cost about US$1 billion and Taiwan would require at least 10 units to cover 70 per cent of its territories.

He made his formal proposal to build the TMD system at the ruling Kuomintang's central committee meeting on Aug 18.

Describing the TMD system as a physical and psychological confidence-booster, Mr Tang said that the low-altitude version of the system would meet the current and future needs of Taiwan.

"We need to have the military force to claim a position of equality with China under the 'special state-to-state relationship'," he added.

President Lee Teng-hui gave the green-light to set up the TMD system at the meeting and instructed Premier Vincent Siew to take whatever steps necessary to facilitate its implementation.

Mr Siew is expected to incorporate the proposal in his next annual policy address when the legislature resumes its session after the summer break.

Mr Tang said that before the TMD system was fully operational, Taiwan needed to rely on its indigenous missile defence system, which focused on the Sky Bow I and II surface-to-air missiles.

According to Major-General Wang Chao-tai, commander of the Army's Air Defence Command, the Sky Bow had been deployed at six army bases, four in Taiwan proper and one each in the offshore islands of Matsu and Penghu.

China has protested strongly against the US attempt to extend its TMD umbrella to Taiwan, saying that it might be forced to readjust its military strategy if the US does so.

Cross-Strait Dispute: China Gives Peace a Chance

28 August 1999

THE Beidaihe retreat provided not just a refuge from Beijing's scorching summer heat, but also helped the Chinese leadership keep a cool mind with regard to dealing with Taiwan after President Lee Teng-hui made his "two states" remarks.

Emerging from the resort, located about 260 km east of the Chinese capital, Beijing, leaders decided to adopt a decidedly more conciliatory approach towards cross-strait problems.

While not renouncing the use of force against Taiwan, Beijing said that it would "try its utmost to achieve reunification peacefully".

This policy was announced on Wednesday at the National Conference on Taiwan. It was the first time since July 9 that China has stressed peaceful reunification, following a month of verbal threats about military action against Taiwan.

One way China defused the volatile situation was to disparage President Lee's theory. Vice-Premier Qian Qichen told a pro-unification Taiwanese group on Monday that China noted no constitutional amendment had been made to give effect to the theory.

As long as this was the case, Beijing would treat Mr Lee's theory as merely his personal opinion that would be shelved as soon as he steps down as president next year.

By playing down the "two states" remarks, Mr Qian provided a chance for China to back down from its previous hawkish position threatening the immediate use of force.

It also gave Taiwan's next president room to disentangle the island from the controversy sparked by Mr Lee.

Thus, an imminent military showdown was avoided.

Mr Qian also reformulated China's long-standing policy on Taiwan, adhering to three principles: the principle of one China; of peaceful reunification under the "one country, two systems" model; and of resolutely defending China's sovereignty and territorial integrity.

He was in fact telling the Taiwanese that there would be no threat of force unless they took definitive action to break away from the mainland.

Although this position is not new, it contrasted sharply with earlier reports that China was so enraged that it thought it might as well make good use of this opportunity to solve the issue once and for all, even if it necessitated the use of force.

Mr Qian also offered Taiwan another chance to return to the 1992 consensus on "one China", by telling the group that Beijing still expected Mr Koo Chen-fu, Taiwan's top negotiator with the mainland, to provide a "genuine" explanation.

This implied that Mr Koo was under pressure not to deviate from Mr Lee's position when he made his initial reply, which was rejected two hours after it was tendered.

Beijing saw the 1992 consensus as the basis for dialogue between the two sides.

It was on this understanding that its top negotiator, Mr Wang Daohan, was scheduled to visit the island in October, making him the highest-ranking official to visit the island in 50 years.

The promulgation of the "two states" theory made his visit highly unlikely, for it could be construed as a tacit endorsement of Mr Lee's departure from the "one China" policy.

Despite this, Mr Wang echoed Mr Qian's call for a "genuine explanation" by saying that he had never said he would cancel the visit.

Both officials' statements showed that despite strong internal opposition to the visit, Beijing was still keeping this option open.

All these are positive developments emerging from the Beidaihe retreat.

Sources said that at the retreat, the Chinese leaders examined every aspect of the Taiwan issue and concluded that war was not yet the last resort.

One significant issue they examined was the American attitude. They wanted to ascertain whether the US was behind or supported the "two states" theory.

They also debated the so-called even-handedness of the US in general terms and at this particular juncture. They wanted a more positive role from the US to force Taiwan back to the "one China" principle.

Most importantly, Beijing wanted to know whether the US would intervene should a war break out, and whether Japan would activate its bilateral defence pact with the US and put Taiwan under the pact's umbrella.

The likelihood of a tripartite military alliance between the US, Japan and Taiwan was also studied.

The leaders decided that during the forthcoming Apec summit, Chinese President Jiang Zemin would seek clarification from US President Bill Clinton on these issues.

The Beidaihe meeting also studied the Taiwanese situation.

In particular, the leaders wanted to know whether Mr Lee would amend the Constitution to enshrine the "two states" remarks.

They also studied the attitudes of all the four presidential candidates towards the "two states" theory and how likely Mr Lee's legacy would be perpetuated.

A lot of time was devoted to cross-examining the likelihood of a military retaliation by Taipei, in view of its recent claim that it could strike Shanghai and Hongkong.

The strengths and weaknesses of Taipei's army were thoroughly examined, including its nuclear and missile capacity and its ability to replenish military hardware.

Domestically, although the leaders were confident of whole-hearted support from the people to claim the island, even by force, they still asked themselves whether there were alternative options to the "one country, two systems" model.

The ability of the economy to support a major war should it become protracted was also thoroughly studied.

The source said, without specifying details, that after weighing each of the factors, they came to the conclusion that there was still room for peace.

It was added that thanks to literally hundreds of researchers who turned out good data and recommendations at short notice, the leadership was able to make a balanced and unemotional decision, which was to give peace a last chance.

Annex
The Members and Their Think-Tanks

AT BEIDAIHE, each member of the Leading Group on Taiwan Affairs of the Politburo, the supreme decision-making body on Taiwan issues, was backed up by a think-tank.

The Group was headed by President Jiang Zemin himself, with Vice-Premier Qian Qichen as deputy.

Members included Zeng Qinghong, Mr Jiang's confidant; Chen Yunlin, top executor of cross-strait policies; Wang Zhaoguo, responsible for united front tactics; Xu Yongyao, the intelligence head; Xiong Guangkai, representing the military; and Wang Daohan, the top negotiator.

The think tanks assisted in fact-finding, policy research and brain-storming to arrive at a more balanced recommendation for their respective bosses.

Credit should be given to them for helping to defuse a potential calamity, sources said.

HEAD OF THE GROUP
Jiang Zemin

THE DEPUTY
Qian Qichen
Institute of International Issues

THE MEMBERS
- Zeng Qinghong
  Central Policy Research Unit
- Chen Yunlin
  Research Bureau, Taiwan Affairs Office
  Institute of Taiwan, the China Academy of Social Sciences
  Institute of Taiwan, Xiamen University
- Wang Zhaoguo
  Policy Research Unit, United Front Department
  Policy Research Unit, National Taiwan Studies Association
  Policy Research Unit, National Taiwan Liaison Association
- Xu Yongyao
  Institute of Modern International Relations
  Institute of Taiwan, the China Academy of Social Sciences
- Xiong Guangkai
  Institute of International Strategic Studies
  Institute of Peace and Development
- Wang Daohan
  Institute of Asia-Pacific Studies, Shanghai Academy of Social Sciences
  Institute of Taiwan Studies, Shanghai
  Institute of International Issues, Shanghai

Lee Teng-hui Backs Plan to Join TMD

19 August 1999

PRESIDENT Lee Teng-hui yesterday backed a decision for Taiwan to join the proposed US-Japan Theatre Missile Defence (TMD) system to protect the island from China's growing missile threat.

The move is certain to add to the current tension with Beijing, which has condemned the anti-missile system and is already incensed by Mr Lee's "two states" remarks.

The Taiwanese leader gave his full support after a briefing by Defence Minister Tang Fei, who told top officials of the ruling Kuomintang that it was necessary for Taiwan to be part of the high-tech TMD project "for the sake of national self-defence".

Describing the TMD system as a physical and psychological confidence-booster, Gen Tang said that the low-altitude version of the system would meet the current and future needs of Taiwan.

"We need to have the military force to claim a position of equality with China under the 'special state-to-state relationship'," he said.

"In the long run, we also need to modernise our military to prepare for high-tech wars. A low-altitude TMD system is a good way to start this long-term process," he added.

According to KMT spokesman Huang Hui-jen, Mr Lee said that TMD not only met the needs of the current situation, but was also in line with the island's long-term interest.

The President said that every effort for the system "deserved praise" and ordered government agencies to work with the Defence Ministry on the plan, which could cost Taiwan billions of dollars.

"Where possible, our defence budget should be augmented to generate the necessary resources for the system," he was quoted as saying.

Meanwhile, China attacked a US-Japan agreement signed on Monday to research an anti-missile system as a poorly masked attempt to dominate the Asia-Pacific region, news agency reports said.

"People can feel that Japan and the United States are further seeking military primacy in the Asia-Pacific area," a People's Daily commentary said yesterday.

"If this situation is going to develop further, it will seriously affect the whole area's peace and stability," it added.

Beijing, which views Taiwan as a renegade province, opposes the TMD system as a tool to contain China.

It has denounced proposals to include Taiwan in the system as "encroachment on China's sovereignty and territorial integrity and interference in China's internal affairs".

China Will Avoid Military Action

14 August 1999

CHINA will refrain from launching any major military offensive against Taiwan before the island's presidential elections next March, even though its military is confident of "landing on the island within a day and putting down all resistance".

This is a conclusion that can be drawn from the recent meeting at the Beidaihe summer retreat of the top Chinese leadership.

In other words, Beijing is giving Taipei a last chance "not to break away", even though it has the military's assurance that the Chinese army has the ability to take the island by force.

According to a source close to the meeting, a military leader claimed that once the political decision was made, "our army can land on the island within a day and put down all resistance".

This assertion seems to contrast sharply with current analysis that China lacks the ability to take Taiwan by force, especially when doing so risks the intervention of the United States.

The source said that Chinese confidence was based on its own strength.

"Most people, including the US, have grossly under-rated China's military capability," the source said, adding that a military official who gave an assessment at the summer retreat had indicated that "without US intervention, taking back Taiwan is just like picking up something from your own pocket".

"The fatal weakness of Taiwan is that it lacks an indigenous defence industry and its army lacks major war experience," the military official said.

Said the source: "With American intervention, the war would be a lot more costly, but it does not mean we will not win.

"We had fought directly with the US in Korea and indirectly in Vietnam, and our military capability at those times was far more backward than it is now.

"In Korea, we pushed the US troops, who came close to the Chinese border near the Yalu River, back to the 38th parallel.

"In Vietnam, we helped the Vietnamese to drive the US out of the country."

Quoting the military official, the source also said: "The US knows perfectly well that once it is involved in an armed conflict with China, it will enter into endless troubles.

"The best scenario is for a war to be avoided. If not, we will win."

Concern for the Taiwanese people was what had been holding back Beijing.

"Had we not been concerned with the loss of life and property among our Taiwanese compatriots, we would certainly have taught Lee Teng-hui a lesson, because what he did had already breached our tolerance limit," the military official said.

According to the source, the Beidaihe gathering agreed that Mr Lee's "two states" theory had increased the threat of national disintegration.

Although China is aware of the growing influence of the independence movement, most people have thought that it will not present a real threat until 2004 or 2008, or about one or two presidential terms after Mr Lee's tenure.

But the danger is more imminent now. And Chinese authorities consider Mr Lee a highly provocative offender.

Sources recalled that shortly after the bombing of the Chinese embassy in Belgrade on May 8 — which shocked and angered China — Mr Lee, on May 19, launched his book Voice of Taiwan, which advocated breaking up China into seven parts.

Instead of sharing the bitter feelings of the Chinese people, Mr Lee added substance to a long-standing suspicion of a US attempt to turn Taiwan into the Kosovo of the east.

Two months later came his open call for "two states".

Beijing saw this as sabre-rattling.

Chinese President Jiang Zemin reportedly said that "the struggle against Mr Lee is not one over differences in ideology or political systems, but one of defending China's sovereignty and territorial integrity".

On issues of this nature, China was prepared to go all out regardless of the costs involved, he said.

To avoid hurting the feelings of the Taiwanese, sources said, China's latest stance on the Taiwan issue following the Beidaihe retreat was to: *pi* (to criticise); *kan* (to observe); and *zhunbei* (to prepare).

This means that China will step up its massive criticism campaign against Mr Lee and his "two states" theory, but it will also wait and see if there is any hope for a peaceful solution.

According to the source, this will depend on whether Mr Lee codifies his theory through constitutional amendments; on the attitude of the next president towards reunification; and on the American stance.

However, China will make all the preparations necessary to ensure military victory should circumstances dictate a non-peaceful solution.

From the regional security point of view, this means that there is still room for a last-ditch peace effort, because infuriated though it is, China is clearly showing great restraint.

China Lacks Vision Over Taiwan

13 August 1999

THE issue of Taiwan's independence has always posed a serious challenge to the Chinese leadership, all the more so in this decade.

The independence movement took root at the end of the last century, when China lost a war to the Japanese and was forced to cede the island province in 1895. Japan surrendered the island to the Allied Forces 50 years later.

To the Chinese people, therefore, recovering Taiwan was — and remains — their legitimate right, something the international community does not challenge.

However, the half century under Japanese rule convinced a section of the Taiwanese population that a reunion with the motherland was not good for the island's future.

Such thinking was not surprising. After all, the fact that Japan could defeat China and take away its territory meant that it possessed overall superiority "militarily, economically and culturally" at that time.

This superiority was reflected in the governance of the island, which fared better than the mainland in those days.

Professor Peng Ming-min, dubbed Taiwan's "father of independence", wrote in his memoirs that his first trip back to China in the 1920s disappointed him so much that he concluded the island was better off separated from the mainland.

The embryonic notion of separation that began in the last century was shaped further by the Cold War that arose after the end of World War II.

Taiwan, situated at the tangent of two belligerent camps led by the United States on one side and the Soviet Union on the other, was Washington's "unsinkable aircraft carrier" in the encirclement of the Soviet-led bloc, including China.

The result — Taiwan's split from the mainland was prolonged for another half a century.

During this period, Soviet-leaning Beijing and US-leaning Taipei took diametrically opposite development paths, which only accentuated the differences between them further.

The independence movement in Taiwan, which gained new strength because of the Cold War, is likely to gain further momentum in the next century because it will become a policy tool of the US.

The biggest problem for the US-dominated world in the next century is how to manage a rising China. This subject has dominated political discussions in the 1990s, with policy recommendations oscillating from containment to engagement.

China has embarked on major reforms since 1979. Two decades of rapid growth since then has resulted in a China which is strong enough not only to survive the meltdown of the Soviet bloc, but also to emerge as a world-class power in its own right.

One of the options suggested to "manage" a rising China was to bring about its disintegration, so that a downsized China would not present any threat. This was first suggested by a US official in 1991.

When a host of sanctions imposed after the Tiananmen Incident of 1989 failed to bring China to its knees, a US official lamented that perhaps "the ultimate sanction is to bring about its disintegration".

This view first appeared in a "Foreign Affairs" essay in 1991, and the idea was soon taken up by Japan.

In 1992, Japanese writer Mineo Nakajima, currently president of the Tokyo University of Foreign Studies, published an article "On the Federal Republic of China" in which he suggested that the country would best be divided into 12 parts. A dismembered China would present much less of a threat to its neighbours, the article argued.

Such open discussion on the dismembering of China reflected latent American and Japanese fears of a strong China emerging in the next century. So any disintegration plan would best start with the Taiwanese, some of whom harbour separatist notions.

The independence movement in Taiwan was quick to seize this opportunity.

In 1995, pro-independence writer Wang Wen-shan published "The Seven Heroes of Peace" in which he proposed cutting up China into seven pieces, with each having its own sovereignty.

The discussion culminated in a recently-published book by Taiwanese President Lee Teng-hui — in which he also called for China to be split into seven blocs to speed up development — and in his controversial "two states" theory.

The Taiwan issue can turn explosive in the next century.

The Chinese leadership would need exceptional statesmanship and far-sighted strategic vision if it wants to extricate Beijing from such a situation.

Unfortunately, these attributes seem to be lacking at the moment.

Only two options are open so far: reunification under Beijing's terms or the use of force.

It would be extremely naive of Beijing if it were to assume that Taipei could accept the "one country, two systems" model.

Taipei would never enter into negotiations which would relegate the island to a subservient position.

Few people doubt China's ability or determination to regain Taiwan by force, or question its legitimacy in doing so.

But doing so will surely create a phantom that will haunt the Chinese race for the next 100 years.

The June 4 Incident has haunted the Communist Party for the past 10 years.

A military takeover of Taiwan and the expected loss of innocent lives will create lasting ill-feeling and bitterness and pose as a real stumbling block to China's aspired national revival.

Unfortunately, between war and peace under Beijing's terms, there is no alternative. This lack of strategic vision is really a tragedy.

Beijing should be able to see that once the country resumes its previous position as a strong nation with irresistible cultural charm, the reunification problem would be resolved naturally.

In its 3,000-year history, China had been the pre-eminent country in the world for 70 per cent of the time, when countries far apart felt honoured to be associated with it.

The setback it suffered in the last 150 years was but a minor and temporary hiccup.

Therefore, in order to solve a problem that straddles three centuries, China should take an extremely long-term view, focusing first on regaining its original position: a country that is among the strongest in the world.

Unfortunately, the present leadership is much too bogged down by petty politics and temporal concerns.

For example, the real reason that Beijing refuses to treat Taipei on the basis of equality is the deep-rooted disdain it has for the island.

Politicians argue that since it is physically much smaller than the mainland, there is no reason to accord it a position equal to that of Beijing.

The military argues that since Taipei's Kuomintang government was defeated by its troops in 1949, there is no reason to accord it equal rights at the negotiating table.

As long as the leadership in Beijing is stuck in this mind-set, there is no chance of solving this three-century-old problem.

Chinese Jets Crossed Strait's Mid-Line Twice, says Taipei

11 August 1999

TAIWAN yesterday admitted for the first time that military tension over the Taiwan Strait had increased with Chinese fighters crossing the mid-line of the strait twice.

President Lee Teng-hui confirmed the incursions personally, but he appealed to the people to keep calm.

According to the Ministry of National Defence (MND), two J-7 fighters crossed the mid-line by 5 km on July 25 and two J-8 fighters crossed it by 10 km on July 30.

China's J-7 fighters are basically copies of the Russian MiG-21 while the J-8s are locally-developed aircraft.

The MND spokesman said that they did not issue any press statement then because they did not want to cause unnecessary panic, adding that the flight profiles of the aircraft were not hostile.

According to a press statement issued by the MND, the Chinese fighters had swerved back immediately when they found that they had crossed the mid-line.

The sorties were isolated and were not followed by others.

The statement said the aircraft crossed the mid-line probably because the pilots were flying too fast and were also trying to avoid thick clouds.

"In any case, their flights were monitored closely by our fighters in the vicinity, so there is no need to panic," it said.

According to Mr Chung Shen-ling, deputy head of the Operations Bureau of the MND, Su-27 fighters had also been spotted near the mid-line.

"They flew in pairs and since there were no other aircraft to provide cover or support, we concluded they were not on any offensive mission," he said.

He added that since the announcement of the "two states" theory, Chinese J-7 and J-8 fighters deployed in Fujian province opposite Taiwan had flown close to the mid-line.

Recently, Su-27 combat aircraft deployed in Anhui and Guangdong provinces had also flown similar sorties, he said, adding that they usually flew a north-south path for about 15 nautical miles (27.7 km) to 30 nautical miles along the Chinese coast.

"As we did not detect any mass concentration of troops at the opposite side, we concluded that these sorties were mainly aimed at applying psychological pressure on us," he said, dismissing reports that an attack was imminent.

An MND spokesman said that in response to the increased sorties, the Taiwanese air force had been told to "avoid provocation without showing weakness".

As long as the state of alert remained unchanged, the policy was to avoid triggering a conflict, he said.

Taiwan's Profile Raised, says Teng-hui

11 August 1999

TAIWAN President Lee Teng-hui yesterday said it was good that his "two states" theory had aroused so much international attention as it would raise the island's international profile.

He also confirmed for the first time that Chinese fighters had crossed the mid-line of the Taiwan Strait on two occasions.

Mr Lee was speaking to senior party cadres of the ruling Kuomintang when he departed from the prepared speech and made the above remarks.

He said that since he made his "special state-to-state relationship" remarks, the whole world seemed to roar.

"Very good, the more they roar, the better the whole world knows our plight. More people are aware that the Republic of China is being pushed to the corner," he said, referring to Taiwan by its official name.

He explained that what he had done was to define clearly Taiwan's status so that whoever succeeded him would not be bothered by an ambiguous existence.

He told his senior cadres that there were three key elements to ensure the island's continued survival and growth: a clearly defined status as a sovereign state; a stable cross-strait relationship; and a pragmatic diplomacy.

The most important was the first, he stressed, adding that he was proud to have based Taiwan's development on these three buttresses which ensured a stable transformation amid rapid economic development.

"My ultimate aim is to transform China, to let the Taiwanese experience blossom there.

"The two former presidents, Chiang Kai-shek and Chiang Ching-kuo, aimed at taking back the mainland by force. Unlike them, I am going to peacefully transform it with the Taiwanese experience. Chinese unification required Taiwanese democracy," he said.

Mr Lee also played down the military threat from China. "There had been lots of reports of Chinese fighters crossing the mid-line. In fact, there are only two such incidents, once by 5 km and another by 10 km.

"As the mid-line is not a clearly demarcated one, and fighters fly fast, they accidentally crossed it. As soon as they were aware of it, they swerved back. So you don't have to take it too seriously," he said, urging the people not to panic.

Following Mr Lee's comments on the Chinese fighters, Hongkong's Hang Seng Index fell 348.76, or 2.7 per cent, to 12,596.71, its biggest decline in a month, led by China-related shares.

The Defence Ministry earlier said there had been increased air sorties and training in the strait by the Chinese army.

Air force major-general Hu Yuan-chieh said the Chinese fighters did not cross the mid-line. But a Defence Ministry statement later in the day confirmed that Chinese fighters had crossed the mid-line twice.

Mr Lee, claiming to be familiar with China's military strategy, said that the Chinese would strike if they had the upper hand in the balance of power. Otherwise, they would back down.

"If we are strong, they will not come; if we are weak, they will…. In 1996 they hurled missiles at us. As soon as the USS Independence came, they stopped," he said.

Mr Lee said on July 9 that relations between Taiwan and China should be considered as "special state-to-state" ties.

Yesterday, Mr Benjamin Gilman, head of a US delegation which visited Taipei, said his group backed Mr Lee's statement. He said the two sides should "engage in a dialogue as equals".

Teng-hui Adamant About 'Two States' Demand

10 August 1999

TAIPEI — Taiwan's President Lee Teng-hui yesterday re-affirmed his commitment to the "two states" theory amid speculation that he had backed down from his own formulation following strong pressure from the United States.

He told a visiting seven-member US congressional delegation that from a historical, legal and realistic point of view, the relationship between China and Taiwan was a "special state-to-state" relationship.

"I am just stating a fact. This fact is undeniable," a presidential office statement quoted him as telling Mr Benjamin Gilman, chairman of the US House of Representatives' International Relations Committee.

"This is to further clarify and assert that relations on both sides of the Taiwan Strait are equal," he added.

He stressed that meaningful cross-strait dialogue could only be conducted on the basis of equality.

He said that the Beijing authorities had repeatedly insisted that "they are the central government and we are a local government".

This was by no means acceptable, the statement quoted him as saying.

"What is more, it is not reality," he added.

Mr Lee told his guests that now that cross-strait relations had been set on the basis of equality, there was nothing that could not be discussed between Beijing and Taipei.

He also extended his invitation to Mr Wang Daohan, China's top negotiator, to visit the island.

Mr Wang, president of the Association for Relations Across the Taiwan Strait, was scheduled to visit Taipei next month or in October.

But Mr Lee's "two states" theory, which China saw as an attempt towards independence, had made his visit highly unlikely. Beijing, however, has not ruled out such a trip.

Mr Lee's remarks to the visiting US delegation indicated that he was not returning to the "one China" policy, which some pro-independence Taiwanese had feared.

Following tremendous pressure from the US, the Mainland Affairs Council (MAC), Taipei's decision-making body on mainland affairs, had issued a much toned-down explanatory memorandum.

It said that Taipei remained committed to the 1992 consensus reached with Beijing on "one China" with different definition.

This was widely seen as an attempt to back down in view of strong negative international response to Mr Lee's theory.

The local media said that the President himself was not satisfied with the MAC memo, but in order not to make the situation worse, he had decided to adopt it. But his remarks yesterday showed otherwise.

Mr Gilman said his visit was part of a two-week fact-finding mission.

"I have been following events in the Taiwan Strait very closely for the past few weeks and have come here to gain a fuller understanding of the situation."

Cross-Strait Ties: The Numbers Game

26 July 1999

WHETHER US envoy Richard Bush's visit to Taiwan is productive at all remains to be seen but it has certainly resulted in a proliferation of political jargon beginning with a number.

Deciphering these numerical jargon can reveal important political messages.

When US President Bill Clinton sent envoys to Beijing and Taipei, he solemnly expounded the "three pillars of China" policy, which means one-China principle, peaceful solution and cross-strait dialogue.

In fact, the three can be reduced to two.

The "one-China" pillar forbids Taiwan to attempt independence and thus defines Taiwan's policy limit.

On the other hand, the "peaceful-solution" pillar restricts China's policy options to non-force ones.

Together, these two pillars define the room for manoeuvre for both sides.

In response, China's charge d'affaires in Washington sums up China's policy in terms of the 1-3-3 principles — meaning one China, three joint communiques and the three-nos policy of the US.

The three-nos policy — no to Taiwan independence, no to "one China, one Taiwan" or "two Chinas", and no to Taiwanese membership in organisations requiring statehood — was articulated by Mr Clinton last year during a visit to China and brought tremendous pressure on Taiwan.

To counter it, Taipei has been lobbying the US to add a fourth no: No to the use of force by China on Taiwan.

Now Taiwan has got it.

In addition to the "three pillars", Mr Bush has modified it to become the "four principles" by singling out the Taiwan Relations Act (TRA), under which the US pledges to help Taiwan in case of attack.

The first three are identical, while the fourth says the US remains committed to the TRA.

Previously, the TRA was treated under the "one China" principle. Now it has been "upgraded" into a separate principle in its own right.

This has the effect of meeting Taiwan's demand that a "fourth no" be added to Mr Clinton's original three.

In other words, the usefulness to China of the "three nos" is somewhat diluted by the addition of the "fourth no".

It immediately draws severe criticism from China.

The explanation of the so-called "special state-to-state relations" is also heavily laden with jargon beginning with a number.

Taiwanese President Lee Teng-hui stresses one no: no to independence. This is perhaps the most welcome gift for Mr Bush.

Vice-President Lien Chan explains the new concept in terms of "four Ps": pragmatism, parity, progress and peace, which makes Mr Lee's formulation look less provocative.

Finally, the Straits Exchange Foundation head Koo Chen-fu has come up with his own numerical jargon: "Four no changes", meaning no change to the basis of exchange, no change to established policy goals, no change to plans for their implementation and the most important of all, no change from the goal of a unified China.

Most likely, the last "no change" is to provide the assurance Beijing needs to resume talks with Taipei.

No Plans to Break Away, Taiwan Assures US

26 July 1999

THE top United States official in charge of Taiwan affairs, Mr Richard Bush, said that Taiwan now had a better understanding of the US position in the cross-strait row sparked by President Lee Teng-hui's remarks.

The head of the American Institute in Taiwan, sent as an emissary to Taipei to ease cross-strait tension, made the comments at the end of his four-day visit yesterday.

He reiterated that the "one China" policy had been "the cornerstone of US policy" for more than 20 years.

He said that, as a result of the discussions he had with Taiwanese officials, Taipei now had a better grasp of the US viewpoint.

Sources said that, when Mr Bush stated this position, he was reading point-by-point from a carefully-prepared note, stressing the US commitment to the "one China" principle.

Beijing was furious after Mr Lee told a German radio station on July 9 that cross-strait ties should be regarded as "special state-to-state relations".

Taiwan's two largest newspapers, the China Times and the United Daily News, both reported that Mr Lee responded to the US position by telling Mr Bush on Friday that Taiwan would not declare independence nor revise its Constitution to that effect.

China Times even quoted Mr Lee as telling Mr Bush solemnly: "I strongly oppose independence."

He reciprocated by saying: "The US remains committed to faithful implementation of the Taiwan Relations Act (TRA)."

He also told his host that he came "not to exert pressure, but to understand".

He reassured Taipei: "The friendship between the American people and the people in Taiwan is rock solid. All the elements of the administration's policy towards Taiwan remain in place."

Having stated the two commitments — to one China and to the TRA — which defined the limits of American tolerance, the US tried to avoid taking sides.

"How to define the 'one China' principle specifically and how to realise it concretely are best left to the two sides of the strait on a mutually-acceptable basis.

"How to promote cross-strait dialogue, exchanges and cooperation is up to the two sides," he said.

He also sought an assurance from Mr Koo Chen-fu, chairman of the Straits Exchange Foundation (SEF), that unification on the basis of democracy remained unchanged.

Mr Bush wanted to know how Mr Koo would answer his Chinese counterpart, Mr Wang Daohan of the Association for Relations Across the Taiwan Strait.

Mr Wang had sought a clarification from Mr Koo who, toeing the President's line, said exchanges between SEF and Arats were inter-state in nature.

The Arats chief said this position undermined the basis for exchanges — the "one China" principle — between them.

In the strongest indication by Beijing so far that Mr Wang's visit to Taiwan could be jeopardised, China said yesterday that there was no longer any basis for talks with Taiwan since its decision to drop the "one China" policy.

The Taiwanese President's "two states" theory had damaged cross-strait ties to the extreme, according to a commentary in the official Xinhua news agency.

"The basis for Wang Daohan's visit to Taiwan no longer exists," said the commentary.

Taiwan Backs Down Over Revising Constitution

22 July 1999

TAIPEI — Taiwan yesterday said that it would not revise its Constitution to legalise President Lee Teng-hui's formulation of "special state-to-state relations".

"There are no plans now to revise the Constitution," top government spokesman Chen Chien-jen told a press conference.

The National Unification Guidelines would also be left untouched, he said.

The spokesman also said that Taiwan would treat cross-strait ties as "special state-to-state relations".

He acknowledged that Cabinet officials, after several days of debate, had decided to drop some terms perceived in Beijing and even in Washington as provocative.

The phrases "two states", "two Chinas", "one China, two states", "one nation, two countries" and other similar formulations had been considered, and even used publicly by some officials, but would now be dropped, he said.

"We don't want to do anything to create confusion or misunderstanding," Mr Chen said. "We think special state-to-state relations is good enough."

The spokesman's statements appeared to be a further backing down for Taiwan.

After Mr Lee announced his new theory two weeks ago, the Taipei government said it planned to go ahead with constitutional revision.

But when an inter-party group met yesterday to iron out specific proposals for constitutional reforms, it decided finally not to raise the issue in view of the extremely volatile situation at present.

Sources close to the presidential office also said that the National Unification Guidelines, which spelt out a three-stage approach towards reunification, might have to be scrapped.

However, Mr Chen confirmed yesterday that the guidelines would remain unchanged.

He said that Taiwan shared China's goal of eventual reunification, but reiterated Taipei's insistence that Beijing first liberalise its political system.

He also repeated Taiwan's three core objectives in its policy on China: dialogue and exchanges with the mainland; a win-win policy in cross-strait relations; and the goal of a peaceful, democratic, united China.

On Tuesday, an unnamed Chinese official on Taiwan affairs warned Taipei not to revise its Constitution to legalise Mr Lee's formulation.

He said: "Divisive forces in Taiwan are attempting to revise the so-called 'Constitution' and 'law' of Taiwan in line with the 'two states' theory, and realise the 'independence of Taiwan' in the name of the so-called 'Republic of China'.

"It is a matter of grave concern, a more dangerous step and a severe challenge to the reunification cause by peaceful means."

The official warned divisive forces in Taiwan to stop playing with fire, or "you will end up perishing in fire".

Why Teng-hui Toned Down 'Two States' Declaration

21 July 1999

PRESIDENT Lee Teng-hui has no other choice.

In the face of strong negative responses from Beijing and Washington following his formulation of a "two states" theory, he had to tone down his formula by appending a "one China" commitment and a "no independence" pledge to his original proposal.

The reasons for making these two additions were obvious.

A strong military threat from Beijing, open criticism from Washington, as well as plummeting share prices at home all testified to the negative reception the proposal received.

US President Bill Clinton's telephone call to his Chinese counterpart added pressure on the Taiwanese leader.

After all, hotline calls were made only in a crisis situation.

The fact that Mr Clinton was forced to make the call indicated that, by Washington's reckoning, the Taiwanese leader was responsible for starting the crisis.

Mr Richard Bush, the most senior US official handling relations with Taiwan, was expected to arrive in the capital this weekend to seek an explanation from Taipei.

The writing was on the wall: It was up to Mr Lee to tone down his remarks or face greater international isolation.

What he could not do was withdraw his statement, which would mean political suicide.

The only way out was to reiterate his own position, but to dress it up with two additional pledges.

These two additions make no significant changes to his original proposition.

Even the opposition Democratic Progressive Party (DPP), which advocates independence for Taiwan, said that it accepted Mr Lee's re-formulation totally — in view of the difficult situation at home and abroad right now.

However, Mr Chiu I-jen, the DPP representative to the US, said the important thing was that by reiterating the "two states" position yesterday, Mr Lee has left no room for a fall-back to the "one China" position.

One can expect that this re-formulation will be the position that Taiwan's top cross-strait negotiator Koo Chen-fu takes when he offers the clarification sought by his Chinese counterpart Wang Daohan, whose visit to Taiwan later this year hangs in the balance.

Annex
Toning It Down

WHAT HE SAID THEN...
What Taiwan President Lee Teng-hui told Germany's Deutsche Welle station on July 9:

'Since we made our constitutional reforms in 1991, we have redefined cross-strait relations as nation-to-nation, or at least as special nation-to-nation relations.'
'The relations between China and Taiwan is one between countries, instead of one between a legitimate government and an illicit one, or a central government against a local one.'
'Since we define cross-strait relations as relations between countries, there is no need to declare Taiwan's independence.'

...WHAT HE SAYS NOW
What Mr Lee said in a speech at a Rotary Club function yesterday:

'The authorities here have redefined cross-strait ties to nation-to-nation, or at least special state-to-state since constitutional reforms were launched in 1991.'

'Our dealings with communist China must be conducted on an equal status in equal attitude. We will push for dialogue and negotiations between the two sides on an equal footing and promote further exchanges with caution. I did not say this to declare independence.'

'One China does not exist now, it is only possible in the future after reunification under the basis of democracy.'

Clinton Phone Call Helps Defuse Tension

20 July 1999

UNITED States President Bill Clinton's telephone call to his Chinese counterpart Jiang Zemin — in which he reiterated Washington's commitment to the "one China" policy — went a long way to help defuse cross-strait tension and might even make Beijing reconsider the need for a military response against Taiwan.

It showed that the US had nothing to do with Taiwan President Lee Teng-hui's redefinition of the island's status. China has been suspicious of American backing for Mr Lee.

The US involvement in the Kosovo crisis has worried China, which feared that it would set a precedent for "interference" in its Taiwan problem.

Therefore, it was watching closely to see if there was any sign of US-led intervention to help Taiwan achieve independence.

China's fears are not groundless. When Taiwan announced its mammoth US$300 million (S$510 million) aid to the Kosovo reconstruction effort, it was done with US acquiescence. Taiwanese Premier Vincent Siew admitted that he had discussed the matter with the US when he made a stopover in New York, en route to Central America in April.

Hence Beijing's concern that Mr Lee's "two states" formulation might also have had American backing.

Mr Clinton's call on Sunday dispelled this concern.

With the US reaffirming its commitment to "one China", it means that the "two states" policy could hardly get out of Taiwan, thus confining the damage within the island.

The call came at a time when China was about to decide what to do with the Taiwanese leader.

Chinese President Jiang Zemin had just returned from his state visit to Mongolia and planned to call an expanded meeting of the Politburo. The US leader's reassurance could therefore subtly guide Beijing towards formulating a less militant decision.

The telephone call, which was made at the US President's initiative, also came at a time when China had yet to recover from the wounds of Nato's bombing of its Chinese embassy in Belgrade.

It presented a good opportunity for Washington to show its goodwill towards Beijing.

Past experience has shown that whenever Sino-American relations were good, the Taiwan issue could be handled more leniently.

Mr Jiang's reply to his US counterpart was to reiterate China's position on Taiwan.

Despite the strong language used against Mr Lee, he did not threaten the use of force against Taiwan right away, a much toned-down approach compared to what pro-China media had depicted.

Crisis Team in Taipei as Tension Mounts

19 July 1999

Taiwan moved further into crisis mode yesterday with the setting up of a high-level team to handle the tense situation that has developed as a result of President Lee Teng-hui's "two states" concept.

Announcing the formation of a trans-ministerial crisis management team, Taiwanese Premier Vincent Siew said: "The need for quick response and fast-track action in an exceptional period required such a team to be set up."

This latest move came a day after the Defence Ministry set up a military task force which has drawn up 13 operational contingency plans to counter any form of Chinese military threat.

Mr Siew said that the high-powered team included heads from the national defence, finance, economic affairs, interior, transportation and communications, and foreign affairs ministries.

More alarming reports surfaced in Beijing and Hongkong yesterday, with China's Life Times Daily claiming that the Chinese military has begun large-scale military exercises in an unnamed location.

"Several special forces detachments of the People's Liberation Army have gathered and are holding large-scale military attack exercises in a certain military region," it reported.

Hongkong's Beijing-backed Wen Wei Po published a front-page photograph showing waves of amphibious vessels and vehicles making beach landings.

"Beijing will not renounce force to counter Taiwan independence," said its headline.

But Taiwan's defence ministry denied media reports saying the PLA had stepped up training drills and even sent jet fighters deep into the Taiwan Strait.

Said military spokesman Kung Fan-ting: "We've detected nothing abnormal.

There is no abnormal troop concentration and their aircraft and ships have not crossed the middle line in the Taiwan Strait."

Mr Siew's trans-ministerial team will meet for the first time today. Sources close to the Executive Yuan, Taiwan's Cabinet, said the Ministry of Finance, for example, will find additional ways of stabilising the financial sector, especially the stock and the foreign exchange markets.

It has set up a national stabilisation fund (NSF) with a targeted pool of NT$500 billion (S$25 billion) to cope with panic selling on the local bourse.

The funds came mainly from the government's civil service pension, labour insurance, labour pension and postal savings, with the remaining NT$20 billion being drawn down from the budget.

As a backup, the ministry may include the national insurance scheme, similar to Singapore's Central Provident Fund, into the NSF.

Other options, such as selling state land and freezing year-end bonuses for civil servants, have also been considered.

Finance Minister Paul Chiu said he would consider every means possible, including the more drastic one of closing the stock market.

The Interior Ministry will step up anti-espionage activities and enhance the capability of every city to handle calamity and salvage operations.

The Ministry of Economic Affairs will secure the supply of basic necessities and industrial ingredients.

If the situation worsens, it will consider rationing basic goods.

It will propose both high incentive as well as strong deterrent fiscal measures to make sure there is no capital flight from the private sector.

The Ministry of Transportation and Communications will ensure that transportation access, such as railways and sea lanes, and means of telecommunication do not break down in an emergency.

The Ministry of Foreign Affairs will try to ward off diplomatic pressures from abroad and will send senior government officials to assure the United States and Japan that President Lee's "two states" policy, which infuriated Beijing and led to the current strained cross-strait relations, does not amount to a policy change on reunification with China.

The ministry was disturbed when Washington instructed US Treasury Undersecretary for International Affairs Timothy Geithner to cancel his scheduled meeting with President Lee.

Mr Geithner was here yesterday to attend a meeting between American Institute in Taiwan and the Taiwan Economic Cultural Representative Office, two bodies representing the US and Taiwan in the absence of formal diplomatic ties.

Teng-hui Acted on His Own, Many Believe

19 July 1999

On paper, it was a group of experts who advised President Lee Teng-hui to replace the "one China" principle with a "two states" formula.

In reality, many people believe the Taiwanese leader acted on his own.

A presidential source said that Mr Lee was responding directly to United States President Bill Clinton's public statement of "Three Nos" in Shanghai during his visit in June last year.

That policy — "No" to Taiwan independence, "No" to "two Chinas" or "one China, one Taiwan", and "No" to membership of Taiwan in organisations requiring statehood — was articulated by a US President for the first time.

"Mr Lee realised the gravity of the impact of Mr Clinton's statement on Taiwan and decided to find a way to circumvent it," the source said.

The official view is that the "two states" position came about following a year-long study by the "Select Group on Strengthening the Sovereignty Status of the Republic of China", headed by Mr Huang Kun-huei, secretary-general of the Presidential Office.

Other members of the task force included Mr Yin Tsung-wen, secretary-general of the National Security Council, Mr Lin Bih-jaw, deputy secretary-general of the Presidential Office, Mr Su Chi, chairman of the Mainland Affairs Council (MAC), and several other international law experts.

Although heads of major policy branches were aware of the work the select group was doing, nobody knew when and in what manner Mr Lee would choose to present the results of its study.

So when the President made the announcement on July 9, all the policy branches were at a loss.

To make sure that top officials understood what he had in mind, the President called emergency meetings in his office on July 10 and 12 so that he could brief them.

Premier Vincent Siew then called an emergency Cabinet meeting on July 13 to study ways to explain the decision to the public, both at home and abroad, and the steps required to handle any emergency situation.

Confusion was evident when officials tried to tone down the provocative nature of Mr Lee's original statement.

For example, Mr Lee stated his "two states" theory without mentioning "one nation".

To tone it down, the MAC chairman capped it with "one nation".

Then Mr Siew assured the Taiwanese that there were no changes to the policy of eventual reunification with China.

The uncertainty was also clear when officials failed to find an apt translation for the President's new concept.

The MAC issued at least two different versions — "inter-state relations" and "two states in one nation" — before settling for the latter.

A day later, it issued a note to stress that the term "nation" should not be taken to mean "country".

In Chinese, both words can be used interchangeably, but the word "nation" can also mean people with the same ethnicity.

The difficulty of finding an exact translation reflected not the lexical incompetence of the officials involved but their inability to really understand their own President.

As a newspaper commentary said: "Lee Teng-hui's frog-leaping style of thinking is difficult for others to follow."

Most of the officials had an extremely difficult time following the President's announcement. For example, Mr Su was in Washington pleading with the US not to pressure Taipei into an interim agreement with Beijing on the Taiwan issue.

Two days later, the entire picture changed and he had to shout aloud for such an agreement.

Mr Siew also had a headache. He had to find NT$500 billion (S$25 billion) for the National Stabilisation Fund at short notice, to prop up the stock market in case there was a sharp fall.

This actually took place on Saturday.

Finance Minister Paul Chiu complained that, given the short notice, he could raise NT$300 billion for the fund at most and could not be sure how to get the rest of the money.

The Standing Committee of the Central Committee of the ruling KMT, which was supposed to vet major policy proposals, was not consulted at all.

Nor was the National Unification Council, a trans-party organisation responsible for forging consensus over the issue of unification.

No one could understand Mr Lee's move — nor predict his next one.

Taiwan Ready to Step Up War Readiness

16 July 1999

TAIPEI — Taiwan's armed forces will step up their state of war preparedness if the Chinese air force continues to intensify its flight activities, a Defence Ministry source said yesterday.

Although Taipei does not anticipate an immediate military attack from China, it has not ruled out other forms of military intimidation from the mainland following President Lee Teng-hui's shock announcement on Monday to scrap the "one China" policy.

A Defence Ministry official has confirmed the detection of more intense flight activities along the south-eastern coast of China in the past two days. But he played this down, saying they were exercises conducted by the Chinese in preparation for their National Day celebrations on Oct 1.

Military sources in Taiwan said that radar spotted Chinese MiG-21 fighter jets deviating several times from their usual flight paths along the Taiwan Strait and veering close to Taiwan.

In one incident, a sortie was detected heading towards the Penghu Islands. This forced Taiwanese fighter jets to scramble.

In normal circumstances, both sides would have exercised extreme self-restraint in adhering to the tacit "mid-line of the Strait" by not crossing it.

The sources described the feints as attempts by the Chinese to test the war preparedness of the Taiwanese navy.

Taiwan's Penghu Islands lie close to the mid-line. At their nearest point, they are only 81 km from China. It takes just five minutes for a Chinese MiG-21 fighter to reach Penghu from Putian, the largest air force base in south-east China.

As a result of the abnormal activities, Taiwanese air force units based in Penghu used the opportunity to conduct exercises simulating a Chinese attack.

Visitors from Penghu also reported frequent take-offs and landings by Taiwanese air force planes in the past few days. They added that servicemen no longer roamed the busy street of Makung, the main town on the islands.

On Wednesday, Chinese Defence Minister Chi Haotian issued a strongly-worded statement warning against any attempt to separate Taiwan from China. He said the Chinese military was determined to thwart any such attempt.

Most strategists interviewed dismissed the possibility of an imminent attack from China as Beijing faced many constraints. Most important of all was their view that Washington would not subscribe to the "two states" formula.

Their worst fear is that President Lee announced his plans after he had obtained tacit endorsement from the United States, as this would complicate the issue.

Another factor that restrains Beijing from choosing the military option is the possibility that such a move might backfire again.

Its 1996 missile tests to protest against Mr Lee's visit to the US had angered Taiwanese and alienated them from their Chinese counterparts.

This resulted in a sharp increase in the number of Taiwanese who no longer considered themselves "Chinese". Previously, most regarded themselves as "both Chinese and Taiwanese".

The missile exercises were also a key factor that led to the strengthening of the US-Japan defence pact and a follow-up plan to build an anti-missile Theatre Missile Defence system, which will include Taiwan.

The Taiwan stock market, which saw a steep 7 per cent drop in the first two days following Mr Lee's announcement, halted its slide yesterday, closing up 0.4 per cent.

The Hongkong bourse, which had also been hit, closed up 1.4 per cent.

In Beijing, Foreign Ministry spokesman Zhang Qiyue urged Taipei to "size up the situation soberly, rein in at the brink of the precipice and cease all separatist activities immediately".

She made the remarks when asked if it was correct to link a report in an army-published newspaper that China stood ready to use force with the revelation that Beijing has neutron bomb technology.

"Whether it is right to connect these two things, I am not in a position to comment on that," she said.

A Chinese government think-tank scholar said that China has postponed discussions about military action against Taiwan until after a meeting next month that will decide the direction of its US policy.

MFA: 'Only one China'

"SINGAPORE recognises that there is only one China and that Taiwan is part of China. The Government of the Republic of Singapore recognises the Government of the People's Republic of China. This has been our consistent policy and it remains unchanged."

The Foreign Ministry, in a statement responding to media enquiries on Singapore's views on Taiwanese President Lee Teng-hui's recent comments on cross-strait relations.

Taiwan Moves to Sell 'Two States' Policy Worldwide

15 July 1999

Taiwan will launch a major diplomatic offensive to sell its "two states" policy to the international community, the ruling Kuomintang (KMT) announced yesterday following a meeting of the standing members of its central committee.

It will also take precautionary measures to stabilise the economy, shocked by President Lee Teng-hui's controversial new proposal announced on Monday.

The Taiwan bourse has witnessed two consecutive days of steep decline, with the main TWSE Index sliding 315.84 points, or 3.9 per cent, to 7,888.66 points yesterday, its largest single-day fall in six months.

The KMT initiative included despatching the chairman of the Council for Economic Planning and Development, Mr Chiang Pin-kung, to attend the Apec meeting in September, where he will explain the "new principle" to the gathering of world leaders.

Taipei will also ask its allies in the United Nations to help explain its "two states" concept whenever they address the international assembly.

In addition, it will ask them to co-sponsor a motion that will allow Taiwan to join the UN. Previously, its bid to re-enter the world body was made by asking for a repeal of UN Resolution No 2758 of 1971, which gave the seat to China.

But this strategy will be changed. Taipei will now ask for permission to join the UN as a new, separate state, using the so-called German model to support its motion.

It will also instruct all its foreign representative offices to explain to their host governments the applicability of the German model, which was embodied in the "Grundlagenuertrag", or Fundamental Treaty of 1972, between the two Germanies.

According to Mr Su Chi, chairman of the Mainland Affairs Council, who made the report at the KMT meeting, Taiwan could draw several similarities from the German treaty.

It did not set any specific future scenario, with one side recognising the other as an equal entity and neither side claiming itself as the sole legal government of Germany.

On the domestic front, the KMT meeting also instructed various departments to take precautionary measures to stabilise the economy. The Ministry of Finance is to speed up its plan of setting up a NT$500 billion (S$25 billion) Stability Fund to meet any contingency.

The KMT meeting disclosed that the "two states" concept was the product of a year-long study by the "Select Group on Strengthening the Sovereignty Status of the Republic of China", which was headed by the secretary-general of the Presidential Office, Mr Huang Kun-huei.

Separate Statehood? Most are Not for It

15 July 1999

President Lee Teng-hui's "two states" proposal is hurting where it matters most — the home ground. Most Taiwanese are not in favour of it.

Although the locals interviewed said that, theoretically, a separate statehood would be good for Taiwan, none of them thought it was feasible or absolutely necessary, given the political reality.

Their unreceptive mood tallied with the results of numerous opinion polls carried out by government and academic organisations over the last few years, which showed that the vast majority of people preferred maintaining the status quo.

For instance, a public-opinion poll commissioned by the ruling Kuomintang showed over 60 per cent backing the categorisation of Taiwan-China relations as "special state-to-state" ties rather than as "political entities". But when these respondents were asked if Taiwan should break with China officially and change its name from the Republic of China to the Republic of Taiwan, only 20 per cent said Yes.

Professor Lin Yu-fong of Tamkong University said: "Any visitor to the Mainland Affairs Council would be treated to a slide presentation showing that the vast majority of the people surveyed over the last decade opted for no change."

"This fact is frequently used by the government to justify its 'no unification' policy. Yet when Lee Teng-hui and the Democratic Progress Party members pushed for independence, they disregarded the same figures which also said people do not like independence," he added.

The latest controversy also raised questions about Mr Lee's style of leadership.

Back in 1991 when he started constitutional revision, Taiwanese were told that the move was aimed only at speeding up democracy.

Now — a decade later — he had conceded that it was a premeditated move to create an independent Taiwan.

China Times had a commentary headlined: "Taiwan — is there anyone else we can believe in?"

After documenting numerous recent scandals and lies from the island's public figures, the paper lamented that politicians, law-enforcers and military personnel had all deceived the people.

"Now, even the head of state is not trustworthy," said the article.

Agreeing, Prof. Lin said: "When the national unification guidelines were drawn up in 1991, a consensus was reached after thorough deliberation among people of all political shades. Yet the collective decision of about a hundred people was scrapped overnight by one single person.

"Is he still worthy of the title of Mr Democracy?"

Even the man in the street seemed resigned to the President's antics.

A taxi-driver lamented: "Insecurity will be with us willy-nilly. What else can we do?"

But the locals also appeared to be immune to fears of a military threat from China.

"We are used to shocks," said the taxi driver.

But Mr Lee's "two states" proposal has found clear support in the pro-independence camp, which has been extremely upbeat.

Forerunners in the independence movement like opposition leader Peng Ming-min, 76, said this was the rare moment that he had been waiting for.

"It reinforced my belief that I can live long enough to see an independent Taiwan," he said.

The DPP has taken active steps to bolster Mr Lee's statements.

It has proposed a set of revisions in the Constitution to give effect to the "two states" status.

Some DPP members have also openly called for scrapping a number of important China-related institutions like the MAC. The party had also set up a small group for crisis-management to cope with any threat from China.

To the majority of people who were burnt in the Taiwan stock-market crash in the last two days, their common complaint was why Mr Lee could not wait to discuss the issue with Mr Wang Daohan behind closed doors, as the top Chinese negotiator was due down later in the year.

If Mr Lee had waited for the right moment, they argued, he could well put forth the new idea as Taiwan's opening position in cross-strait negotiations.

Teng-hui Pushing Changes to Constitution

14 July 1999

DESPITE strong criticism of his controversial "two states" proposal, Taiwanese President Lee Teng-hui is pushing ahead with constitutional amendments to give his plan a firm legal foundation, sources close to the presidential office said yesterday.

This is expected to take place together with a major overhaul of the constitutional and legal framework when the National Assembly resumes its session in a few months' time.

"The overhaul represents the most arduous task in the decade-long process of constitutional reform first launched by the President in 1991," a presidential source said.

The review is expected to cover all aspects of laws ranging from the definitions of state and institutions to territories and people.

Under the present Constitution, Taiwan is referred to as the "freedom area of China" while the mainland is described as "Republic of China (ROC) territories other than Taiwan".

Amendments are needed now to confine ROC territories to Taiwan proper, Penghu, Kimmen, Matsu and other islands.

All government decrees, notices, memoranda and propaganda materials, including websites, would be revised to reflect the new status. Government ministries were told to draw up a full list of documents that needed amendments.

Sources said the revamp would be a formidable task that would take several years to accomplish.

President Lee restated his claim to national sovereignty yesterday, saying that the Republic of China (Taiwan's official name) has always been a sovereign state, not a local government.

He said that Beijing had been blinded to historical and legal realities, adding: "Since we launched constitutional reforms in 1991, we have defined cross-strait relations as state-to-state, or at least special state-to-state."

His shock announcement on Monday has been blasted by both Chinese and Taiwanese media. It has also drawn veiled threats from Beijing, caught Washington and Tokyo off guard and sent Taiwan's buoyant stock market into a tailspin.

The official Xinhua news agency yesterday described President Lee's "naked separatist remarks" as an intentional attempt to destroy cross-strait relations.

In a commentary, it said he chose this particular moment when cross-strait tensions have shown signs of easing to utter his separatist words — just as he did in 1995 when he went to the United States to advocate "two Chinas" and "one China, one Taiwan".

The United States also reaffirmed its one-China policy in response to Mr Lee's declaration, a signal that his position was contrary to American policy.

"Our policy is unchanged. Our one-China policy is longstanding and certainly well known," said State Department deputy spokesman James Foley. He urged both sides to engage in "a meaningful, substantive dialogue".

Japan, echoing Washington's position, reaffirmed that it recognised that "one China" ruled from Beijing and expressed hopes that both sides would work out their problems peacefully. Both the Taiwanese and Chinese bourses reacted negatively to Taiwan's "two states" policy.

Taipei stocks plunged 3.1 per cent to 8,204.50 points on panic selling.

China's stock markets also closed sharply down as investors unloaded shares on worries over rising tension.

The Shanghai B share index slumped 3.648 points, or 7.39 per cent, to 45.711 while Shenzhen's B index tumbled 6.88 points, or 6.76 per cent, to 94.91.

Some investors were concerned that the row could affect China's trade and economy and might even lead to armed conflict, brokers said.

On the military front, Taiwanese troops went on alert yesterday, with a defence ministry spokesman saying that "the military is keeping a close watch on any development".

Lee's 'Two States' Proposal Was a Long Time Coming

14 July 1999

PRESIDENT Lee Teng-hui's shock announcement of a "two-states" proposal on Monday may have come as a shock to many. But to the policy's mastermind, it has been a long time coming, following a decade of deliberate, painstaking preparations.

The heightened sense of urgency in his unpopular proposal, despite accusations of wrong timing by his critics, was in fact the tail-end of Mr Lee's plan to lay the groundwork for political independence — before his term in office expires next year.

Pro-unification New Party (NP) legislator Fung Hu-hsiang has noted that the hasty move should be set against the backdrop of Mr Lee's decade-long effort to dislodge Taiwan from China.

Seen in that light, it was no rush-job decision but a carefully worked out programme waiting for the right moment to make its appearance.

To the NP, which has been highly suspicious of his constitutional reforms, the latest proposal was no more than a logical sequence of preparations to achieve this objective.

Since the 1991 constitutional revision, the forerunners of NP had warned Taiwanese voters that the revision would endanger the status of the Republic of China (ROC).

Indeed, the revision had led to the founding of the NP in 1993 with the explicit aim of "defending the ROC".

Mr Fung had said that few people had been able to see Mr Lee's ulterior motive then.

Almost a decade on, the President finally admitted to a German press delegation that the 1991 and 1992 Constitution revisions were aimed at giving Taiwan "separate-state" status, thus confirming the NP's fears.

The process of diminishing the ROC continued with another constitutional amendment that scrapped the province in the administrative hierarchy, which was completed last year.

"With these processes completed, he attempted to turn Taiwan's de facto independence into a de jure one," Mr Fung noted.

In 1993, Mr Lee, a Christian, told the late Japanese author Ryotaro Shiba that he saw himself as the Moses of Taiwan.

Mr Fung read this to mean the splitting of Taiwan from China, since Moses led his Jewish people out from Egypt.

But time was not on Mr Lee's side. With 10 months to go before stepping down, he was hard pressed to finalise the legal framework needed.

Since revising the Constitution and other laws take time, the countdown dictated that the process had to commence right now.

"That accounted for the seeming hastiness," Mr Fung said.

Dr Chen Yuchun, professor at the Graduate School of American Studies of the Chinese Culture University, offered another explanation.

He thought that American pressure might be a factor.

Dr Chen noted that since the missile crisis in 1996, the US had departed subtly from its previous non-mediatory role to one advocating an "interim agreement" between Beijing and Taipei.

Under such an agreement, which is supposed to last 50 years, Taipei would not declare independence while Beijing would renounce the use of force.

This proposal has developed gradually from an academic suggestion to one pursued actively by the US government.

The pressure for Taiwan to enter into political talks with China was so great that it had to send Mr Su Chi, its Mainland Affairs Council chairman, to Washington to plead for a more lenient US approach.

This strong American pressure backfired.

To solve the matter once and for all, President Lee took a calculated risk by declaring Taiwan a bona fide state, thus scrapping the one-China concept that was his perennial nightmare.

Another popular theory relates to next year's presidential elections.

According to opinion polls, former governor James Soong (35 per cent) leads all other candidates by a wide margin, including the DPP's Chen Shui-bian (26 per cent) and Vice-President Lien Chan (14 per cent).

However, it is believed that Mr Lee is unwilling to hand the presidential seat to Mr Soong, who has mainland origins and whom he finds too unruly.

Unfortunately, his hand-picked candidate Lien is unable to muster even the threshold support.

Therefore, the only way to deal Mr Soong a lethal blow was to undermine the trans-party support he enjoys currently.

By abandoning the one-China principle, it would be difficult for the former governor to take sides.

If he opposes the new formulation, it would cost him the votes of indigenous Taiwanese.

And if he supports it, he would lose voters with mainland origins.

Observers have pointed out that Mr Su Chi-cheng, deputy secretary-general at the presidential office, had once said that Mr Lee could easily cut Mr Soong's support with a "deadly weapon".

Many people are now convinced that the mastermind's "two states" policy is the so-called deadly weapon.

Teng-hui Sets Back Cross-Strait Relations

13 July 1999

Taiwanese President Lee Teng-hui's declaration that China and Taiwan are separate countries would inevitably affect cross-strait relations as well as the outcome of the island's presidential elections next year.

At the international level, his statement — made in an interview last Friday — would affect US thinking on the trilateral relationship among Beijing, Taipei and Washington.

Beijing has already issued a strongly-worded statement warning Mr Lee not to play with fire.

Referring to him by name, the warning was the strongest issued since his 1996 US visit led a furious China to conduct a series of military exercises and missile tests near Taiwan.

But the statement did not say if the scheduled visit to Taiwan by top Chinese negotiator Wang Daohan, chairman of the Association for Relations Across the Taiwan Strait (Arats), would be affected.

It also reiterated China's traditional wish to work with the Taiwanese towards peaceful unification.

This showed that Beijing was targeting only Mr Lee, who has challenged its one-China policy repeatedly.

Beijing has also tried to minimise damage to cross-strait ties by keeping the door open for dialogue with other political forces that are not pro-independence.

But observers say the possibility of Mr Wang's visit being called off cannot be ruled out. After all, Arats' No 2 man, Mr Tang Shubei, had indicated that the present mood was not encouraging.

Cancellation of the trip would be a major setback for China-Taiwan relations.

Mr Lee's redefinition of cross-strait ties could also affect the outcome of Taiwan's presidential elections.

It was tantamount to him, chairman of the ruling Kuomintang (KMT), endorsing the political programme of the opposition, the pro-independence Democratic Progressive Party (DPP).

The DPP was quick to point out that Mr Lee had finally adopted its position on Taiwan's status.

Its presidential candidate, Mr Chen Shui-bian, thanked the President openly and said he was ready to work with him towards building an independent Taiwan.

One who could lose out is the highly-popular formergovernor James Soong, who is expected to break away from the KMT to run as an independent in the polls.

While he opposes reunification on Beijing's terms, he also opposes independence.

He has criticised Mr Lee's decision-making as being rough, hasty and with little consideration of Taiwanese interests in preserving cross-strait stability.

The opposition New Party (NP), which supports reunification, saw Mr Lee's redefinition of ties as a case of dumping likely KMT presidential candidate Lien Chan, who is the Vice-President, to help the DPP's Mr Chen.

Said NP analyst Cheng Long-shui: "Knowing that Mr Lien would have no hope of winning the election, Mr Lee is trying to persuade KMT voters to vote for the DPP instead of giving their support to Mr James Soong.

"Mr Lee has let the people know that he is on the side of the DPP as far as the status of Taiwan is concerned.

"Faced with a situation in which the ruling party's candidate has no hope of winning the presidential election, he is encouraging his KMT supporters to cast their votes for the DPP man instead of the more popular Mr Soong," he added.

He said the same thing happened in the 1994 Taipei mayoral election, which saw the DPP's Mr Chen winning the race against the ruling-party candidate and a former KMT man.

Given this precedent, Mr Cheng said, Mr Soong's election chances would be adversely affected.

Mr Lee's controversial remarks have also caused grave concern in the US as it challenged Washington's one-China policy, a bipartisan consensus evolved over more than two decades.

Mr Richard Bush, who heads America In Taiwan (AIT), a semi-official organisation handling bilateral relations in the absence of diplomatic ties, was said to have asked for a full transcript of Mr Lee's statement and an official explanation of its content.

While refraining from making a formal statement, the US had obviously been caught by surprise.

Assistant Secretary of State Stanley Roth was detailing his proposal of an interim accord between Beijing and Taipei to visiting Mainland Affairs Council chairman Su Chi just two days before Mr Lee made his shocking comments.

It was like a slap in Mr Roth's face.

At a time when Sino-US relations was at a low, due to the bombing of the Chinese Embassy in Belgrade, Washington had hoped that a warming of cross-strait ties, symbolised by the Arats chairman's visit, would reduce pressure on the trilateral relationship.

Mr Lee put paid to these hopes.

Washington has been warning Taiwan against provoking China. Its response to a highly-provocative new policy would determine its future attitude towards Taiwan.

Taiwan to Scrap 'One China' Policy

13 July 1999

TAIWAN yesterday announced that it would scrap the "one China" principle following President Lee Teng-hui's redefinition of relations with China as "state-to-state" ties, drawing a stern warning from China against "playing with fire".

Speaking at a press conference in Taipei, the chairman of the China policy-making Mainland Affairs Council (MAC), Mr Su Chi, put the blame on the mainland, which he said answered repeated friendly overtures with hostility.

He said that Taipei formulated the National Unification Guidelines in 1991 so as to create more room for co-operation with Beijing.

It also acted unilaterally to end hostility towards China, promoted bilateral exchanges and drafted a law governing civil contacts.

In return, he told reporters, China mounted verbal attacks against Taiwan, conducted missile tests in waters near the island and kept squeezing its international space.

Asked if this meant that Taiwan would no longer uphold the "one China" principle and support reunification, Mr Su's reply was that Taiwan saw cross-strait relations as "special relations" between two Chinese states, stressing that Taiwan strove for "two states in one nation". He avoided using the term "two countries", emphasising that "state" would be a more appropriate term than "country".

In Beijing, a Chinese Foreign Ministry spokesman, warning Mr Lee against playing with fire, said that he had taken an "extremely dangerous step" towards splitting China.

"We can clearly see that he has gone a long way down the road of playing with fire," state television quoted Mr Zhu Bangzao as saying.

"We sternly warn Lee Teng-hui and the Taiwan authorities not to underestimate the Chinese government's firm determination to uphold the nation's sovereignty, dignity and territorial integrity," he was quoted as saying.

China has never renounced its aim to retake Taiwan by force if the island, which Beijing views as a renegade province, declares independence.

"Don't underestimate the courage and force of the Chinese people to oppose separatism and Taiwan independence," the spokesman said, adding that reunification was "the will of the people".

On the reunification issue, Mr Su cited pre-unification Germany as a classic case of "two states in one nation".

He said that the fact that Germany was divided did not prevent its eventual unification, stressing that when "conditions are ripe", nothing can stop reunification.

Mr Su said that the timing was ripe now for President Lee to redefine cross-strait relations.

The short-term purpose was to prepare for the upcoming visit by Mr Wang Daohan, chairman of the Association for Relations Across the Taiwan Strait (Arats), he explained.

The longer-term purpose, he added, was to create a new framework for Taiwan's relations with China in the next century.

Mr Wang, China's top negotiator on ties with Taiwan, is scheduled to make a landmark visit to the island later this year at a date to be fixed.

Observers have expressed doubt that the atmosphere after Mr Lee's declaration that Taiwan is a separate state would still be conducive for a visit by Mr Wang.

Mr Wang, reacting to Mr Lee's statement, has said that the "one China" principle has served as the basis for dialogue and co-operation between the Arats and the SEF, the two semi-official bodies handling matters between China and Taiwan in the absence of formal ties.

In an interview with a German radio station last week, the Taiwanese President said that as of 1991, Taiwan had ceased to exist as part of China.

"Since we conducted our constitutional reforms in 1991, we have redefined cross-strait relations as nation-to-nation, or at least as special state-to-state relations. Under such special state-to-state relations, there is no longer any need to declare Taiwanese independence."

Taiwan a Separate Country: Teng-hui

11 July 1999

Taiwan President Lee Teng-hui has made a controversial declaration that there are two separate "countries" on both sides of the Taiwan Strait.

In an interview on Friday with Mr Dieter Weirich, Chief Executive of Voice of Germany — the world's third largest broadcasting company — Mr Lee said that as of 1991, Taiwan had ceased to exist as part of China.

According to him, two separate countries have existed since then.

Never before had the President been so stark in calling Taiwan a separate country.

His comment represented a major departure from the official position of the ruling Kuomintang (KMT). According to the party's National Unification Programme, Taiwan and China are "two equal political entities within the one-China framework", although in practice, it talks aloud about "separate political entity" and is almost tight-lipped on "One China".

Mr Lee said that in the 1991 constitutional revision, he had already restricted the jurisdiction of the Taiwanese constitution to the present-day islands of Taiwan, Penghu, Kinmen and Matsu.

The revision also acknowledged that the People's Republic of China was the legitimate ruler in the mainland instead of a "rebellious clique", as it used to be called by Taiwan.

While the 1991 revision stated that both the legislature and the National Assembly were to be constituted by people elected from Taiwan, the 1992 revision said that both the president and vice-president were to be elected by the people in Taiwan.

"Therefore we never claim ourselves to be representative of the whole of China. We derive our legitimacy to rule from the people in Taiwan only, and there is nothing to do with people in China," he explained.

"Therefore since 1991 we have already defined clearly bilateral relations across the strait as relations between country and country, or at least a special relation between country and country," he stressed.

"The relation between China and Taiwan is one between countries, instead of one between a legitimate government and an illicit one, or a central government against a local one."

Mr Lee's unprecedented declaration showed his ultimate motive in the 1991 and 1992 constitutional revisions, which were to provide the necessary constitutional basis for the existence of Taiwan as a separate country.

"Since we define cross-strait relations as relations between countries, there is no need to declare Taiwan's independence," he added.

As expected, his view was highly commended by the independence-minded Democratic Progressive Party. But others were worried it might mar the forthcoming visit by China's top negotiator Wang Daohan.

Taiwan Helps Itself by Helping Kosovo

15 June 1999

Taipei's recent pledge of a huge aid package for Kosovo refugees has raised questions about whether it is to benefit Kosovo or Taiwan itself.

The US$300 million (S$513 million) aid was equivalent to 0.1 per cent of Taiwan's gross domestic product (GDP) or 1 per cent of the total estimated cost of post-war reconstruction required by Kosovo.

Being the largest aid package Taiwan has ever made, it far exceeds that pledged by any Nato member. For example, the total Nato aid to Kosovo refugees in Macedonia was about US$1.26 billion. Taiwan's donation alone was a quarter of that amount.

Its generosity also dwarfed the efforts of the UN High Commissioner for Refugees (UNHCR), which tried to raise a total of US$470 million from 185 member states for Kosovo.

The sheer size of the aid shocked the Taiwanese. In local currency terms, it was close to NT$10 billion, equivalent to total social welfare subsidies in fiscal 1999-2000. At a time when the budget deficit stands at NT$700 billion while accumulated government debt is at a staggering NT$7 trillion, people are concerned about whether they can afford such a commitment.

What disturbed the Taiwanese more was the decision-making process, which led people into thinking that it was a one-man decision.

According to the secretary-general of the presidential office, the decision was made after only two top-level meetings: first on May 24 when President Lee Teng-hui made the proposal and then on June 7, when he announced the package.

Legislators pointed out that normally, budgetary expenditure of this size would require lengthy debates and reviews by parliamentary sub-committees. Furthermore, no one seemed to know how the amount was arrived at.

Two hours before Mr Lee announced the aid package, Foreign Minister Jason Hu briefed the legislature on the aid and promised that it would in no way exceed US$10 million. The minister was shocked when, two hours later, the package turned out to be 30 times bigger, suggesting there was a serious problem with the decision-making process.

None of the ministries involved directly in the aid package was aware of its size. Neither Mr Wei Duan, head of the Directorate General of Budget, Accounting and Statistics of the Executive Yuan, responsible for drawing up the Budget, nor Finance Minister Paul Chiu, responsible for generating the required sum, knew how that amount could be sourced.

As to the use of the funds, Mr Hu could not even tell who exactly the recipients would be.

All these anomalies suggested that it was a pet project of President Lee. Critics claimed that it was meant to snag the Nobel Peace Prize. Mr Lee had been named twice for this honour.

Against these criticisms, the President stressed the need for Taiwan to reach out to the international community now that it had the wherewithal to make its presence felt.

While the domestic uproar could be easily quelled, Beijing's suspicion would be hard to dispel. Although Mr Lee stressed the humanitarian nature of his aid package, Beijing saw it as another trick to implement the "two Chinas" or "one China, one Taiwan" policy.

In the past decade, Taiwan has been trying every possible means to break its diplomatic isolation.

Apart from "dollar diplomacy", in which Taiwan offered huge sums of aid to needy countries in return for their diplomatic recognition, it also tried "recreation diplomacy", with top leaders going for "holidays" in foreign countries.

These would provide a good chance for high-level bilateral contacts with countries with which Taipei had no diplomatic relations.

However, neither was effective. While "recreation diplomacy" proved to be too troublesome for the host countries (by inviting protests from Beijing), "dollar diplomacy" proved to be too unreliable because recipients could switch their loyalty easily with a change in government or following bigger bait from Beijing.

This was how "humanitarian diplomacy" came about. Taiwan thought the emphasis on humanitarian grounds would make it difficult for China to oppose the aid or for recipient countries to reject it.

The Taiwanese Foreign Ministry did not deny the fact that the aid was meant to increase the island's international visibility. "Compared with spending about the same amount of money in winning the diplomatic recognition of a small country in God-knows-where with dubious loyalty, the aid would project a much better international image of Taiwan," said a Foreign Ministry official.

In his report to the Legislative Yuan, Mr Hu claimed that the aid could help Taiwan make a major diplomatic breakthrough in Eastern Europe. In the Kosovo crisis, Nato had largely ignored China, he said, and this created an opportunity for Taiwan to make its influence felt. The aid provided the right channel, as witnessed by the positive response from the United States and international organisations, he added.

"Through this aid package, we hope to develop some sort of dialogue between Taiwan and Nato, and to establish some concrete ties with international organisations," he said.

Mr Hu disclosed that three East European countries, including Czechoslovakia, were keen to enhance their relations with Taiwan. Moreover, three to five international organisations had expressed their willingness to help Taiwan channel its funds into the region.

It is clear, therefore, that the Kosovo aid is a roundabout way for Taiwan to help itself break out of diplomatic isolation.

Taiwan's smug calculation may end up as no more than wishful thinking, as China is turning the Nato bombing of its embassy in Belgrade into a trump card to force Nato to return to the UN framework, where China has veto power.

China's record of exercising its veto power in the UN Security Council — twice so far — has been because of the Taiwan factor. In both incidents, China vetoed proposals to send UN peacekeeping forces to the Republic of Guatemala in 1997 and to Macedonia this year because the two nations maintain diplomatic relations with Taiwan.

If past patterns are any guide, Beijing may well threaten to exercise its veto power again when the issue of sending UN peacekeeping forces to Kosovo is tabled to ensure that neither Nato nor the UNHCR will provide a springboard for Taiwanese penetration into the Balkan area.

The Hidden Cost of Tiananmen: Unification Deferred

30 May 1999

Perhaps the biggest "hidden cost" of the June 4 incident 10 years ago is the negative impact on unification, one of the cherished dreams of the Chinese people.

According to Mr Chang Jung-kung, director of the Mainland Work Committee of the ruling Kuomintang (KMT), both China and Taiwan were on the verge of a democratisation process around the period from 1987–89.

In China, the ruling Chinese Communist Party (CCP), under the leadership of then-party secretary Zhao Ziyang, announced a major political reform plan at the party's 13th National Congress in 1987.

In the same year in Taiwan, then-President Chiang Ching-kuo lifted martial law that had been in force for four decades.

The political systems of the two sides were not that different at the time, but the Tiananmen incident in 1989 was to propel them in opposing directions, Mr Chang said.

While democratic reform was scaled back in China after 1989, it picked up speed in Taiwan.

"The CCP had not been able to return to the consensus on the need and form of political reform reached in 1987," he said.

"As for the KMT, it had since then transformed the political system of Taiwan radically."

The result is that the gulf between the two sides widened. When Beijing made the first unification proposal in 1979, objections raised were based mostly on economic (the wealth gap) and social (differing lifestyles) grounds.

Today, the barrier is a political and ideological one. Different attitudes towards human rights, democracy and freedom make the obstacles formidable.

Said Mr Chang: "If unification is delayed or rendered impossible, then the June 4 incident was certainly a contributory factor. It could prove to be the biggest hidden cost of the crisis."

Professor Andy Chang of the Graduate School of China Studies at Tamkang University agreed.

He recalled that democratic movements in both countries started at roughly the same time, in the late '70s.

By about 1987, both governments, under intense public pressure, launched initiatives to liberalise their political systems.

The Tiananmen incident nipped China's democratisation process in the bud, but acted as a catalyst for that in Taiwan.

Said Prof. Chang: "Students at that time pointed to Beijing's brutality to push their demand for speedy reform. They demanded a dialogue with President Lee Teng-hui, who finally agreed to call a national meeting on democratic reform. The incident was therefore an important catalyst.

"Taiwan is now preparing for its second presidential elections and a strong opposition is posing a real challenge to the ruling KMT.

"Yet in China, people could still be put in jail simply because they want to exercise their constitutional right to form political parties."

In such circumstances, he said, the natural reaction for any Taiwanese would be to reject unification altogether.

"Democracy, freedom and respect for human rights have now become intrinsic values for the Taiwanese and we all agree that these values transcend national boundaries and supersede sovereignty. This diametrically different value system is the single largest stumbling block on the road towards unification," he said.

Subsequent developments, such as the disintegration of the Soviet Union, which contrasted sharply with the stability and phenomenal economic growth the Chinese people enjoyed, seemed to justify the drastic actions taken at the time.

Beijing's position, however, was rejected totally by the Taiwanese.

Taiwan enjoyed a decade of stability and speedy growth while overhauling its entire political system, pointed out Dr Pan Shi-tang, director of the Graduate School of China Studies at Tamkang University.

"After seizing political freedom away from the people, the CCP had to pacify and compensate them with greater economic freedom. This is what they called 'leftism' in politics but 'rightism' in economics, and it explained the rapid growth," he said.

"Stability is achieved by silencing dissenting views and this is rationalised through appeals to nationalism. The CCP keeps telling its people that the dissident movement is a wedge driven by the US to bring about China's disintegration, similar to what happened to the Soviet bloc."

He added that it was doubtful whether the post-Tiananmen growth and stability could be sustained in the long run.

"The policy of practising 'leftism' in politics but 'rightism' in economics would accentuate the problems created by reforming the economic system but leaving the political system intact," he said, warning that postponing badly-needed political change would only bring about a greater cost of reform in the future.

Queries Rife on Teng-hui's Observations

19 May 1999

Even before its official launch today, President Lee Teng-hui's book, titled "Voice Of Taiwan", has raised controversies, including his criticism of Singapore's Senior Minister Lee Kuan Yew.

Several legislators have asked President Lee to clarify his proposal that China be divided into seven parts, which could be seen as an attempt to break up the country.

They also wanted him to explain his remark on the political legacies of both SM Lee and himself.

In the book's last chapter, entitled Taiwan After Lee, the Taiwan leader quoted US political scientist Samuel Huntington's remarks predicting that Taiwanese democracy would continue to be practised even after President Lee dies, while Singapore's political system will perish with SM Lee's demise.

Prof Huntington had said in 1995: "The freedom and creativity that President Lee has introduced in Taiwan will survive him.

"The honesty and efficiency that Senior Minister Lee has brought to Singapore are likely to follow him to his grave.

"In some circumstances, authoritarianism may do well in the short term, but experience clearly shows that only democracy produces good government in the long run, as in America."

President Lee said that as a friend of the Singapore leader, Mr Huntington's remark evoked mixed feelings in him.

The convener of the New Party, former legislator Lee Ching-hua, disagreed, pointing out that Singapore's Mr Lee had established a clean political system and a civil service based on meritocracy, while President Lee's system was far from politically clean.

He also said that President Lee had pushed for several rounds of constitutional amendments which resulted in an all-powerful President not accountable to anyone.

"The Taiwanese system was therefore democratic in name but autocratic in substance," he added.

Presidential office official Ting Yuen-chao stressed that Mr Lee had no intention of criticising SM Lee.

"He was merely quoting what Mr Huntington said to stress the importance of establishing a democratic system. Only a sound political system could survive a great political leader."

Drawing even stronger criticism was President Lee's suggestion that China be divided into seven blocs.

New Party boss Lee recalled that the first open proposal to break China up was put forth by Japanese writer Mineo Nakajima in 1992. He suggested then that China should best be divided into 12 parts to pose less of a threat to its neighbours.

This idea was picked up by Taiwanese separatist writer Wang Wen-shan, who proposed cutting up China into seven sections, each having their own sovereignty and all would co-exist peacefully.

It is known that President Lee had made Mr Wang's book a "must-read" for his senior officials.

All the heads of policy branches involved in cross-strait matters denied Mr Lee intended to divide China.

They stressed that what he really meant was the need for a delegation of power to the local authorities.

President Lee also told the International Press Institute on Monday that he was merely addressing a management problem, and there should be no further political speculation on it.

Said Mr Lee Ching-hua: "Both the mainland and Taiwan remained to be convinced."

Traditional Taiwan Looks More Chinese Than China

16 May 1999

The most colourful event in Taiwan last month was the annual parade of Matsu, or Goddess of the Sea, along a 280-km route in central Taiwan that attracted an estimated half a million fervent followers.

It was undoubtedly a most spectacular religious carnival, one that is unlikely to be found in China.

The size and zeal of the parade suggested that, perhaps, traditional Chinese culture was better preserved and developed in Taiwan than in China itself.

Though essentially an offspring of the Chinese heartland, folklore in Taiwan is much more developed in terms of scale and sophistication than similar activities in China.

Folklore apart, other cultural habits confirm this impression. In writing, for example, traditional Chinese characters are still used, while in China, these were abandoned almost half a century ago.

Instead, a simplified form was created by Beijing to facilitate speedy learning.

Traditionally, all Chinese writings was arranged vertically from top to bottom. Taiwan stuck to this method of writing, but in China, it was changed to one arranged horizontally from left to right. Even broadsheet newspapers, which are typically laid out horizontally, are arranged in a vertical format in Taiwan.

In China, classical Chinese is almost extinct as a working language and has become a cultural relic studied only by researchers or the literati.

Everyone uses vernacular Chinese now. In Taiwan, however, one is amazed to find classical Chinese still being used in official documents. For example, presidential decrees are all written in standard classical Chinese.

Taiwan still sticks to the traditional way of numbering the years.

In old China, years were numbered first with the dynasty, then the emperor and finally the number of years that particular emperor had been in power. Thus the year 1900 would be recorded formally as the 26th year of the Emperor Guangxu of the Great Qing Dynasty.

In China, this obsolete way was abolished after the communists came to power in 1949. Yet in Taiwan, it is still preserved.

Although the AD (Anno Domini) system is also acceptable, the formal way to number a year in Taiwan is to use the founding of the Republic of China (ROC), which is 1911, as the reference year.

Thus 1999 would become the 88th year of the ROC.

To show deference in classical Chinese writings, especially in official documents, the writer had to start a new line whenever the name of an emperor was mentioned.

When the names of any dignitaries lower in status than the emperor were mentioned, spaces equivalent to two Chinese characters had to be left blank.

This format is no longer observed in China but is still practised in Taiwan.

For example, whenever the name of the founder of ROC, Dr Sun Yat-sen, is mentioned, it starts with a new line. When the names of former presidents Chiang Kai-shek or Chiang King-kuo are mentioned, blank spaces are left.

More traditional Chinese rituals are observed in Taiwan than in China.

For example, all Chinese people honour Emperor Huangdi (or the Yellow Emperor, circa 3,000 BC, believed to be the first emperor in Chinese history) as their common ancestor.

In the past 2,000 years, there has been an annual memorial service dedicated to him. It was a major event in feudal China and was adhered to faithfully, unless interrupted by war.

When the communists took over China in 1949, this annual ceremony was stopped on grounds of weeding out feudalism.

Surprisingly, it continues uninterrupted in Taiwan, though on a much smaller scale.

As with past practices, the No. 1 man (the emperor in days of old but now President Lee Teng-hui) has to face westward (towards the Chinese heartland) and make offerings to Huangdi and recite a solemn oration in dedication to him.

It is interesting to note that for political reasons, the communist government in China has revived quietly this traditional practice in recent years.

They see this as a good "united front" tactic to woo overseas Chinese. Thus the provincial authorities in Shaanxi (where Huangdi was believed to have been buried) were told to hold annual dedications to Huangdi as a means to revitalise Chinese nationalism.

One reason that Taiwan preserves more of traditional Chinese culture than its mainland counterpart is that the island is relatively free from extremist political ideologies.

Since the communist takeover in 1949, strict ideological control has been imposed on the people in China.

All cultural relics, including traditional performing arts, were regarded negatively and were to be eradicated.

This obliteration of traditional things went on uninterrupted for three decades (1949–79), culminating in the so-called Cultural Revolution, which saw a widespread sweeping away of past practices.

If people were forbidden from taking pride in their own traditions, it was natural that traditional culture would wither away.

It was not until the mid-eighties, after the communist authorities relaxed ideological control over the people, that folk activities were revived.

In Beijing, for example, the traditional Temple Festival was revived only in 1986, after a ban that lasted three decades.

Taiwan, which was spared extreme ideologies, has been able to preserve traditional Chinese culture.

So it is rather interesting to note that Taiwan, while trying to break away from the influence of China, is in fact more Chinese than China in many aspects, not least in the preservation of traditional Chinese culture.

Reunify? Democratic reforms first, says Taipei

9 April 1999

Taiwan President Lee Teng-hui yesterday set democratic reform in China as a pre-condition for Taiwan's reunification with the Chinese mainland, the first time Taipei has made its position official.

He also reiterated his call for a summit between leaders of both sides of the Taiwan Strait and for the creation of a mechanism to promote peace and stability in the region.

"It is my earnest hope that the two sides would engage in top-level visits and constructive dialogues, bringing stability and welfare to the people on both sides of the strait," he said in his opening address to the island's National Unification Council.

Democratisation as a precondition for cross-strait reconciliation is a theme first developed by Mr Koo Chen-fu of the semi-official Straits Exchange Foundation during his ice-breaking trip to China last October.

"Only when China accomplishes quickly its social diversification and political democratisation can the two sides gradually establish consensus regarding future developments on the basis of democracy and freedom," Mr Lee said.

He also hinted at a possible expansion of cross-strait exchange aimed at building mutual confidence.

But the Taiwan leader criticised China's threats of force against Taiwan and the more rapid deployment of missiles along the Taiwan Strait, saying that these delayed normalisation of cross-strait ties and threatened Asia-Pacific security.

His calls yesterday represented a re-packaging of his six-point policy for promoting cross-strait relations, which he promulgated four years ago in response to Chinese President Jiang Zemin's eight-point programme for reunification.

In fact, Mr Lee made it clear that the six points made in April 1995 were still valid.

Nevertheless, he introduced some new elements to the original six points.

On his call for a summit meeting, he dropped his previous precondition that it be held at an international venue. The peace-promoting mechanism echoed recent calls to set up confidence-building measures across the strait.

On restraining Taiwanese investment in China and on the issue of establishing the three direct links of trade, transport and post, the Taiwan leader stood by his "no haste, be patient" policy, despite mounting pressure at home for a change in the policy.

Observers said that if Mr Lee's original six points did not impress Beijing, neither would his latest modifications because there was not a single reference in his entire speech to the principle of "one China".

TAIWAN President Lee Teng-hui's six-point programme for cross-strait relations announced in 1995:

- Pursue China's unification based on the reality that the two sides are governed respectively by two governments;
- Strengthen bilateral exchanges based on Chinese culture;
- Exchange trade and economic relations to develop a mutually beneficial and complementary relationship;
- Ensure that both sides join international organisations on an equal footing and that leaders on both sides meet in a natural setting;
- Adhere to the principle of resolving all disputes by peaceful means; and
- Jointly safeguard prosperity and promote democracy in Hongkong and Macau.

Trade-Offs Needed to Give Cross-Strait Talks a Push

25 October 1998

UNLESS one side is prepared to make a major concession, the recent visit to China by Mr Koo Chen-fu, chairman of the Taiwanese Straits Exchange Foundation (SEF), would at best be remembered for identifying cross-strait problems but not resolving them.

At the most basic level, working towards a return visit by Mr Wang Daohan, chairman of China's Association for Relations Across the Taiwan Strait (Arats), SEF's counterpart, seems to be the obvious starting point.

But both sides would want more to extract maximum mileage from that, so some trade-off is inevitable.

Taiwan's strategy for future dealings with the Chinese is clear, judging from the international propaganda it served up following last week's visit.

To counteract Beijing's "one-China" principle, it intends to develop the theory of "a divided China" which will help justify its claim for a position of equality — even though it is physically smaller.

This would also reinforce Taipei's ongoing efforts to expand its global presence.

Taiwan will most likely prefer a democracy model as an alternative to the "one country, two systems" model for reunification. If accepted, this would give Taipei moral strength when negotiating with Beijing.

More importantly, by setting China's democratisation as a precondition to reunification, it gives the island's administration ample breathing space, since such a process will take decades to accomplish.

The island would then be able to give practical issues priority over abstract political ones.

Meanwhile, it also possesses a useful card for contingency use — the power to restrain Taiwanese investments from growing in the mainland.

But the future does not look smooth-sailing for the Taiwanese. For a start, it is difficult to anticipate breakthroughs in the "one-China" issue and in the preconditions for reunification.

Arats vice-chairman Tang Shubei made his anger clear at a press conference when he heard "Republic of China", which is how Taiwan refers to itself.

Chinese Vice-Premier Qian Qichen did not hesitate to tell Mr Koo that Beijing would continue restraining Taiwan's quest for a higher international profile.

The Chinese Foreign Ministry also issued a statement barring Taiwan's participation in a Kedo (Korean Energy Development Organisation) project, which Mr Koo raised during his meeting in Beijing.

Also, Beijing scorns at the idea of democratisation as a precondition for reunification. It showed open displeasure by denying the participation of Mr Kang Ning-hsiang — described as "witness of Taiwan's democratisation" — in Mr Koo's meeting with Chinese President Jiang Zemin.

But all is not lost. Beijing has to honour its pledges that once political dialogue is launched, full-scale bilateral exchanges between SEF and Arats will resume.

Therefore, it is reasonable to expect China to soften its position on whether talks should focus on practical or political issues.

On Taiwan's side, it is under tremendous domestic pressures to change its mainland policies. Although Premier Vincent Siew reiterated the long-standing strategy of restraining investment in China and barring direct links with it, he did not rule out the possibility of a change provided that there was "an indication of goodwill" from the Chinese side.

For Beijing, the most it can achieve in the years ahead is an agreement with Taipei to end hostility. Such an agreement might entail a tacit commitment by Beijing to steer clear of military means as long as Taipei does not declare independence.

In return, Taipei might have to undertake not to break away.

The sealing of such an agreement will surely provide good substance for a summit between the Presidents of the two sides.

Taipei Happy With Outcome of Talks

23 October 1998

The Wang-Koo meeting, despite committing Taiwan to negotiation with China on political issues, has produced results which delight Taipei.

Taiwanese President Lee Teng-hui has hailed the outcome of the meeting as "extraordinary" and "marvellous".

The Mainland Affairs Council (MAC), an executive arm responsible for China-related issues, on its part admitted that the island's top cross-strait negotiator Koo Chen-fu's trip had achieved more than expected.

MAC vice-chairman Lin Chong-pin said Taiwan managed to "shout aloud" the existence of the Republic of China (ROC), the name Taiwan calls itself.

He added that China had assumed that ROC was obliterated in 1949, when the communists drove the Kuomintang to Taiwan. Based on this assumption, it tried to squeeze Taiwan out of the international arena.

However, he said, Mr Koo's trip drove home the historical fact and political reality that the island never ceased to exist.

Any negotiation with Taiwan should start from a recognition of this reality, he added.

As Mr Koo, chairman of the Straits Exchange Foundation, put it: "It will be ridiculous to negotiate with something which did not exist."

Mr Lin noted that China, to make Mr Koo's trip possible, had modified its stand slightly, even though it stuck to its one-China definition, and even as Chinese Vice-Premier Qian Qichen suggested that the diplomatic embargo of Taiwan would continue.

He also said that China had quietly changed one of the three sentences in its formal statement of the one-China principle.

The sentences used to read: "There is only one China in the world.

"Taiwan is part of China.

"The People's Republic of China (PRC) is the lawful representative of China."

But the third sentence now reads: "The sovereignty and territorial integrity of China is inalienable."

This modification made its one-China definition much more acceptable to Taiwan, Mr Lin said, adding that the chances of a real rapprochement between the two sides would be much higher if this definition could be applied in the handling of international issues.

The Straits Times learnt that the Chinese leadership had told Washington of its changed policy towards Taiwan even before US President Bill Clinton's visit to China in late June.

The change included the concept that "one China can be many Chinas in one", as well as the country having two armies.

Sources said that at one point, Mr Koo was overcome with emotion when he told the Chinese leaders that for the past 350 years, China had never once taken good care of the island.

Instead, time and again, it inflicted great pain on Taiwan, he reportedly said. Yet, until recent years, most Taiwanese had remained loyal to the mainland.

If Beijing continued its policy of pushing Taiwan into a corner, it would be held responsible if the island was forced to declare independence eventually, Mr Koo was quoted as saying.

It was through such frank exchanges that Taiwan made known its bottom line for negotiation: recognition of the ROC's existence.

According to Mr Lin, the term ROC had been taboo not only in China, but also at most international functions.

Taiwan has had to avoid it when taking part in multilateral affairs.

Thus, the fact that for the first time in half a century, Beijing was forced to recognise tacitly the existence of the ROC was no small success for the island.

War Awaits Taiwan If It Rejects Talks, China Hints

22 October 1998

THE most important message to have come out from Beijing during the revived Wang-Koo talks which ended on Monday is that political discussion holds the key for Taiwan to tackle the reunification issue — if it wants to avoid military conflict.

In his meeting with Mr Koo Chen-fu, chairman of the Straits Exchange Foundation (SEF), Chinese Vice-Premier Qian Qichen told his guest that if Taiwan wishes to settle the unification issue peacefully, "the only way is to enter into political negotiation".

The unspoken words are understood: If Taiwan rejects political talks, then war awaits the island's authorities.

He told Mr Koo emphatically that Taiwan should "take the interests of the people and nation seriously". Beijing did not hesitate to drive home this dire fact even if it was delivered in a congenial manner.

From all the public statements, it was clear that China saw anti-separatism (the need to prevent Taiwan from breaking away) as more urgent than reunification and was prepared to use force if necessary.

However, as long as Taiwan adhered to the "One China" principle, Beijing was willing to wait until the time was ripe for reunification.

This was clear in Beijing's reaction to Taiwan's two preconditions for political discussion on unification.

The first was that Beijing must recognise the fact that China was currently divided and that the Republic of China (ROC) was in effective control of part of the Chinese territory.

Mr Koo stressed that recognising this fact would provide a basis of equality on which to conduct negotiation. He went into history at some length, citing the 1945 Postdam Declaration that ended World War II to prove that Taiwan was returned to ROC under that declaration, not the People's Republic of China (PRC), which did not even exist at that time.

The second precondition was that unification should be accomplished only after the mainland achieved its democratisation. Without it, the gap between both would not be narrowed and there would be fears among neighbours of an aggrandised China.

Mr Koo said he expounded this point at length during his meeting with Mr Jiang. He saw the effective operating of a multi-party system as an indicator of democratisation.

Beijing reacted fiercely towards the idea of recognising the ROC. It was so annoyed by Mr Koo who brought up what he called a "historical fact and political reality".

Mr Koo was told by his host that once Taiwan returned to the principle of One China, then "anything could be discussed", including expanding Taiwan's participation in international bodies like the Asia-Pacific Economic Cooperation and the Asian Development Bank.

Addressing Taiwan's precondition on democratisation, Beijing was a lot more accommodating. Though dismissing it as "unrealistic", Mr Qian nevertheless said: "Let us both make progress first and discuss unification later."

Knowing that unification talks would be a protracted process, Beijing was willing to allow Taiwan ample time for it to achieve domestic consensus.

"Should Taiwan still find it difficult now to enter into preparatory talks on procedural matters leading to full-fledged political negotiation, we could start with academic forum first to exchange views," Mr Qian told his guest.

Beijing's strategy was crystal clear. Step one was to compel Taiwan on political negotiation, even if the latter was reluctant to do so.

By implying war should there be no political negotiation, Mr Qian did not leave Taiwan any alternative. By unilaterally declaring that political dialogue had already started, Mr Tang forced upon his counterpart, SEF vice-chairman Shi Hwei-yow, a route of no return.

Any subsequent contacts between the SEF and the Arats would be construed as part of this political-dialogue process.

Step two was to define China's bottom-line — the "One China" principle. This was expounded in three sentences: There is only one China in the world; Taiwan is part of China; and the sovereignty and territorial integrity of China are inalienable.

Mr Tang explained that the third sentence, which previously read "The PRC is the only lawful representative of China" was changed to make the principle less objectionable to Taiwan.

Step three was to resume full-scale cross-strait exchanges by both the SEF and the Arats, which had been suspended for more than three years, after arrangements were made to start off political dialogue.

Taiwan was thus left without any choice but to embark on the unwilling road of political negotiation. It might influence the pace but not the direction of this arduous journey.

China and Taiwan Find New Way to Engage

19 October 1998

THE defreezing efforts by both sides of the Taiwan Strait have created a new platform for future dialogue, despite the fact that China and Taiwan still differ sharply on the meaning of "one China" and on ways to achieve reunification.

The five-day visit by Mr Koo Chen-fu, chairman of Taiwan's Straits Exchange Foundation (SEF), to China at the invitation of its counterpart, the Association for the Relations Across the Taiwan Strait (Arats), is the highest-level exchange between the two sides in almost 50 years.

Although differences still abound, the visit produced a four-point consensus — stepped-up dialogue to include political issues, resumed exchanges between Arats and SEF at all levels, giving greater concern to functional issues and a return visit to Taiwan next year by Mr Wang Daohan, chairman of Arats.

There are reasons to believe that this new framework of exchange would be more effective than the previous one established in Singapore in 1993, when Mr Wang and Mr Koo conducted their first talks.

Firstly, under the new framework, Beijing has engaged a reluctant Taipei on political talks, which was a taboo in the 1993 framework.

Arats vice-chairman Tang Shubei said last week: "We have decided to increase dialogue, with the contents covering all aspects — economic, political and so on."

As both sides have set forth their sharp political differences in a very candid manner during the current visit, this paves the way for consultation over politically-sensitive issues.

Secondly, Mr Koo's visit would go a long way towards creating a more amicable relationship between the sides.

As SEF vice-chairman Shi Hwei-yow put it, such direct exchanges at senior level could greatly reduce the likelihood of misinterpretation and miscalculation.

Thirdly, with Taiwan agreeing to hold political dialogue, China is ready to settle "functional issues" of greater urgency raised by Taiwan.

In other words, after a sharp reverse in ties, both sides found a new way to engage each other.

Mr Koo confirmed, after his meeting with President Jiang Zemin, that the Chinese leader was in full endorsement of the consensus.

Still, there are many issues which need to be ironed out.

Foremost is the principle of "one China".

Beijing has spelt out its position in three sentences: There is only one China in the world. Taiwan is part of China. The sovereignty and territorial integrity of China are inalienable.

Taiwan claims that it has never deviated from the "one-China" principle.

To Taiwan, recognising that China is divided and that each has its own right to secure a place in the international arena does not constitute a "two-China" policy.

It maintains that "the fact that China is divided is both a historical fact and a political reality".

Any practical efforts towards reunification must take off from this starting point, it said.

Mr Koo said the Republic of China, which Taiwan calls itself, had never ceased its existence as a legal and political entity since 1911.

On ways to reunify, he stressed the Taiwanese view that reunification not based on democratisation would cause only hardship to the people and concern to neighbouring countries.

He expounded this point at great length during his meeting with Mr Jiang.

This, of course, was unacceptable to his host, who thought that Taiwan was creating unnecessary obstacles.

Both sides clearly failed to narrow their diametrically opposed positions during Mr Koo's "ice-thawing" visit.

Fortunately, the door for political dialogue has been opened.

As Mr Koo put it in his press conference: "Spring will come and by then everyone will get cheered up, but before that, one has to be prepared for the deep winter cold."

This perhaps sums up the result of his trip.

Kinmen Opts for Links With China, the Tourism Way

8 September 1998

KINMEN, one of the most fortified islets in the world at the height of tensions between China and Taiwan, is being turned into a major theme park, with the recently de-commissioned military installations its biggest attraction.

Held by the Kuomintang (KMT) government since its withdrawal to Taiwan in 1949, the island was the scene of many bloody clashes between the KMT and the Chinese Communist Party, the most famous being the so-called August 23 Artillery War 40 years ago.

Kinmen is only about 134 sq km in area, about one-quarter the size of Singapore. But its strategic location — 10 km off Xiamen in south-eastern Fujian province, but 277 km from the nearest point in Taiwan — made it an ideal front-line defence for the KMT.

On Aug 23, 1958, China began the bombardment of the island which was to last for 44 days. Within that time, some half a million — 474,000 to be exact — artillery shells were fired at it.

The strategic intention of the August 23 War was interpreted differently by both sides.

Taiwan saw it as an attempt by China to capture Kinmen to prepare for a major attack on Taiwan itself.

Seen this way, Taiwan claimed its successful defence against the communists paved the way for a prolonged period of peace and stability in the Taiwan Strait, which was vital for the impressive economic growth that later took place.

Thus the 40th anniversary of the war this year was celebrated with much fanfare in Taiwan.

China's intention was to stop American pressure on Taiwan to abandon the islet.

In the late 1950s, the KMT government came under great American pressure to abandon both Kinmen and the Matsu islands. The US told Taiwan that it would not defend any place west of the middle line in the Taiwan Strait.

Taipei, under President Chiang Kai-shek, refused to buckle.

Beijing saw the islands as forming a natural bond between Taiwan and the mainland. If this link was severed, then there would be a greater likelihood for Taiwan to separate from the mainland.

(It turned out that Beijing was right, as, 40 years after the war, pro-independence Taiwanese actually suggested abandoning these islands. The first formal proposal to do so was tabled by pro-independent Democratic Progress Party Chairman Sze Ming-teh, in 1995).

To ward off US pressure on the KMT, Chairman Mao Zedong made the decision to bomb Kinmen. As expected, the move helped put a stop to US pressure.

According to the communists' version of events, capturing the island had never been Chairman Mao's intention.

The fierce resistance put up by President Chiang during the bombing was said to have impressed Mao, prompting him to say: "I feel at ease with Taiwan under Chiang."

The Chinese leader had sensed that he had something in common with his arch enemy: both were staunch defenders of the principle of "one China".

During his historic meeting with US President Nixon in 1972, Chairman Mao told him, on record, that with Taiwan under President Chiang's government, he was prepared to wait 100 years for the reunification problem to be resolved.

Thus Beijing saw the August 23 War as a means to stop American attempts to bring about a permanent separation of Taiwan from the mainland by breaking the symbolic bond between the two sides.

While the true reason for the war may never be known, it is gratifying to see that Kinmen has been demilitarised since 1992, thanks to a gradual relaxation of tensions between both sides.

Progress in military technology also reduced the significance of Kinmen and Matsu as forward defence bases for Taiwan.

The demilitarisation has led to an influx of tourists, all eager to visit the previously highly-secretive installations. In fact, a National Park, Taiwan's sixth, was set up there in 1995 to preserve some of the war-related installations as cultural monuments.

The latest to be de-commissioned include a huge underground waterway capable of hiding a whole fleet of 10 gunboats and an underground artillery base which was instrumental in blockading several small harbours along the coast.

The popularity of Kinmen as a tourist attraction — thanks to the proliferation of military facilities — can be gauged from the high frequency of air traffic between Kinmen and Taiwan island.

Domestic airlines operate eight flights from Taipei and three flights from Kaohsiung daily. With a small civilian population of 30,000 on Kinmen, such a high frequency of flights would not be viable if not for the huge inflow of tourists.

Another amazing thing is that although Kinmen was a battlefield 40 years ago, there is little enmity now between residents in Kinmen and those in Xiamen, from where the shells were launched.

Indeed, vociferous have been the calls by Kinmen residents to Taipei for their own "three mini-links" with China. The "three links" are direct shipping, postal and business links across the Taiwan Strait, which Beijing is pushing hard for.

Reasoned Mr Chan Ching-bao, the legislator representing Kinmen county: If the "three links" for the whole of Taiwan are not feasible soon, why not have "three mini-links" between Kinmen and Xiamen first?

He pointed out that the nearest points between Kinmen and Xiamen were only 1.8 km apart and a trip between the two ports took only 40 minutes by boat.

But as Taiwanese are not allowed to go there direct, they have to spend at least a full day detouring through Taipei and Hongkong.

Mr Chan admitted that even though the government disallowed direct contacts, it was no secret that most Taiwanese flouted the ban.

So while Kinmen residents welcome the tourist dollar, they find that there is more money to be made from smuggling in mainland goods or produce, which cost a fraction of those from Taiwan. Such illicit exchanges are their main source of income.

A "smuggler" shopkeeper, pointing to the high frequency of flights between Kinmen and Taipei, declared proudly: "We are brokering for those in Taiwan who do not have direct access to the mainland."

With the gradual normalisation of cross-strait relations, Kinmen, the island that used to be shrouded in a veil of military mystique, can have a new lease of life.

Taiwanese Parties Forced to Adjust to New Realities

5 August 1998

PRESIDENT Bill Clinton's reiteration of the United States' "three no's" policy on Taiwan is forcing the nationalist island's major political parties to re-adjust their approaches towards China.

The ruling Kuomintang (KMT), for one, finds that it has to accept political negotiation earlier than it would have liked to.

Before the two summit meetings between Mr Clinton and Chinese President Jiang Zemin, the KMT's strategy was to engage China in talks on functional issues while avoiding political matters.

The rationale for this was that success in settling practical problems would pave the way for handling the more difficult political issues.

Beijing, however, preferred to settle "matters of principle" first, its position being that as long as both sides agreed to the "one China" principle, all practical issues could be solved easily.

The KMT was forced to concede on this. In a National Unification Council (NUC) meeting held to take stock of the Beijing summit in June, Mainland Affairs Council chairman Chang King-yuh warned that Taiwan should be "psychologically prepared for political negotiation".

President Lee Teng-hui agreed to "hold consultations based on the reality of a divided China and sign a cross-strait peace agreement, thereby ending the state of hostility and promoting harmony in cross-strait relations".

This proposal to sign a peace agreement is similar to that made by Mr Jiang in his programme for cross-strait ties announced in 1995.

However, there is one significant difference.

Mr Jiang proposed that the peace treaty be signed under the "one China" principle, while Mr Lee's counter-proposal was that it be signed "based on the reality of a divided China".

The rhetoric of "one China" versus "one divided China" reflected the diametrically opposing positions taken by China and Taiwan. Yet, both agreed that it could be the starting point for political negotiation.

As for the largest opposition party, the pro-independence Democratic Progressive Party (DPP), it is also feeling the pressure to speed up dialogue with the Chinese Communist Party.

The party's policy had been one of "strengthening our own base while moving westward". After the Clinton shock, the DPP was forced to review its priorities.

Party secretary-general Chiou I-jen paid a four-day visit to Xiamen on July 24. To quell internal opposition, he did not go in his official capacity and avoided political centres such as Beijing and Shanghai deliberately.

Mr Chiou, who used to dub any Taiwanese politician visiting China a "traitor", returned from the trip in quite an upbeat mood.

He defended his mainland trip, describing it as a brave move. He insisted that, as the international environment was worsening for Taiwan, it would be fatal if the island continued to reject exchanges with the mainland.

He also said that the DPP had been playing the role of a "black sheep" (hampering cross-strait exchanges) and that it was now time for it to become the "white sheep" (promoting exchanges).

The DPP's outgoing chairman Hsu Hsin-liang recently advocated the concept of "one system, one country" as a means to break the present impasse.

According to this concept, Taiwan would wait until China undertook political reforms to close the gap between the two sides. Only then would they have more common ground to hold discussions on "one country".

This represented a major departure from the party's pro-independence programme.

Mr Hsu also expressed his wish to visit Beijing if he could secure a meeting with Chinese Premier Zhu Rongji.

Given his stature in the opposition movement, the DPP heavyweight's change of mind came as a surprise to many.

The third largest party, the New Party (NP), used to advocate "one China" on Taiwanese terms. It has since changed its tack to call for "peaceful negotiation to protect Taiwan and reject independence".

Its spokesman for mainland affairs announced that the party planned to set up a Beijing office to facilitate this exchange.

It is clear from the above that all the three major parties have been adjusting their cross-strait policy carefully to the new reality.

The worst hit were the pro-independence advocates because Mr Clinton's "three no's" policy obliterated their political space entirely.

As expected, a strong sense of being cornered forced them to adopt a more drastic and militant approach.

The Taiwan Independence Party (TAIP), for example, advocated holding a referendum on independence immediately. While it is a small party, its reaction underlined another fact: intensified international pressure could prove counter-productive.

Past opinion polls have shown that there is a strong correlation between external pressure and Taiwanese support for independence.

The latest opinion poll conducted to gauge public reaction to the Sino-US summit again confirmed this correlation.

It showed, for the first time, that support for "eventual independence" (44 per cent) exceeded support for "eventual unification" (34 per cent) by a significant margin.

This finding was something the political parties also could not afford to ignore.

SECTION

Trilateral Balance: Beijing, Taipei & Washington

Korean Detente Could Set Off Arms Race in Asia

12 June 2000

THE first summit between the two Koreas in five decades has raised hopes that detente on the Korean peninsula will set in motion a general disarmament process which will, in turn, lead to enhanced peace and security in North Asia.

There are grounds for such optimism.

The Korean peninsula was the battleground of a fierce war between China and the United States in the early 1950s.

As the contact point between rival camps led by the US and the former Soviet Union, it became the world's most fortified place after World War II, and it remains so even though the Soviet empire is no more.

Any detente, therefore, would cut the ground for the US to continue stationing troops in the region and to develop the Theatre Missile Defence (TMD) system.

It would also weaken Japan's desire to rebuild its military forces.

A general easing of tension would ensue, although it would be more in the psychological rather than real sense.

Unfortunately, the strategic location of the peninsula itself makes it difficult, if not impossible, for lasting peace to come by.

Jutting from the Chinese mainland like an arrow pointed at Japan and with Russia slicing into its northern border, Korea had been a target of major powers for the past 150 years.

In the 19th century, being stuck between a crumbling ancient Chinese empire and a rising new Japan led to its annexation by the latter.

In the 20th century, it was the contact zone for the rival ideologies of two camps.

For this reason, Korea was divided arbitrarily along the 38th Parallel, which became, literally, the world's most fortified border.

At the beginning of the new millennium, the Koreans have decided to take matters into their own hands.

Instead of accepting whatever is prescribed for them by the four major players in the region — the US, Russia, China and Japan — the two Koreas are seeking their own rapprochement.

Their reasons for doing so are different.

Stripped of superpower patronage by the former Soviet Union, North Korea stands exposed to global trends that do not favour rigid and narrow economies.

On the other hand, growing affluence in the South has created a strong desire to reunify with the North — and to send their guests — about 37,000 American soldiers — home.

The strong US troop presence is a daily reminder to the South Koreans that their fate is not entirely theirs to decide — a special irritant to a people scarred deeply by Japanese colonisation.

Without this spontaneous effort by the Koreans themselves to achieve national reconciliation, any peace arrangement imposed on them will not last long, as evidenced by past experiences.

So there are some grounds for cautious optimism this time round that a more durable peace might result from the summit starting tomorrow. Yet the impact of inter-Korean detente on security in North Asia should not be overstated.

Without a change in the American mindset, lasting peace will not be forthcoming.

During the Cold War, rivalry between the two Koreas mirrored that between the US and the Soviet Union, and provided the Americans with a strong excuse to station its troops in the Far East.

In the post-Cold War era, the threat from Russia receded but the US found a new source of threat, the so-called "rogue states", which renewed support for a strong American military presence in the region. North Korea was on this blacklist.

With Pyongyang now apparently ready to start talking about coming to terms with Seoul, as well as indicating a strong desire to rejoin the world community, one would think that, perhaps, the US no longer has a strong excuse for its huge forward deployment.

Unfortunately, this is not the case. Washington has just completed an assessment of its defence needs in the next two decades and the conclusion is that a military build-up is needed to counter "peer competitors".

This is contained in "Joint Vision 2020", a Pentagon policy paper that was published on May 31.

Even without mentioning any country by name, it is obvious that the report is referring to China.

"China is the new Beltway buzzword," observed Mr Dov S. Zakheim, a former Pentagon official who is an adviser on defence policy to Republican presidential candidate George W. Bush. To defeat such an enemy, the policy paper called for building up a military might that would ensure the US "full-spectrum dominance", which includes conflicts involving the employment of strategic forces and weapons of mass destruction, major theatre wars, regional conflicts, and smaller-scale contingencies.

Mr Thomas Ricks of the Washington Post disclosed that when Mr William Cohen became Defence Secretary in 1997, the first question he asked Pentagon officials was: "How can we change the assumption that US troops will be withdrawn after peace comes to the Korean peninsula?"

This showed that even with peace in the Korean peninsula, the US will find new excuses to keep its troops in the region. The Pentagon paper confirms this.

According to Mr Ricks, the attention on a possible military competition with China is also reflected in two long-running, military-diplomatic efforts.

The first is a drive to re-negotiate the US military presence in North-east Asia.

This is aimed at ensuring that American forces will still be welcome in South Korea and Japan after the North Korean threat disappears.

The second is the negotiation of the US military's re-entry in South-east Asia, 25 years after the end of the Vietnam War and almost 10 years after the US withdrew from its bases in the Philippines.

These developments will certainly not promote durable peace in the region even with detente in the peninsula.

Quite the contrary, they could just spur another arms race in East Asia.

Quoting former National Security Adviser Zbigniew Brzezinski, Mr Ricks noted that the effect of a build-up against China "would be felt immediately by the Chinese and would presumably precipitate a build-up".

That, in turn, "could provoke India to beef up its own nuclear forces, a move that would threaten Pakistan". A Chinese build-up also could make Japan feel that it needed to build up its own military, he added.

In drawing up its "Joint Vision 2020", the Pentagon disregarded findings showing that China was not that strong a force.

An assessment by the US National Defence University surmises that China's military in 1998 was "probably two decades away from challenging or holding its own against a modern military force".

Mr Paul Goodwin of the National War College puts "the window for China becoming one of the world's major military powers at somewhere between 2020 and 2050".

Surveying the prospect worldwide, Mr Russell Travers, an analyst at the Defence Intelligence Agency, concluded that "no military or technical peer competitor to the US is on the horizon for at least a couple of decades".

So why this obsession with threats?

Messrs Carl Conetta and Charles Knight, co-directors of the Project on Defence Alternatives at the Commonwealth Institute in Cambridge, Massachusetts, concluded that there was a mechanism within the Pentagon that "invents threats".

They noted in a paper that it was a remarkable admission for a chairman of the Joint Chiefs of Staff to say: "I'm running out of demons. I'm down to Kim Il Sung and Castro."

They concluded that unless the threat-invention mechanism was dismantled, detente on the Korean peninsula alone would not bring lasting peace to the North Asian region.

US Trade Vote No Big Deal

28 May 2000

THE United States' vote to give China permanent trade benefits helped reverse a dangerous downward spiral in Sino-American ties, but in no way did it resolve the deep-rooted differences between the two nations.

If anything, the debate process showed that there would be no shortage of conflicts in the years to come.

Many members of the House of Representatives hailed Thursday's vote as one of the most important in the history of the US Congress.

As Representative David Dreier put it: "This may, in fact, be the most important vote cast in the 213-year history of the US."

Agreeing, Mr Bill Archer said that the vote "will affect American generations to come".

Yet the case should be viewed more soberly.

Sheer common sense dictated that the US should grant China permanent normal trade relations (PNTR) status and so the whole debate is meaningless if viewed from a purely trade angle.

First of all, PNTR is not a legal prerequisite for China to enter the World Trade Organisation (WTO) and the American public was certainly misled into thinking this was the case.

After studying all the relevant WTO and US domestic laws, Messrs Clyde Hufbauer and Daniel Rosen, two senior fellows at the US Institute for International Economics, concluded that "China will become a full-fledged member of the WTO, once the remaining bilateral agreements are concluded, whatever Congress decides on PNTR".

Based on this finding, all anti-PNTR arguments become invalid.

Secondly, the WTO accession agreement China reached with the US is lopsidedly in favour of the latter.

Mr Stanley Roth, Assistant Secretary of State for East Asian and Pacific Affairs, admitted this point in a congressional hearing.

"The deal does nothing to improve the access of Chinese companies to the US market. Regardless of whether China joins the WTO, regardless of whether the US Congress grants PNTR to China, Chinese companies will have the same access to the American market which they have had," he said.

However, he added: "The deal will significantly advance opportunities for American companies to export goods and services to China. In trade terms, then, the case is clear: China's WTO accession overwhelmingly benefits the US."

To reap this benefit, the US needed to grant China permanent trade relations.

Said Mr Roth: "There is one large caveat: we will not enjoy these benefits unless the Congress grants PNTR to China upon its accession to the WTO.

"If it does not, these advantages, so skilfully negotiated by Ambassador Charlene Barshefsky and her team, will go to our competitors in other nations.

"They will be able to sell their services to China, while we will not. They will be able to use WTO mechanisms to resolve disputes with China, while we will not. Clearly, that makes no sense."

Messers Hufbauer and Rosen also confirmed in their legal studies: "Chinese membership in the WTO will not automatically mean that China extends its WTO obligations to the US."

Hence, a vote against PNTR, or no vote at all, means that the US would miss out on the most valuable elements of China's concessions, they argued.

So why all this heated debate over a "common sense" issue? How did such an issue become so divisive as to split the American society?

"To understand this, the debate should be set against the overall background of managing a rising China," said Mr Chen Zhong-wei, director of the China International Relations Institute in Beijing.

"The American society is split over this and it led to a decade-long debate over whether the US should contain or engage China."

The PNTR vote was but a continuation of the same debate, he stressed.

In American politics, this containment-engagement divide is sometimes expressed in terms of the dichotomy between idealism and pragmatism.

The idealist, who places more importance on "values" such as democracy and human rights, would like to contain China.

The pragmatist, on the other hand, focuses more on "interests" such as business opportunities and would prefer to engage China.

Although the Clinton administration tended to be more pragmatic, it sometimes had to succumb to pressures from the idealists, Mr Chen explained.

The pragmatists want to grant China PNTR because they see this as the best way to further their strategic objective, which is to make China play by a set of agreed rules.

Defending the administration's PNTR stance, Mr Roth said that US strategy on China is "to integrate China into regional and global institutions, helping it become a country that plays by the accepted international rules, cooperating and competing peacefully within those rules".

He therefore described PNTR status for China as a "win-win-win" situation. China benefits from WTO entry. The US benefits by gaining access to a huge market. Finally, the strategy of integrating China through engagement also wins.

Judging from this manifestation of US intentions, Mr Chen concluded that future US policy towards China would shift from the "hard power" approach, which was characteristic of the Cold War era, to one adopting "soft power".

He defined "hard power" as confrontation over military power and "soft power" as confrontation over ideals and values.

He predicted that in the next five to 10 years, the US would expend greater energy into building up American-led global frameworks in political, economic and social arenas in which human rights and humanitarian issues would be used more frequently as a pretext for intervention into other nations' domestic affairs.

"It is not surprising, therefore, that while the Congress granted PNTR to China, it also attached a stipulation — the Levin-Bereuter provision — requiring the President to report to the Congress on China's human rights situation."

The whole PNTR debate reflected a dire fact: the imminent rise of China is creating great strategic and psychological pressures for the Western world, according to Mr Chen.

"In the next 10 years, China will move closer and closer to the centre of international politics and the forefront of international economics. This is a natural result of its own growth," he said. "Yet this natural growth will inevitably have an impact on others' spheres of interests."

He said it was logical to expect Western developed countries to close ranks in their overall strategy to delay this process.

"To China, this means that the external environment is becoming more hostile. But it nevertheless reflects a change in the relative rise and fall of players in the international stage," he said.

"So while we welcome the decision to grant PNTR to China, we should be vigilant about the future battleground: the test of strength in soft power," he concluded.

US Trade Vote Eases Tension But Real Peace Remains Elusive

26 May 2000

MUCH hope has been attached to the passage of permanent trade benefits for China by the US Congress as a means to reducing cross-strait tension.

Some observers even link Beijing's rather restraint response to the inaugural address of Taiwan's President to its bid for the trade status.

It certainly helps, but the permanent normal trade relations (PNTR) deal can hardly lead to true peace across the Taiwan Strait.

The trade Bill helps reduce tension in two ways. First of all, it patches up shaky Sino-American relations. As former US national security adviser Brent Scowcroft has pointed out, China is paranoid about American intentions.

The US decision to allow Taiwan's President Lee Teng-hui to visit Cornell University in 1995, the Taiwan Strait missile crisis of 1996, the aborted visit of Chinese Premier Zhu Rongji last year and the bombing of the Chinese embassy in Belgrade last May all contributed to Chinese suspicions that the US was more a foe than a friend.

"If we turn down PNTR now, it feeds into this paranoia about what the US is up to. I think it would be the event that made the Chinese decide that we are fundamentally hostile to them and their progress," Mr Scowcroft said at a seminar organised by the Nixon Centre, a think-tank on national policies.

According to him, the PNTR goes a long way to prove that the US is basically friendly and sympathetic to the Chinese. This gesture of goodwill makes China more at ease in managing the Beijing-Washington-Taipei trilateral relations.

Secondly, it facilitates the entry of China into the World Trade Organisation (WTO) and, by tacit understanding, of Taiwan in its wake.

Although the PNTR is not a legal prerequisite for China's accession to the world body, it nevertheless serves as a lubricant, smoothening the entry of both Beijing and Taipei.

It helps remove an American nightmare. A State Department official said privately that should PNTR be blocked, Beijing might retaliate by blocking the entry of Taiwan.

In theory, it can do so because according to the understanding between China and WTO, Beijing would enter the world body ahead of Taipei.

Once in it, Beijing could request Taiwan to state its compliance to the "one-China" principle as a precondition for its membership. This possibility, though highly unlikely, cannot be ruled out totally.

With the PNTR passage, the prospect of such a retaliation is greatly reduced. With both brought into the world body, Washington hopes that their differences could be reduced through expanded exchanges and dialogue.

This is also the reason why Taipei is willing to support PNTR status for Beijing. Taiwan wants to develop cross-strait relations, especially the so-called "three direct links", within a global framework instead of a bilateral one.

Within a global framework, Taipei feels more at ease because the rules governing the behaviour of each of the members are set collectively and there is no fear of being bullied by Beijing.

Moreover, in a global framework, Taiwan has a greater sense of equality vis-a-vis Beijing. After all, security and equality have been the two most salient elements that Taipei insists on, in its dealings with the Chinese.

Taiwan hopes that with enhanced security and dignity, it could handle cross-strait problems with greater confidence.

"This will lead to greater exchange between Beijing and Taipei and hopefully both sides could learn how to handle their differences," said Dr Julian Kuo, who teaches politics at Taiwan's Soochow University.

In due course, these exchanges will gradually prepare the ground for both sides to enter into talks over more difficult issues, added Dr Kuo, who also advises Taiwan's President Chen Shui-bian.

Thus, to some extent, PNTR helps reduce tension. But its impact must not be exaggerated.

Cross-strait tension is a direct result of Taiwan wanting to break away from China. To defend its territorial integrity, Beijing is prepared to use every possible means, including force. Unless this root cause of tension is removed, no interim measures, no matter how ameliorating they are, could make for real peace.

PNTR is helpful only to the extent that it facilitates both sides to enter WTO as smoothly and early as possible, and thereby opens up the opportunity for bilateral exchanges within the WTO.

How both sides are going to make use of this opportunity remains the key issue. If it leads to the lifting of the ban on "three direct links" as well as the "no haste, be patient" restrictions by Taipei so that cross-strait exchanges could develop unfettered, then the prospect for an integration acceptable to both sides might emerge.

Yet if concurrent membership in the world body leads to enhanced efforts by Taiwan to assert a separate statehood, then the outlook will be extremely bleak.

Sino-US Summit Smooths Over Cross-Strait Tensions... for Now

16 September 1999

LAST Saturday's Sino-US summit on the sidelines of the Apec conference in Auckland succeeded in preventing a crisis, triggered by Taiwan President Lee Teng-hui's "two states theory", from escalating into a war.

Yet a durable peace is still not in sight.

China saw Mr Lee's statehood remarks as a big step towards declaring independence and threatened to use force to preserve its territorial integrity, while the United States saw his move as a unilateral and an abrupt attempt to upset the delicate trilateral relationship.

Thanks to the meeting between Presidents Jiang Zemin and Bill Clinton, a military confrontation was avoided, at least for the time being, because China and the US were able to patch up their relations, which have spiralled downwards since late last year.

Both sides emerged from the summit much satisfied.

The Americans announced that bilateral relations were "back on track" while the Chinese said that the meeting "laid a strong foundation for bilateral relations in the next century".

To crown the summit, Mr Clinton pledged his support for Chinese membership in the World Trade Organisation (WTO) openly. The intent of the world's most powerful country was embodied in the Apec declaration immediately.

Past experience showed that whenever Sino-US ties were strong and sound, cross-strait tension was reduced. This pattern repeated itself this time.

Ironically, it was Taiwan which helped reverse the downward trend in Sino-US relations.

Mr Lee's "two states theory" created a crisis that forced both Beijing and Washington to mend ties immediately to address the matter jointly.

In his summit with Mr Jiang, the US President concurred that Mr Lee had created trouble for Sino-US relations.

He reassured Mr Jiang of his commitment to the "one China" principle. He also told the Apec forum that the US recognised only one China. This US position ensured that the "two states theory" would not get any support internationally.

These three gestures satisfied China and helped to clear Chinese suspicion that Mr Lee made his remarks with US blessings.

Mr Jiang reciprocated by reiterating China's long-standing policy to solve the Taiwan issue peacefully, but would not rule out re-taking the island by non-peaceful means.

He was quoted as telling Mr Clinton that while he did not like war, he was answerable to 1.2 billion Chinese who were very concerned about Taiwan's separatist tendencies.

In other words, as long as Taiwan abided by the "one China" principle, there would be no war.

Thus a potential conflict was averted, at least temporarily, to the great relief of the Asia-Pacific countries.

Taipei, as usual, stressed that the outcome of the Apec summit did not harm its relations with Washington, yet most observers in Taiwan agreed that Mr Lee's theory had clearly backfired on the island.

His claim to statehood, even though justifiable from Taipei's point of view, had nevertheless upset the "one China" principle that, for all of its shortcomings, had served the three parties well since 1971.

It brought about more than two decades of peace and stability to the region, which underlined the rapid economic growth in China and Taiwan as well as the whole region at large.

However, this important principle had never been defined clearly.

Beijing took "one China" to mean the People's Republic of China (PRC) while to Taipei, it was the "Republic of China" (ROC).

Washington maintained equally strong relations with both. This was an ambiguity that all sides have tolerated since 1971, because none of them had the power to dictate its own definition to the others.

As long as Taiwan did not attempt to break this ambiguity, China could tolerate it long enough to let time solve the problem.

Washington saw eye to eye with Beijing on the fact that Mr Lee's claim to separate statehood was a clear attempt to break from the "one China" principle and that this could have serious implications.

As a result, the US was forced to tilt towards China by spelling out the three pillars of its China policy: the "one China" principle, cross-strait dialogue and peaceful solution.

In upholding the "one China" principle, the US departed from its long-established neutralist stance that "people on both sides of the Taiwan Strait agree that there is only one China and the US does not dispute it", as worded in the 1971 Shanghai communique.

In recent years, Beijing talked more about the "one China" principle while Taipei shied away from it. By upholding the "one China" principle, Washington was siding with Beijing.

On cross-strait dialogue, too, the US departed from its previous commitment to Taiwan not to mediate between both sides or to force the island into negotiations with China.

This commitment was one of the "six assurances" it made to Taipei when it signed the third communique with China in 1981.

On cross-strait dialogue, while Beijing wanted to have "political talks" to set a general framework for handling bilateral relations, Taipei proposed "functional talks" so as to avoid political ones.

Long before Mr Lee's formulation of the "two states theory", there were already calls from Washington urging Taipei to enter into "substantive talks" with Beijing. Washington was clearly slanting towards Beijing.

The "two states theory" made things worse for Taiwan. Washington seemed to be suggesting that the "one country, two systems" formula proposed by Beijing for the eventual settlement of the Taiwan issue could be considered.

For instance, Mr Clinton made reference to Hongkong, a former British colony unified under the "one country, two systems" formula, when he showed his displeasure at Mr Lee's theory.

Not long afterwards, Deputy Assistant Secretary of State Susan Shirk called openly for a "one country, three systems" formula.

Although it was premature to conclude that the US accepted the Chinese formula, such references at least showed that it did not find it unfavourable. This was an obvious change in American attitude.

On peaceful solution, too, the onus was not just on China.

In his address to Apec business leaders, Mr Clinton urged both sides to refrain from making moves that would escalate the tense situation across the Taiwan Strait.

In other words, Washington thought that both Beijing — which threatened the use of force — and Taipei — which provoked Beijing into making the threat — were to blame for the current crisis.

Observers also pointed out that Mr Clinton told Mr Jiang that the recent US$5 billion (S$8.4 billion) sale of arms to Taiwan was one made on a case-by-case basis.

Never before had any US president said that military sales mandated by the Taiwan Relations Act (TRA) were made on such a basis.

One could deduce that the words held the hidden message that Taiwan should not take US military sales to the island for granted.

On the surface, therefore, the nomenclature or terminology of America's China policy remained unchanged, but there were discernible tilts in favour of Beijing.

These were the results of how the "two states theory" has backfired on Taiwan.

Though war has been averted temporarily, sustainable peace is still not in sight because China and Taiwan have so far failed to work out a way to settle their differences. They have depended on American "arbitration" this time round to avoid open conflict — but such arbitration, in the long run, could only perpetuate the state of separation and leave the problem unresolved.

And as long as the Taiwan issue remains unresolved, there will be no lasting peace.

Soothing Chinese Nerves at Apec

10 September 1999

THE Jiang-Clinton meeting, which takes place this weekend on the sidelines of the Apec summit in Auckland, is certain to overshadow the conference since few other issues are as important to this region as Sino-US relations.

A stable bilateral relationship between the two countries has been the cornerstone of prolonged peace in the region and this has, in turn, underpinned the region's extraordinary economic growth.

The prospect of a conflict between China and the US, which loomed large in recent months, was perhaps more alarming to Asia-Pacific leaders than the financial crisis that swept the region.

It was therefore a great relief to many that Presidents Jiang Zemin and Bill Clinton agreed to patch up their relations at the Apec summit.

Topping the agenda of their talks will be China's accession to the World Trade Organisation (WTO) and the crisis sparked by Taiwanese President Lee Teng-hui's "two states" theory.

Beijing sees this new claim to statehood as a move towards independence and vows to use force to prevent any separatist move by the island.

Defusing the Taiwan crisis thus has more urgency than China's WTO bid.

There are indications that the US would try to solve the first — and easier — issue first, so as to create the right atmosphere for tackling the more difficult one.

Washington has indicated that it would push through a proposal at the Apec forum calling for WTO membership for both Beijing and Taipei before the end of this year.

It hopes that doing so will ease the extremely tense atmosphere across the Taiwan Strait since Mr Lee made his "two states" remarks two months ago.

The US also needs badly a political "quid pro quo" for China in order to compensate for Nato's bombing of the Chinese embassy in Belgrade, which plunged bilateral relations to its lowest point since 1979, when they established diplomatic relations.

The US intention to solve the WTO accession problem for Beijing and Taipei was reflected in a report drafted by senior Apec officials for their ministers.

The officials recommended that the ministers take steps to encourage the admission of China and Taiwan into the WTO "at the earliest opportunity, if possible before the third WTO ministerial meeting in Seattle" in November.

Echoing the US, WTO director-general-designate Mike Moore also said that he would do all he could to facilitate the entry of China and Taiwan into the world trade body before the end of the year.

Judging from the American move as well as the eager cooperation from Apec member countries, it is logical to assume that the WTO issue would be largely resolved when Presidents Bill Clinton and Jiang Zemin meet.

Solving the WTO issue, which will go a long way to improve US-China relations, would create a more congenial atmosphere for tackling the Taiwan issue.

China wants to secure from the US an unambiguous statement that it does not support the "two states" theory.

While Mr Clinton was quick to reiterate the three pillars of Washington's China policy soon after Mr Lee made his "two states" remarks, the US had not condemned the Taiwanese leader or his theory.

Instead, Mr Clinton approved the sales of E-2T early warning aircraft as well as advanced equipment for F-16 fighters to Taiwan.

A Pentagon delegation went ahead with its trip to Taiwan, suspended after the "two states" theory was announced, to assess the island's needs for theatre missile defence (TMD).

At the same time, the US Congress adopted a resolution on July 21 urging Beijing to renounce the use of force against Taiwan, and was mulling over the Taiwan Security Enhancement Act, which calls for the US to provide Taiwan with a host of modern weapons.

China saw these inconsistencies as arising from the Taiwan Relations Act (TRA), which dictates a non-military solution for the Taiwan issue while at the same time mandating the US administration to provide sufficient war material for the defence of Taiwan.

Although the formal defence pact between Taiwan and the US was scrapped way back in 1979, the TRA works in much the same way as one.

China claims that as a result of the protective cover offered by the TRA, Taipei is able to resist reunification with the mainland.

Beijing feels that Washington's "strategic ambiguity" is hampering a peaceful solution as it misleads Taiwan into thinking that it can hide behind the US and continue to provoke China without risking punishment.

This ambiguity, in China's view, has complicated the Taiwan issue.

The most difficult task facing Mr Jiang Zemin when he meets his US counterpart is to clear up this US ambiguity.

Specifically, Beijing wants Washington to be unequivocal in refuting the "two states" theory.

When the Chinese leadership decided at their Beidaihe retreat last month to postpone a decision on military action against Taiwan, one of the reasons was this week's Apec conference.

If Beijing could secure an unambiguous statement from the US against the "two states" theory, the risk of a conflict would be much reduced.

China Believes TMD Could Trigger Another Arms Race

3 September 1999

IN A Pentagon report on Theatre Missile Defence (TMD) options for the Asia-Pacific region in May, the United States recommended an integrated architecture called "the TMD family of systems" (FoS) for Taiwan.

But the TMD system which Taiwan plans to build will be a modified version of that recommended by the US.

According to the military report, the FoS approach is required to provide multi-tier defences which are necessary to increase system robustness, or kill probability, and efficiency against the enemy's large inventories of short-range missiles as well as longer-range ones.

The report justified the option based on Taiwan's key geographical feature, which is a narrow sea between the island and the mainland.

Short-range missiles — with ranges below 300 km — could fly over that barrier and remain within the atmosphere for the entire flight. With China's size, an attack utilising such missiles could come from multiple directions.

But China's theatre ballistic missiles — which come with longer ranges of up to 3,000 km — would require defence systems that feature early warning surveillance to cue the defending missiles to the incoming threats.

Four systems, both land and sea-based, have been recommended to intercept attacking missiles from inside (endo-atmosphere) and outside (exo-atmosphere) the atmosphere.

The Pentagon report estimated that Taiwan would need 12 land-based and 11 sea-based units — or lower-tier units — to intercept short-range missiles.

It would also need one sea-based unit and one land-based unit to guard against long-range missiles.

For the FoS to function effectively, the boost phase, as well as upper and lower-layer defences, will be supported by an early-warning and battle management/command, control and communications system.

The lower-tier units alone would cost at least US$20 billion (S$33.6 billion), as each individual unit costs about US$1 billion to install.

But with budgetary resources only half of what was required, Taiwan had to make several modifications to the original recommendation.

Defence Minister Tang Fei announced last week that the island was going to spend NT$300 billion (S$15 billion) over the next eight years to install the system.

The revised Taiwan plan includes postponing the decision on the upper-tier units until 2006, reducing total coverage of its territories to 70 per cent, and making more use of its indigenous Sky Bow (Tien-kung) missiles, which are said to be as efficient as the US-made Patriots.

China is strongly opposed to the TMD and its extension to Taiwan.

Ambassador Sha Zukang, director-general of the Foreign Ministry's Department of Arms Control and Disarmament, said that by extending TMD to the island, the US had violated one of the three conditions for normalisation of Sino-US ties, which was to scrap the defence treaty between the US and Taiwan.

The other two conditions were cessation of official diplomatic relations and withdrawal of US troops in Taiwan.

Beijing saw TMD sales to Taiwan as the first step towards the re-establishment of a de facto military alliance between Washington and Taipei.

China argued that TMD was substantially different from other weapon systems because it required significant military cooperation between the US and Taiwan.

Such cooperation would come in the form of early warning satellites, long-range ground-based radar and, possibly, space-based sensors for cueing purposes.

In addition, Taiwan would have to rely on the US for much of the training to use it, leading the US to assume certain obligations to defend Taiwan.

By extending the TMD to Taiwan, China said, the US also violated a 1982 joint communique commitment which stated that the quantity and quality of arms sales to Taiwan would not exceed the level at the time the communique was signed.

To pass on to Taiwan an advanced weapons system was therefore a blatant breach of the commitment.

The extension of TMD to Taiwan could also send a dangerously wrong signal to the island that it could rely on US assistance to neutralise Beijing's military superiority, and therefore resist reunification forever.

Beijing's objection to the TMD was not confined to Taiwan.

It viewed the whole TMD issue as an overall attempt to contain China.

Responding to the US argument that TMD was developed as a strategic response to China's missile tests near Taiwan in 1995 and

1996, and North Korea's missile test last year, Mr Mu Changlin, a senior research fellow with the China Institute of International Strategic Studies, called it a flat lie.

According to him, long before the claimed missile firing by China and North Korea, the US Congress had passed the Missile Defence Act in 1991 under which it approved and appropriated funds for research into a Global Protection Against Limited Strikes (GPALS) programme.

GPALS envisioned three phases: (1) TMD systems to be developed and deployed concurrently with (2) the national missile defence (NMD), after which (3) a Global Protection System (GPS) would be developed and shared globally.

Since then, the US had been lobbying Japan, South Korea and Taiwan to join the TMD and share the costs.

All these took place long before the Chinese and North Korean missile tests, according to Mr Mu, who said the real reason underlying the TMD issue was that China survived the collapse of the Soviet bloc and emerged stronger, becoming the only country in the world that could say "no" to the US.

To manage a rising China militarily, the US needed to have an NMD system to protect its own territory and a TMD system to protect its key allies in Asia.

By intercepting any attacking missiles, both systems hope to neutralise China's nuclear deterrent and counter-strike capability.

Moreover, although the US had stressed that TMD was basically defensive in nature, Chinese military experts showed that the system could be modified easily into an offensive one.

If the TMD was converted into an offensive system, it would immediately upset the military balance in East Asia, said Mr Mu, arguing that Japan would be enticed to re-embark on a militarist route while Taiwan would forever refuse reunification.

"This will trigger another arms race," he said.

Uphill Task for Obuchi

7 July 1999

THE timing of Japanese Prime Minister Keizo Obuchi's visit to China could not be worse.

Since Chinese President Jiang Zemin made his unfruitful summit trip to Japan last November, the soured bilateral relations had been marred further by developments in both Japan and the international arena.

The best result that Mr Obuchi could hope to achieve during his three-day trip is to slow down the slide, there being little hope of a major breakthrough.

The Chinese leader's failure to secure a satisfactory Japanese apology for its war atrocities and its non-commitment to the "Three No's" principle — no to Taiwan independence, no to two Chinas, no to Taiwanese membership in international bodies requiring statehood — had prompted an infuriated Mr Jiang to raise the lessons of history at almost every public occasion during the visit.

Unfortunately, this approach backfired because it only made the Japanese more hostile.

The Japan Forum on International Relations (JFIR), a private think-tank, for example, drew up a Foreign Policy Recommendation, co-signed by 78 influential scholars, opinion leaders and Diet members, calling for a review of Japan's foreign policy.

On China, it stressed the need to "eliminate disagreements between Japan and China over historical understanding".

Such a recommendation suggests that the Japanese disagree with China over historical issues in the first place.

A separate group of professors made a similar presentation to the Japanese government, stressing "the compelling need for an overall review of the basic stance of Japan and Japanese foreign policy without being bound by the past".

Such an open attempt to dispute historical facts was certainly not acceptable to China.

The JFIR also recommended a firm Japan-US stance on the so-called "fourth no" — no use of force by China to re-claim Taiwan, which the mainland regards as a renegade province.

The recommendation read: "Japan's basic position goes no further than the idea of 'fully understanding and respecting the position of the Chinese government' as set out in the Joint Japan-China Communique of 1972.

"Of course, 'fully understanding and respecting' is not the same as 'approving'.

"Should military tensions arise in the Taiwan Strait and hostilities erupt, such a position would not force Japan to stand by and do nothing.

"Japan and the US should therefore co-ordinate and maintain a firm stance on 'no use of force by China to liberate Taiwan' and should be careful not to send any wrong signals to the Chinese in this regard."

In China's view, this was an attempt to curtail its sovereignty over Taiwan, which it regarded as a domestic issue.

On the international front, developments were also not conducive to improving Sino-Japanese relations.

China saw some major changes in the international environment following the Kosovo crisis and Nato's bombing of its embassy in Belgrade.

Foremost is the worldwide expansion of American hegemony which was helped by the eastward expansion of Nato and the strengthening of the Joint US-Japan Defence Pact.

Then, "human rights" was given priority over and above "nation's rights" or sovereignty. Military aggression against a sovereign state could be justified on the pretext of safeguarding human rights.

Third, the United Nations framework as a means of resolving international dispute was cast aside. This upset totally the modus operandi on handling international relations since its establishment half a century ago.

The Chinese called these three major changes in the international environment the "Kosovo model".

"If the Kosovo model became a norm, then China is not far from it," noted a Chinese expert on international affairs, Professor Wang Fuchun of the Institute of International Relations of Beijing University.

"The bombing of our embassy served merely to demonstrate in a highly dramatic way that China could be a victim of the model," he said.

With China highly wary of the Kosovo model, any explanation by Mr Obuchi to ease Chinese fears over the revised Joint US-Japan Defence Pact would not be accepted easily by Beijing.

In fact, short of an unequivocal statement to exclude Taiwan from the pact, any explanation would be futile.

An editorial in the Liberation Army Daily, a newspaper reflecting the Chinese military's views, claimed that the pact was a "strategic plot to pursue hegemonism" and that "Japan is trying, by relying on the strength of superpower America, to realise its dream of first becoming a great political power and then a military power".

The pact, thus, had destroyed the strategic balance in the whole Asia-Pacific region, the editorial said.

"It may hollow out the state treaties and documents signed between China and the US and between China and Japan, and cast a shadow over Sino-US and Sino-Japanese relations," it warned.

The spectre of the Kosovo model was obviously having an effect on China's foreign policy thinking.

Yet, the Japanese are not so pessimistic.

According to a Japanese diplomatic source, Mr Obuchi's visit tomorrow deserved attention because the Japanese prime minister would be the first leader from the Group of Eight (G-8) major powers to visit China after the Cologne summit.

During that summit, Japan was pushing subtly for expanding the G-8 to include China.

"At a time when China sees itself threatened by a US-led bloc, such a move could help alleviate its fear and is therefore very meaningful," the diplomatic source said.

Moreover, given the fact that China needs a stable international political environment desperately in order to carry on its own economic development, Beijing's basic diplomatic orientation is to promote stable ties with other major nations in the region.

Thus, China's need for a stable international environment plus Mr Obuchi's G-9 effort could bring the two nations closer than would be the case, the source concluded.

Questions About Hard Evidence

4 June 1999

THE Cox Report, which accused China of stealing US military technologies when it was released last week, further strained Sino-US relations already frayed by the bombing of the Chinese Embassy in Belgrade.

Unfortunately, the 700-page report, lengthy though it is, has provided little solid evidence of Chinese wrongdoing. This impression is one shared by many observers who have read the report.

That such an exceptionally-strong allegation was made without hard facts to support it simply fuelled suspicion in China that the charge was fabricated for political purposes.

The report claimed that China had systematically conducted a 20-year intelligence-gathering programme.

The methods used included espionage, review of unclassified publications and extensive interactions with scientists from the US Department of Energy's national weapons laboratories.

Observers were quick to point out that, espionage excepted, there was nothing wrong in obtaining information through the other two channels.

"Even espionage activities should be considered a norm rather than an exception," said a US security analyst who declined to be identified.

"It is just common sense that countries conduct espionage activities against each other, whether they be friend or foe. In the notorious Jonathan Pollard case in the mid-80s, an American was found spying for Israel, a US ally.

"The onus of counter-espionage rests with the host country. Since the report admitted that the counter-intelligence programme at the national weapons laboratories failed to meet even minimal standards, then it is time to take remedial actions, not blame others," the analyst said.

While the Cox report accused China of espionage against the US, the information contained in the report could also be turned into evidence of US espionage against China, said a scholar specialising in Sino-US relations at the China Academy of Social Sciences. He did not want to be identified.

For example, the report detailed the three programmes underway to turn China's silo-based inter-continental ballistic missiles (ICBMs) into mobile ones.

These included the road-mobile and the submarine-launched ICBMs, as well as ICBMs with multiple warheads (called multiple independent re-entry vehicles).

It also predicted that the first road-mobile ICBM would be tested this year and be operational by 2002. Such information would not have been available without professional espionage activities.

The report also disclosed that Pentagon officials had previously frowned on the export to China of US mobile-phone technology known as CDMA (Code Division Multiple Access).

It argued that its encrypted format would make it hard for US spy satellites to eavesdrop.

According to the Chinese scholar, all this was evidence of US conducting espionage activities against China and US Representative Christopher Cox, who led the six-month investigation, was fully aware of it.

"So why the double standard?" the scholar asked, somewhat angrily. The report identified four major areas in which significant technology loss allegedly took place: thermo-nuclear, missile, space and high-performance computers (HPCs).

In thermo-nuclear technology, according to the report, China obtained classified information on seven thermo-nuclear warheads and one neutron bomb, all of which represented state-of-the-art US military technology.

However, a Chinese State Council spokesman demonstrated that the so-called classified information was easily available on the Internet.

In missile technology, a guidance system, an electro-magnetic weapon and a detection technique, all too sensitive even to be named, were allegedly stolen by China.

In space venture, technical information arising from investigations by American firms into the causes of failed satellite launches in China were considered classified but were allegedly transferred to China illegally.

In dual-use technologies, China allegedly diverted HPCs bought from the US to military applications, which violated US export controls.

The implications of these technology losses, according to the report, were that the threat to US territory was moved up by about 10 years.

In particular, the threat to forwardly-deployed US troops in the west Pacific and its Asian allies had become more probable now.

Yet the report failed to name even one single incidence showing that the loss of technology was due to unbecoming activities by the Chinese although it did, at one point, mention that President Bill Clinton had withheld information on how technology was stolen on national security grounds.

The bulk of the unclassified version of the Cox report was on space technology, which took up roughly a third of the report.

Mr Cox complained that following three satellite launch failures since 1992, two US manufacturers had helped to investigate the cause of the failure and submitted their findings to China together with classified information on guidance and nose-cone technologies.

He claimed that such information on rocket design, if applied to missiles, could enhance greatly China's capability to launch an attack at American soil.

The two companies — Huges Electronics Corp and Loral Space & Communications Ltd — have denied strongly any wrongdoing.

"Even if they had passed on information, it should not be considered as theft. In a joint investigative effort such as this, it was normal that there would be substantial exchange of views between the satellite manufacturer and the launcher," said the Chinese scholar.

Pure commercial interests dictated that both sides be aware fully of why the satellite launches had failed.

The report also said that dual-use technology, especially the HPCs, was diverted illegally to military uses.

Unfortunately, it based this grave charge on deduction rather than hard facts.

Mr Cox argued that prior to signing the Comprehensive Test Ban Treaty (CTBT), the US conducted more than 1,000 tests to perfect its nuclear arsenal. Yet the Chinese did only about 50 before signing the CTBT.

This, he said, suggested that China must have stolen US computer models and test data so that it could simulate nuclear tests using HPCs.

According to Mr Cox, this was the way China managed to cut short the time needed to attain technological perfection.

The flimsiness of this reasoning stemmed from a gross underestimation by the US of China's ability to develop its own technology indigenously.

Mr Cox lost sight of the fact that even before bilateral relations started to thaw in 1972, China had already exploded its first atomic bomb — in 1964.

Between 1964 and 1972, China exploded a hydrogen bomb, launched its first surface-to-surface missile and sent its first satellite into space.

All these were accomplished under a technological blockade imposed by both the US and the then Soviet Union and at a time when the Chinese economy was much less developed.

"Although no country would sensibly deny acquisition of advanced technology to speed up its own developmental process, to say that the Chinese achieved military modernisation by stealing US technology is outrageously wrong," the Chinese scholar said.

"Fifty years ago, Chairman Mao Zedong told the Chinese that there were two things for which China could never rely on others: food and weapons.

"The people have adhered to this belief to this day," he pointed out.

New Style of Diplomacy?

18 April 1999

A suave Mr Zhu Rongji ended his trip to the United States last week, during which his simple and direct defence of China over thorny issues, combined with doses of humour and quotable quotes, won over the American audience.

By any standard, the visit was remarkably successful. Indeed, some would say he had accomplished a mission impossible by providing new impetus to bilateral relations at a time when anti-China sentiment was running high.

He captivated his hosts, from President Bill Clinton to the average man, quickly, and this became clearer as the tone of media coverage became warmer by the day.

Observers of the nine-day trip said his personality came through in a pervasive, powerful way: His strong charisma, an iron will, a no nonsense approach, a candid but sincere attitude — all helped to make an imprint on the American people.

They were more willing to listen to his exposition of the Chinese position on all issues, delivered usually in a solemn yet suave, serious yet earnest manner.

One thing that endeared him was his ability to speak off-the-cuff, without having to rely on prepared speeches that were predictable and laced with propaganda.

His impromptu style made him look more humane and approachable than most other visiting communist officials.

For example, he told his American hosts publicly that he risked being knocked out of office for the concessions he made in the World Trade Organisation (WTO) accession talks.

He joked that just a few years back, he would have been found guilty of treason, simply for the extent of concessions given.

His personal suffering during the anti-rightist movement lent weight to his words.

At one point in a briefing session by US Trade Representative Charlene Barshefsky, a US journalist challenged her, asking why, given the concessions which China had made, the US was still taking the risk of undermining Mr Zhu by letting him go home empty-handed.

Clearly, he had won the sympathy of the Americans, including many new converts.

He also did not hide his hesitation to make the trip, which, at one point, looked highly likely to be cancelled.

"To tell you the truth, I was really reluctant to come," he said.

"If Ambassador Sasser risked being beaten black and blue just because of preparing for my trip, would my face be turned into a bloody one when I came?"

Starting the visit with this pointed joke, he set clear the gravity of the situation. This forthright way of cutting directly into the issue had worked in his favour, an American journalist said.

The two countries were at odds over a host of prickly issues — he avoided none of them, confronting each head-on.

On the toughest WTO issue, he displayed great statecraft. Against a highly hostile background, he realised there was no hope of getting a final accession agreement to crown his trip.

Yet, he said: "I respect the judgement of your president, but I disagree that this should be the result."

Undaunted, he began to tackle a belligerent Congress. First, he managed to nail Mr Clinton down on a specific statement that the US support China's accession this year — and no later. To him, this was the second-best response from Washington.

Next, he tried to secure an 11th-hour agreement on agricultural products, right before he left Washington. This earned China strong support from the American agrarian states immediately.

Then, in his mid-west tour, wherever he went, he asked people to make sure that their senators and representatives supported China's WTO bid. Turn "China threat" into "China opportunity", he urged.

This tactic delivered the desired result: Mr Clinton felt the pressure from his business constituencies and he telephoned Mr Zhu to resume talks as soon as he returned home.

The Chinese premier also had the gift of reducing a complicated issue to a few simple "fact of life" statements. For example, the trade deficit had been played up as a major issue souring bilateral relations.

He countered with three simple points. He showed that actual deficit was not as great as what the US claimed. Then, he pointed out that it was a US decision to ban high-tech exports to China that caused the imbalance, not China's unwillingness to buy US goods.

Finally, he showed that the total deficit represented only 2 per cent of the US gross domestic product and did not warrant such widespread concern.

His points were stated eloquently and simply and were convincing.

As a communist member, he is a rare leader who does not have the stereotypical thinking expected of an apprentice from the party apparatus. This aspect was clear in the way he handled the human-rights issue.

Most Chinese leaders become defensive whenever such issues are raised, hiding behind strong political jargon. Statements on the subject made by Chinese president Jiang Zemin or former premier Li Peng were therefore highly predictable.

With Mr Zhu, even the language was different. When challenged by CNN, he said calmly that "if you look into our profiles, you will find that we all share a similar personal experience, namely, when we were young, we were all fighting for democracy, freedom and independence".

"It would be unimaginable that those of us who had spent a lifetime fighting to improve the rights of the Chinese people would want to go violate their human rights."

The calmer his tone, the greater was his persuasive power.

The embarrassing issues of military espionage and political contribution provided another test of his wit. He simply denied it categorically. He then added credence to his denial by offering help in their investigations. To diffuse a potentially tense atmosphere attendant with discussions of this sort, he made jokes out of them.

For example, he said China would have to label all weapons going to be displayed in the October parade as "Made in China" and not stolen from the US.

Said an American journalist following his visit: "Zhu is definitely a formidable leader. Compared with Jiang, he has no flowery language or grandiose remark that makes one feel good but slippery.

"Once a friend, he is the guy you can trust. He is a far more effective communicator of China's position."

In the view of Professor Wang Jian of the Chinese Academy of Social Sciences, a new style of Chinese diplomacy may be emerging.

Typical training in basic diplomatic manner includes re-wording differences in euphemistic terms and avoiding a display of displeasure in public. Yet Mr Zhu "had disregarded all these, yet produced a much better result".

At the end of the day, analysts felt that the real measure of his success is whether anti-China sentiments have subsided. The answer to that is definitely "yes".

Zhu Doesn't Expect Much from US Visit

6 April 1999

CHINESE Premier Zhu Rongji sets off today on his US tour, which he has told his countrymen "not to expect too much from", despite intense pressure at home to postpone it.

The decision to go ahead with the trip was a difficult one as the timing could not have been worse.

It takes place amid growing American hostility towards China.

In response to Beijing's alleged nuclear espionage, missile-targeting at Taiwan and breach of human rights, the US has banned satellite sales, threatened to include Taiwan in the Theatre Missile Defence system and initiated a motion to censure China in the United Nations human-rights conference in Geneva.

These measures prompted hardliners at home to call for a re-consideration of the visit.

Recent developments have also worsened the situation.

Despite China's commitment to make substantial concessions in talks with the US over its World Trade Organisation (WTO) accession, it fell short of exacting American demands.

Mr Zhu told US chief negotiator Charlene Barshefsky that America's conditions were just too harsh. The US has warned against expecting an agreement on WTO entry for China to crown the Premier's visit.

Another issue is the Kosovo crisis. Despite Chinese President Jiang Zemin's call for the North Atlantic Treaty Organisation (Nato) to stop its offensive against Yugoslavia during his recent European tour, he was largely ignored.

If Mr Zhu went ahead with the US trip, it would be tantamount to a Chinese endorsement of the US-led invasion.

Beijing sees the Nato operation as a move to encourage the split of Yugoslavia, a result of Nato's eastward expansion after the breakdown of the Soviet Union.

In the Far East, Beijing regards the renewed guidelines of the US-Japan Joint Defence Pact — which legalises Japanese military operations outside its own territories — as the Asian version of a Nato expansion.

Such an expansion, it fears, could lead to similar military moves to frustrate its own claim to Taiwan.

But after balancing the pros and cons, Beijing decided to go ahead with Mr Zhu's visit, regardless of how onerous the mission.

First and foremost, bilateral ties are badly in need of damage-control efforts. Beijing deems Sino-US relations to be the most important ties in its overall diplomacy.

Said a scholar at the Institute of America Studies under China's Academy of Social Sciences: "It is the single most important country in the world that can make or break our modernisation and unification efforts.

"Though it doesn't mean that we are at the mercy of the Americans, we do hope to have as little hindrance as possible in our endeavours."

Secondly, China does not want an impression of a de facto alliance between Russia and China. It has already toed the Russian line closely over the Kosovo crisis.

If Mr Zhu postponed the visit, it would invoke memories of the anti-West Sino-Russian alliance of the 50s.

A third crucial factor for China seems to be US President Bill Clinton's attitude.

Since the espionage issue erupted, the Clinton administration has strongly defended his engagement policy with China.

Cancelling the trip now would be a slap on his face and proof of the futility of his policy.

These long-term interests dictated that the Chinese Premier should go ahead with the visit, regardless of how onerous the mission.

Will TMD imperil Taiwan?

8 February 1999

DESPITE strong objections from China, the United States still plans to extend its theatre missile defence (TMD) umbrella to Taiwan, citing the growing military imbalance in the Taiwan Strait as the main reason.

But neither the US nor Taiwan can say for sure that upon its installation, the island — which China vows it will claim back by force if necessary — will be safer.

The TMD project is intended to protect US forces and its allies and friends from ballistic missile attacks. It dates back to former pre-Ronald Reagan's Strategic Defence Initiative (SDI), or "Star Wars" concept, in 1984. The perceived threat at the time was the Soviet Union's inter-continental ballistic missile (ICBM).

After the collapse of the Soviet Union, the project was shelved until 1996 when China, at the height of the Taiwan Strait crisis, threatened to fire missiles at Los Angeles.

Shocked by this move, the US Congress ordered a full-scale study to assess the ballistic missile threat to the US. The report, which was delivered in the middle of last year, said that China's 1996 missile firings in the Taiwan Strait provoked a sharp confrontation with the US.

During the crisis, a pointed question was posed by Lieutenant-General Xiong Guangkai, a frequent spokesman on Chinese policy, about US willingness to trade Los Angeles for Taipei. This comment seemed designed to link China's ballistic missile capabilities with its regional priorities.

This came as a major embarrassment, since it was the same Clinton administration which said in 1995 that no ballistic missile threat would emerge for 15 years.

The North Korean firing of a missile on Aug 31 last year added greater urgency.

General Henry Shelton, chairman of the Joint Chiefs of Staff, had assured Congress in writing only a week earlier that the intelligence community could provide the necessary warning of an indigenous development and deployment of an ICBM threat by a rogue state against the US. It was unfortunate timing indeed for the general.

Within a week, North Korea shocked the world with a test of its Taepo Dong-I missile, a three-stage rocket with intercontinental potential. It was exactly the kind of threat which the CIA said was 15 years away.

These developments prompted the Clinton administration to re-activate the SDI — which was once seen as a result of Mr Reagan's Hollywood naivete and crude anti-communist attempts to cope with new threats arising from the proliferation of ballistic missiles in states hostile to the US.

Essentially, the TMD consists of five core programmes: the Patriot Advanced Capability-3, the Medium Extended Air Defence System, and the Theatre High Altitude Area Defence, which intercept attacking missiles at low, medium and high altitudes respectively. There are also two ship-borne systems: the Navy Area Defence and the Navy Theatre-wide Defence systems (see chart).

The cost of research and development for these five systems is astronomical.

Between 1990 and 1998, the US spent close to US$13 billion (S$22 billion) and is expected to spend another US$11 billion before the system could be installed by 2005.

Washington has tried to force allies that enjoyed its protection to share the cost. Taiwan, for example, is expected to contribute between US$1 billion and US$2 billion annually for the next 10 years.

China is extremely disturbed by this project, and for good reason. The extension of the TMD to Taiwan represents a de facto joint defence arrangement between the US and Taiwan.

One of the three pre-conditions for the establishment of formal diplomatic relations between China and the US is the abrogation of the Joint ROC-USA Defence Treaty (1954–1979).

The TMD extension therefore restores the joint defence arrangement which existed before the US switched diplomatic recognition to China and amounts to a violation of the principles underlying the establishment of diplomatic relations.

Also, if the development of the TMD and its more general version — the National Missile Defence (which focuses on the defence of the US proper) — proves successful, it will effectively nullify China's nuclear counter-strike capability because any ICBM fired at the US will theoretically be intercepted long before it reaches its target.

It is this hard-won capability that has placed China on par with the US in the area of nuclear threat and deterrence.

To regain this counter-strike capability, China will have to divert scarce resources to upgrade its nuclear and missile technology; this could bog down the entire Chinese economy.

One of the frequently-quoted reasons for the collapse of the former Soviet Union was its attempt to set up its own "Star Wars" programme to respond to the SDI.

Subsequent development proved that the cost of research, development and deployment of such a programme was too heavy for the Soviet economy and could have become the proverbial last straw that broke the camel's back.

Clearly, China sees the same strategy that brought down the Soviet Union being applied to itself. This, perhaps, explains Beijing's stern warning that China would be compelled to re-adjust its military strategy should the TMD be installed and extended to Taiwan.

As for the possible re-adjustment, Dr Chien Chung, a professor with the War College of Taiwan's Armed Forces University, identifies several general areas that warrant special attention.

First, the weaponry.

China would step up developments in areas in which it already possesses decisive supremacy, such as submarines, medium-range missiles (especially the DF-15), cruise missiles and the electro-magnetic pulse devices.

At the same time, greater effort would be applied to upgrading its ICBM technology to bypass TMD interception. All this would mean a vastly expanded military budget.

Second, the tactics.

The extension of the TMD to Taiwan will remove a big unknown in the equation, which is the US role in the event of an armed attempt at unification.

Until now, Washington has been deliberately ambiguous on this point.

If Taiwan is included in the TMD, then by definition (and contractual obligation) the US would race to its defence should a conflict break out, which means China will have to adopt a tactic that will bring about Taiwan's capitulation within hours of the conflict before the US can respond.

Third, in strategic terms, China could counteract by establishing a united front against the TMD with Russia, which is also unhappy to see a similar system installed in the Nato area.

It could also stop acquiescing to US military operations worldwide, using its veto in the United Nations, which would cause considerable tension between the two countries.

On balance, would Taiwan feel safer or more imperilled with the TMD umbrella?

Dr Chung admitted that the missile interception technology is still very raw and far from perfect. Until now, the accuracy rate has been only about 50 per cent. The psychological impact will be far more significant.

The Taiwanese people are not really interested in the TMD's effectiveness, but they want to see the government doing something to enhance the island's security.

Furthermore, knowing that Taiwan has the backing of the US is another reassuring factor.

Yet, from a more global point of view, Dr Chung admitted that the inclusion of Taiwan in the TMD would greatly intensify the arms race in the Taiwan Strait.

In the long run, this is not conducive to Taiwan's security and there is the real possibility that the TMD will imperil the island.

Jiang Finds Japan a Tough Nut to Crack

29 November 1998

CHINESE PRESIDENT Jiang Zemin's state visit to Japan is marked by Beijing's failure to secure a more repentant Japanese attitude towards its war crimes as well as a more affirmative pledge not to meddle in the Taiwan issue, which China considers as an internal affair.

The joint communique, issued after a six-hour delay, fell far short of Chinese demands and did not carry any formal Japanese apology.

Japan merely stated that it "is keenly conscious of the responsibility for the serious suffering and damage that Japan inflicted upon the Chinese people through its aggression against China during a certain period in the past and expressed deep remorse for this".

China had been asking for an apology similar to the one Japan offered a month earlier to South Korea, which read: "(Japan) regarded in a spirit of humility the fact of history that Japan caused, during a certain period in the past, tremendous damage and suffering to the people of the Republic of Korea through its colonial rule, and expressed deep remorse and heartfelt apology for this fact".

Chinese displeasure was obvious when a Foreign Ministry spokesman condemned, after the summit, Japanese war atrocities in much harsher terms.

On the Taiwan issue, the communique failed to commit Japan to the "three no's" which China was seeking — no to Taiwanese independence, no to "two China" or "one China one Taiwan", and no to Taiwanese membership in international bodies based on statehood.

Japan merely restated principles set in past documents (the Joint Communique of 1972 and the Peace and Friendship Treaty of

1978) and acknowledged that there was only one China, and that Japan-Taiwan relations would be of a "private and regional nature".

Again, China had to issue separate statements through the Foreign Ministry spokesman in stronger terms warning Japan not to meddle in China's internal affairs.

Negotiations on the joint communique were held up for six hours and, in the end, it was China which had to give in. The so-called landmark visit by Mr Jiang, therefore, did little to remove or reduce the two biggest difficulties in bilateral relations.

China had been on the verge of getting its way when Mr Jiang postponed his September visit to Tokyo, citing the huge floods in the country. Japan, feeling the pressure, was about to concede. At the time, there were reports in Tokyo about Japanese willingness to include a formal apology and at least two of the three no's in the joint communique.

What made Japan change its mind and maintain its tough stand?

A possible explanation could be Washington's reassurance of its ties with Tokyo. Just days before Mr Jiang's arrival, United States President Bill Clinton visited Japan. A joint statement issued on Nov 20 stated that both countries consulted each other on major international issues, including Russia and China.

"We reaffirmed our two countries' contribution to global peace and security which goes beyond our bilateral relations," the joint statement said.

It went further to say that "the relationship between the US and Japan is the cornerstone of stability and prosperity in the Asia-Pacific region.

"To be the cornerstone, we must continue to carry our weight. We're going to meet our responsibilities first and foremost as allies."

Observers pointed out that contrary to Chinese hopes, Mr Clinton's visit to Japan ensured that the Tokyo-Washington military alliance was boosted to its highest level since the end of World War II.

Two days later, the Pentagon issued its fourth Report on US Security Strategy for the East Asia-Pacific Region in which it attached great significance to Japan.

The report stressed two points:

1. "US bases in Japan will remain the anchor of our regional force presence. In the next century, the US-Japan alliance will remain the linchpin of our regional security policy and must therefore continue preparing to respond to regional threats and to engage in preventive diplomacy."
2. "As our most important bilateral alliance in the region, the US-Japan partnership will remain critical to US and regional interests — as important to Asia's future as it has been to its past. The US sees no substitute for this historic relationship as the region prepares to address old and new challenges into a new century."

These statements reassured Japan, whose nightmare is falling out of US favour.

It still remembers the shock of being told in 1971, just a few hours before the formal announcement, that President Richard Nixon was despatching Secretary of State Henry Kissinger to China. It also cannot forget his statement in 1989 that a strong Japan needed to be contained.

Japan's fears resurfaced when Mr Clinton visited China without making a stopover in Japan. Worried about the shift in the Washington Tokyo-Beijing triangular relationship, Japan had felt obliged to concede to China.

Emboldened by American reassurance that Japan, and not China, is the ultimate ally of the US, Tokyo turned tough against Chinese pressures. This, perhaps, explains its change of mind.

Now that the summit has ended with all the important issues unresolved, it is doubtful whether the so-called "friendship and cooperative partnership" with Japan will endure.

China had hoped to settle all historical problems so that relations with Japan in the new century will not be marred by legacies of the past. But, as it found out to its chagrin, these problems are likely to dog bilateral ties in the future.

For Taiwan, China's "loss" means that it gains a temporary respite. To its relief, the feared "domino effect" — countries following the

US lead in declaring the "three no's" policy — did not take place. So far, the only major country to have done so is Russia, whose relations with Taiwan had never been strong.

Now, had Japan succumbed to Chinese pressure, it could be the beginning of real trouble for Taiwan.

Bumpy Ride Ahead for Sino-Japanese Summit

24 November 1998

THE real test of this week's summit meeting between China and Japan will be whether both sides can resolve the contradictions inherent in the Sino-Japanese peace treaty and the new US-Japan defence guidelines.

While the Peace and Friendship Treaty of 1978 made China a friend of Japan's, the defence guidelines, which were revised last year, turned Beijing into an enemy.

Before Chinese President Jiang Zemin agrees to strengthen bilateral friendship, he will need to be assured by his host, Prime Minister Keizo Obuchi, that the gesture will not be nullified by the new guidelines which were agreed on by Japan and the United States last year.

What a mockery it would be if his efforts to forge "strategic partnerships" with the US and Japan are reciprocated by a fortification of their military alliance against China!

Enough assurances have been given by both Washington and Tokyo that the new guidelines are not directed at China, yet Beijing remains unconvinced.

"A military alliance without a specific target is unheard of," a Chinese Foreign Ministry spokesman has said.

China's foremost concern is possible joint US-Japan military action to thwart its unification with Taiwan should non-peaceful means become necessary.

The new defence guidelines, among other things, legitimise such intervention in "situations in areas surrounding Japan"

It is no coincidence that the decision to revise the guidelines of the US-Japan defence pact was taken in mid-1996, two months after China launched missile tests near Taiwan.

Officially, both the US and Japan have tried to remain ambiguous on the geographic definition of "areas surrounding Japan".

But former Japanese Cabinet Secretary Seiroku Kajiyama has admitted that "it certainly includes Taiwan".

Said a Japanese Foreign Ministry source: "We have been following the definition developed by former prime minister Nobusuke Kishi in February 1960."

According to Mr Kishi, who had presented the US-Japan Defence Pact for parliamentary approval, the concept encompassed a core area stretching from the north of the Philippines to Korea, including areas ruled by the Republic of China (ROC) — the name which Taiwan calls itself — and an outward extension from the core.

China claims that unless the new guidelines exclude Taiwan, they could encourage the nationalist island to take the risk of declaring independence, since it is assured of US and Japanese military protection.

So one of Mr Jiang's tasks at the summit, scheduled for Thursday, is to secure an unequivocal commitment from Japan to exclude Taiwan from the guidelines.

The chances of success, however, are slim.

What upsets China most is that despite all the good wishes expressed in both the 1972 joint communique and 1978 peace treaty, Japan still approaches it with a belligerent attitude.

The US-Japan military alliance was first directed at the Soviet Union.

After the Cold War, its target became China.

US security strategists made it clear that the new guidelines and the eastward extension of Nato constituted two major anchors in the US global security framework in the post-Cold War era.

While the eastward extension of Nato ensures that a collapsed Soviet Union can never stand up again, the new guidelines ensure that a rising China is adequately contained.

When the decision to revise the guidelines was taken, then Japanese Prime Minister Morihiro Hosokawa told his people:

"Over the past 100 years, China has had a history of difficult trials and tribulations. It is a history in which nationalistic impulses have not been entirely fulfilled.

"Hence I think it is necessary to pay sufficient attention to the latent desires of the Chinese state and the instability this introduces to Asia.

"Although one doesn't know with certainty if China itself is aware of this, it is unmistakable that other neighbouring countries are aware of a 'big China' and must inevitably have strong concerns."

These words speak clearly of Japanese uneasiness about a rising China.

China feels that its leniency towards Japan's war crimes, as shown by its voluntary forfeiture of war indemnities, has not been reciprocated by goodwill.

It hurts the Chinese that Japan, which had waged several wars against China in the last hundred years, should consider their country a source of threat to its own security.

Finally, the new guidelines raise the spectre of Japanese re-militarisation.

This is a nightmare not only to China but also to the entire east Asia.

A WAY TO BYPASS THE CONSTITUTION

The guidelines provide for a skilful way to bypass the Japanese Constitution, which bars the country from involvement in military activities of all kinds outside its own territory.

They oblige Japan to take supportive combat operations complementary to American war efforts in regions defined as "areas surrounding Japan".

This constitutes a fundamental change to Japan's defence posture.

A Chinese strategist summed it up as a change from inward-looking to outward-looking in terms of war preparedness.

From passive involvement (the provision of bases and facilities) to active involvement (joint operations with the US).

From the defence of Japanese territories to the invasion of other states' territories.

China sees these changes as evidence of the resurgence of Japanese militarism.

The history of Asia in the past 300 years has never witnessed a China and a Japan being strong at the same time.

For the first time in history, a China that is getting strong is pitted against a Japan that is already very strong.

Can the two strong neighbours co-exist peacefully?

The answer would have been negative in the past.

What about the future?

The way Mr Jiang manages to address his people's genuine concerns this week will be a gauge of his statecraft.

Annex

NEW GUIDELINES: What they are
These are the new guidelines, adopted in September last year, for US-Japan defence cooperation.
Cooperation under normal circumstances

- Basic defence posture: Place Japan under US nuclear protection
- Information sharing and policy consultations
- Develop a number of bilateral programmes:
    — Bilateral defence planning and mutual cooperation planning
    — Establishment of common standards for preparations
    — Establishment of common procedures
    — Bilateral coordination mechanism.

Actions in response to an armed attack

- When an armed attack against Japan is imminent, cooperation in:
  — Intelligence sharing
  — Coordinated responses.
- When an armed attack against Japan takes place, cooperation in:
  — Command and coordination
  — Communications/electronics
  — Intelligence activities
  — Logistic activities (including supply, transportation, maintenance, facilities and medical services)

Cooperation in situations in areas surrounding Japan

- Joint efforts to prevent further deterioration of situations
- Bilateral cooperation in:
  — Japan's logistic support for US forces' activities with the use of facilities and rear area support.
  — Complementary military operations (like mining and de-mining, air space control)
  — Activities for ensuring the effectiveness of economic sanctions (like a blockade)
  — Humanitarian activities, including search-and-rescue and non-combatant evacuation operations.

Jiang to Put Ties with Japan on a New Footing

17 November 1998

CHINA is trying to formulate a new platform for Sino-Japanese relations when President Jiang Zemin makes a landmark visit to Japan later this month, the first ever by a Chinese head of state.

It hopes that bilateral relations will reflect the fact that China has finally come of age and that it will be an influential factor in shaping the world order, especially in the East Asia region.

Their ties are built upon the Joint Communique of 1972, which normalised relations, and the Peace and Friendship Treaty of 1978.

Former Japanese Prime Minister Ryutaro Hashimoto visited Beijing last year, which marked the 25th anniversary of the communique.

President Jiang is returning the visit this year, two decades after the treaty was signed.

In a recent interview with Japanese reporters in Beijing, Foreign Minister Tang Jiaxuan said that Sino-Japanese relations hinged upon two key factors: Japan's attitude towards history (that is, its war responsibility) and its stance on Taiwan.

These are two issues about which Bejing has not been able to secure a more positive attitude from Tokyo since 1972.

At the time, China was still weak, so its main concern was breaking through the United States-led encirclement. The terms on which it established relations with Japan were, therefore, extremely lenient.

On the history issue, for example, Japan stated in the communique that it felt "responsible for the great loss inflicted upon the Chinese people through war".

For this, China waived all the war indemnities for which Japan was liable.

The Japanese statement fell far short of the apology Japan offered to South Korea last month which read: "Japan regarded in a spirit of humility the fact of history that Japan caused, during a certain period in the past, tremendous damage and suffering to the people of the Republic of Korea through its colonial rule, and expressed its deep remorse and heartfelt apology for this fact."

On Taiwan, China merely secured Japanese recognition that the People's Republic of China (PRC) was the only legitimate government of China.

As to Beijing's assertion that Taiwan is an inalienable part of China, Japan stated that it "understands and respects" this stance, but did not commit itself to the Chinese position.

What China has found particularly frustrating since 1972 is that "leniency" towards Japan does not pay.

In the past 25 years, there have been constant efforts, at both official and unofficial levels in Japan, to re-interpret history and dispute the country's war atrocities.

In recent years, some Japanese leaders have even made pilgrimages to the controversial Yasukuni war shrine dedicated to the country's "war heroes", including soldiers executed as war criminals after World War II.

China sees these developments as danger signs pointing to a possible revival of Japanese militarism. It wants Japan to issue an apology similar to that offered to the South Koreans.

Japan's insistence on adhering to Article 8 of the Potsdam Declaration, which was mentioned in the 1972 Communique, gave rise to unnecessary ambiguities over the political status of Taiwan. At the same time, this allowed Tokyo to remain evasive on the subject.

Beijing pushed hard to remove these ambiguities by insisting that Tokyo took a firmer and clearer stand on Taiwan. One way would be for Japan to reiterate the "three no's" as US President Bill Clinton did in Shanghai in June.

Unless Tokyo provides more assurances on these two key issues, neither side will be able to tap the full potential of bilateral relations, Beijing declared.

Japan was unwilling to comply.

China has already accepted Japan's apology contained in the 1972 Communique, it said, adding that the Japanese people would be hurt if Beijing kept asking them to apologise.

As for Taiwan, since Japan no longer has a role to play in the issue, it believes that Beijing should not ask Tokyo for a clear statement.

The Chinese response was to postpone Mr Jiang's September trip to Japan, using the summer's devastating floods as a convenient excuse. Japan got the message.

Prime Minister Keizo Obuchi sent former premier Toshiki Kaifu to Beijing to express Tokyo's willingness to reconsider its position.

From the statements that have been coming out of Tokyo lately, Japan might be willing to re-phrase its apology to China along the lines of that given by Prime Minister Tomiichi Murayama in 1995 to commemorate the 50th anniversary of the ending of World War II.

In that statement, he admitted that "through its colonial rule and aggression, Japan caused tremendous damage and suffering to the people of many countries, particularly to those of Asian nations. I regard, in a spirit of humility, these irrefutable facts of history, and express here once again my feelings of deep remorse and state my heartfelt apology".

According to a Japanese Foreign Ministry official, the exact text may be tailor-made for China.

Japan agrees to reiterate verbally the first two of the "three no's", namely "No to Taiwanese independence" and "No to two Chinas, or one China, one Taiwan".

But it will not budge on the third no — Taiwanese membership in international organisations based on statehood.

The reason Japan is now willing to make some compromise is obvious: Mr Obuchi needs the summit more than Mr Jiang.

While China's economic and political strength has been growing, Japan's has been on the wane. This change is highlighted by the fact that while China can still expect a healthy 8 per cent growth amid the current economic crisis, the Japanese economy is in shambles.

Security issues aside, Beijing is also fast replacing Tokyo as Washington's most important partner in Asia. At the leadership level, too, Mr Jiang's position is far more entrenched than Mr Obuchi's.

All these factors are good bargaining chips for China in its negotiations with the Japanese.

Nevertheless, it is understood that the Chinese President does not want the visit to be confined to the "narrow agenda" of history and Taiwan.

As long as the Japanese side comes up with a solution showing sufficient sincerity, Beijing will not push for further concessions.

Annex

POTSDAM DECLARATION: Loopholes to be manipulated
IN THE Sino-Japanese Communique of 1972, Japan insisted on sticking by a provision under Article 8 of the 1945 Potsdam Declaration inviting Japanese surrender.

The article read: "The terms of the Cairo Declaration shall be implemented and Japan's sovereignty shall be limited to the islands of Honshu, Hokkaido, Kyushu and Shikoku."

The Cairo Declaration of 1943 stated that Japan had to return all Chinese territories seized during previous wars, including northeast China and Taiwan, to the Republic of China (ROC). At that time, the People's Republic of China (PRC) had yet to be established.

In 1951, the Allied Forces concluded a peace treaty — the San Francisco Treaty — with Japan, which codified all the political intentions expressed in both the Cairo and Potsdam declarations.

Unfortunately, this formal legal document merely obliged Japan to relinquish its sovereignty over Taiwan and other occupied Chinese territories, and did not specify to whom Taiwan should be returned.

Hence, adherence to the Potsdam Declaration gave rise to two major ambiguities:

1. That Taiwan be returned to the ROC, not the PRC. This was the position taken by Taiwan in the recent Wang-Koo talks. This interpretation also provides the legal basis for Taiwan to refute Beijing's claim of PRC sovereignty over Taiwan.
2. That Taiwan's ultimate political status is as yet undetermined. This is the theoretical and legal basis for pro-Taiwan independence activists.

Military Links the Way to Manage a Growing China

22 July 1998

THE Sino-US summit in Beijing last month improved bilateral relations substantially, a sharp contrast to the situation in 1996 when the two nations were said to be on the brink of war.

The dramatic change could be attributed to the two presidents, who managed to transcend the divisive Taiwan issue.

The formula was for US President Bill Clinton to reiterate that the US does not support Taiwanese independence, two Chinas, and Taiwanese membership in international bodies based on statehood. This so-called "Three No's" policy quashed Taiwan's hope to separate from the mainland.

Having secured this American reassurance, Beijing was prepared to leave the thorny Taiwan issue aside for the time being in order to strengthen ties with Washington.

Another factor was that the two leaders were able to identify a broad range of common strategic interests. These were later expressed in terms of the 40 or so items of cooperation, ranging from global security to bilateral economic interests.

This helped to beef up the otherwise empty concept of "strategic partnership" advocated by China during President Jiang Zemin's visit to the United States last October.

A closer relationship between China and the US is most welcomed by countries in East Asia, as it will greatly enhance security in the region.

Most important of all, the Sino-US agreement on non-targeting — whereby each side refrains from targeting the other in the deployment of nuclear weapons — spares the region from a nuclear holocaust.

Mr Clinton's change of heart on this was dramatic. In November last year, he issued a new guideline for nuclear targeting in which he allowed "broadening the list of possible targets in the event of a nuclear exchange with China". Barely seven months later, he reached an accord with his Chinese counterpart not to target nuclear weapons at each other.

This showed the tempo at which the two leaders were embracing each other. When they hugged, East Asia relaxed.

Through this non-targeting arrangement, the summit prescribed a norm for responsible behaviour of nuclear countries. It came at a time when a joint approach was called for to contain nuclear proliferation in South Asia.

China's approach to solving international conflict — to talk to, instead of to sanction, an adversary — seemed to be effective in causing a relaxation of US economic sanctions against both India and Pakistan. Such a development would help reduce tension in the sub-continent.

Improved Sino-US relations have also resulted in busy exchanges between the military establishments of both countries.

Engaging the Chinese military has been one of the top priorities of the US' overall engagement policy. According to a US source, the Pentagon mapped out an eight-stage engagement policy for China which, in ascending order of intimacy, calls for:

- One, an exchange of visits between senior military officials;
- Two, an exchange of general staff information;
- Three, seminars held between the two armies;
- Four, military training for Chinese officers in the US;
- Five, joint exercises in military engineering and medical operations;
- Six, small-scale military training;
- Seven, joint military exercises in the field; and
- Eight, Chinese participation in US-held multinational military exercises.

The current status is somewhere between stages three and four. The source did not deny US intention to speed up the process.

In fact, during the recent summit, it was indeed hastened.

Mr Clinton was able to get Mr Jiang's agreement on mutual observation of military exercises on a reciprocal basis as well as on some form of joint military exercises.

Through this eight-stage policy, the US is, perhaps, the only country in the world which has managed to force a degree of transparency on the Chinese military establishment.

China used to be very wary of joint military exercises. A similar suggestion from Russia in the 1950s caused grave misunderstanding and precipitated the sharp rift between the two communist giants. Yet Beijing is now taking up a similar proposal from Washington.

In security terms, a more transparent Chinese military establishment has positive implications for the region.

It reduces the risk of misunderstanding, misinterpreting and miscalculating, a lesson that the US learnt the hard way during the 1996 Taiwan Strait crisis.

Similarly, a strong Sino-US relationship that extends to military areas is welcomed because it will help defuse three potential flash points in East Asia, namely the Taiwan Strait, the Korean peninsula and the Spratly Islands.

While Taiwan might be unhappy with the outcome of the summit, which relegated its status, East Asia, as a whole, was glad to see both China and the US succeed in keeping cross-strait tension under control.

Rapprochement between China and the US also went a long way to stabilising the touchy situation in the Korean peninsula and the Spratlys.

Most Asian countries are faced with a dilemma. While they welcome the rise of China whose strong economic growth would benefit the whole region, they are also anxious that it keeps its muscle within its own boundaries.

A strong Sino-US military relationship will serve exactly this purpose.

In the view of most Asian countries, this was the way to manage a growing China.

Even on economic grounds, the region would welcome strong Sino-US ties.

Beijing, anxious to prove that a strong China was not a threat to the world, was forced to hold its currency steadfast, despite sustaining huge losses. In return, Washington was obliged to put pressure on Tokyo to stop the value of the yen from falling.

This joint move to stabilise the currency situation in East Asia is ample proof that strong bilateral relations between the US and China can only benefit the entire region.

Taiwan Worries as US Policy Tilts Towards China

21 July 1998

DESPITE American efforts to calm Taiwan, the renegade province of China was shocked by the US President's open pledge to uphold the Three No's policy. Mr Bill Clinton was referring to the policy of saying "No to Taiwan independence", "No to two Chinas," and "No to Taiwan membership in international organisations based on statehood".

He gave his pledge in public for the first time on June 30 during a discussion in Shanghai. He later said he was merely reiterating a long-standing American position and that it constituted no change whatsoever in US policy.

Still, he felt obliged to send Dr Richard Bush, his aide on Taiwan affairs, to brief Taiwan on the results of the Sino-US summit. Judging from Taiwanese reactions, Dr Bush accomplished little in dispelling anxiety.

US Secretary of State Madeleine Albright called the Taiwanese anxiety an over-reaction. Yet, the Taiwanese were not alone in feeling outraged. US congressional leaders are trying to enact new legislation that would balance the adverse impact on Taiwan of Mr Clinton's pledge.

The Taiwanese have good reason to worry. Over time, there has been a discernible shift in US policy towards Beijing. Changes have occurred subtly but consistently. Though these changes do not seek to abrogate any standing commitments to Taiwan, the underlying spirit has been eroded.

US commitments to Taiwan were embodied in the Taiwan Relations Act (TRA) of 1979 and the Six Assurances of 1982. These two documents were meant to offset the adverse impact on Taiwan of the second and third Sino-US communiques respectively.

Previously, whenever a major breakthrough in relations between the US and China took place, there were some counterbalancing moves for Taiwan. The two documents are meant to redress the shocks to it.

This time round, there are no counterbalances. This in itself signifies a major tilt in favour of Beijing.

The problem for Taiwan does not end here. A careful study of the results of the summit shows that the spirit of the Six Assurances has been undermined gradually.

Under the Six Assurances, the US will not:

• Alter its position regarding Taiwan's sovereignty.
• Mediate between Taiwan and China.
• Pressurise Taiwan to negotiate with China.
• Alter the terms of the TRA.
• Set a date for the termination of arms sales to Taiwan.
• Consult China in advance about US arms sales to Taiwan.

The reason why Mr Clinton's open pledge to adhere to the Three No's policy caused such a shock in Taiwan is that it undermines the spirit of the first assurance.

The Three No's principle was Beijing's established position written into the first Sino-US joint communique in 1972. In that document, the US avoided committing itself to this principle. Instead, it tried, deliberately, to adopt an ambiguous stance by stating that "the US acknowledges that all Chinese on either side of the Taiwan Strait maintain there is but one China and that Taiwan is part of China. The US government does not challenge that position".

If then US President Richard Nixon found it difficult to accept the Chinese principle in 1972, while Mr Clinton openly endorses it in 1998, the only logical conclusion one can draw is that there has been a shift in American policy in favour of Beijing.

The second assurance was virtually nullified when Mr Clinton made a public appeal in Beijing for Taiwan to come to the negotiation table. In Taipei, this was interpreted as giving up American neutrality in the cross-strait dispute.

The third assurance was rendered void after several Track Two diplomats — former high-ranking US officials — went to Taipei carrying the same message: There would be no unconditional US support for Taiwan should it declare independence.

Although the Clinton administration denied any connection with these messengers, their actions are regarded as a tacit pressuring of Taipei into negotiations with Beijing.

It is therefore obvious that the Six Assurances are not rock solid. This is perhaps the clearest message to Taiwan from the Sino-US summits. But it is not the end of the story. For Taiwan, there are still worries ahead.

Central to the US commitment is the arms sales obligation. This is an important provision in the TRA, and was reaffirmed again in the Six Assurances. However, the Chinese were optimistic that even this commitment would be eroded gradually.

To dislodge this US military commitment, China told the US unequivocally that Taiwan independence meant war. Arms sales to it would encourage independence and thus raise the risk of conflict. In the event of a cross-strait war, the US would be drawn into it.

The consequences of a war between China and the US would be catastrophic, not just for the two countries but for the world as well. Thus, it was in American interests to end arms sales to Taiwan eventually.

The US should seriously consider not allowing the Taiwan issue to drag it into a war with China.

According to strategist Li Jiaquan, former director of the Taiwan Institute under the Academy of Social Sciences, this message was already sent to the US by visiting scholars before the presidential journey, and reiterated during the Jiang-Clinton meeting in Beijing.

He said China did not expect an about-face in the US arms sales policy. Instead, it expected a phased reduction over a period of time. In his words, this was "to leave room for manoeuvre for the US".

Initially, China hoped that the US would honour the promises made in the third Sino-US communique, which was to freeze the sales of weapons in quantitative and qualitative terms at the 1982 level.

"Ever since the signing of this communique, the US hasn't honoured it at all," he said. "If the US agrees to do so, it'd go a long way towards removing a potential factor for war."

China also hoped the US would appreciate the Chinese position that non-peaceful means was an option of last resort for Beijing in the unfortunate event that Taiwan declares independence. Seen this way, the risk of war would come from Taiwan, not from China.

"In the light of this, the US can easily redefine its arms-sales obligation listed in the TRA," said Mr Li.

It is therefore clear that the Chinese strategy is to dismantle, bit by bit, US commitments to Taiwan, patiently, but persistently. The Clinton shock may be just one of a series.

Clinton Visit May Drive Taiwan Mad

By: Ching Cheong, East Asia Correspondent
2 July 1998

AFTER carefully monitoring the performance of Hongkong over the past year after its reversion to China, the US government felt comfortable about sending its head of state there.

President Bill Clinton's trip there today, the first by an incumbent US president, would therefore be seen as an American endorsement of the "one country, two systems" concept as applied in the Special Administrative Region (SAR).

In 1992, the US had enacted the US-Hongkong Policy Act to safeguard its interests in the territory. The Act required the State Department to report annually to the Congress on the post-1997 situation in the SAR and watch out for any adverse developments.

The Americans have substantial interests in Hongkong. As the second largest foreign investor there, direct investment reached US$16 billion (S$26.9 billion) by the end of last year, with exports to the territory totalling US$15 billion.

There are over 1,100 US firms employing 250,000 locals — or 10 per cent of the workforce. Hongkong is also home to about 50,000 Americans and destination to more than 700,000 business and tourist travellers — or an average of 2,000 a day.

In addition to strong economic ties, there are also significant political and military relations. It maintains one of the largest consulates in East Asia, while port calls by the US Navy constitute an important part of its defence strategy in the western Pacific.

Reflecting the importance of its interests there, the US Secretary of State, the Secretary of the Treasury, the Secretary of Commerce, 40 US government delegations and teams, and over 40 senators and congressmen visited Hongkong in 1997, underlying the intense concern of the US on the change of sovereignty.

A year after handover, the US is clearly satisfied. The 1998 State Department Report noted: "There is no evidence of interference from the Chinese central government in local affairs, Hongkong's civil service remains independent, and senior officers, including those who have been critical of the PRC, have been retained.

"Hongkong continues to play an important role as a regional finance centre, actively participating in efforts to address the Asian financial crisis. The Hongkong press remains free and continues to comment critically on the PRC and its leaders, though some self-censorship has been reported. Demonstrations, often critical of the PRC, continue to be held.

"Mainland Chinese companies are subject to the same laws and prudential supervision as everyone else, and the rule of law and the independent judiciary remain in place as guarantees of Hongkong's free and open civil society."

In discussing developments that might affect US interests, the report said that "the most significant development of the year...has been the restraint shown by the central government in Beijing — which has avoided involving itself or giving the appearance of involvement in local affairs.

"The record since reversion has bolstered confidence in both the local and international community that China's leaders intend to keep their commitment to allow Hongkong to remain autonomous and 'let Hongkongers rule Hongkong'."

On top of this positive assessment, the presence of a US president lends greater credence to the feasibility of the concept of "one country, two systems" as a unification model. It would no doubt greatly enhance international confidence in Hongkong.

The impact of Mr Clinton's Hongkong visit does not end there. Taiwan has been watching with concern whether he would go as far as to publicly endorse Beijing's unification model.

Taipei has fiercely rejected the model, which relegated it to a subservient position. If Mr Clinton does so, he would create tremendous pressure for Taiwan.

Still, Mr Clinton's presence has several consequences for the Greater China area: It would strengthen the international status of the SAR, shed positive light on China, and most probably, drive Taiwan mad.

Plugging the Rights Message

30 June 1998

BEIJING — Perhaps the most remarkable feature of US President Bill Clinton's Beijing trip thus far is his zeal in espousing human-rights values to the Chinese.

Central to his message is the non-negotiable respect for an individual's rights and protecting of one's freedom to exercise such rights.

From Day One, he has seized almost every conceivable opportunity to drive home this message.

The attempt to weave human-rights issues into American diplomacy first became apparent during Mr Jimmy Carter's Administration, but few US presidents had assumed this "missionary" role as directly as Mr Clinton is doing during this trip.

Merely two hours after he touched down in Xian, he lectured that "the greatness of any country is measured in its people — in their shared reverence for family and community, for work and learning, and in their individual thoughts, beliefs, and creativity".

He told his Chinese hosts that "a commitment to providing all human beings the opportunity to develop to their full potential is vital to the strength and success of the new China".

By recreating the glamour of Imperial Tang Dynasty for the welcoming ceremony, the Chinese had set out to impress him with the glory of China's historical past.

Cleverly, Mr Clinton seized this opportunity to point out that what made China great in the past was its openness to new ideas brought by philosophers and thinkers from all over the world.

What he was perhaps trying to imply was that its subsequent backwardness has been the result of its closed-door policy.

During the summit, he touched on the sensitive Tiananmen incident, stressing that he believed the use of force and the tragic loss of life was wrong, that freedom of speech, association and religion were the right of people everywhere and should be protected by their governments.

He rejected President Jiang Zemin's justification that "resolute action" was needed for the sake of stability, saying instead that "stability in the 21st century will require high levels of freedom".

"If you are so afraid of personal freedom that you limit people's freedom too much, then you pay — I believe — an even greater price in a world where the whole economy is based on ideas and information and exchange and debate", he said.

His next pitch for freedom was at the Beijing University, where he said: "We do not seek to impose our vision on others. But we are convinced that certain rights are universal...These are not American rights or European rights or developed world rights. They are the birth rights of people everywhere".

He also tackled the notion of swopping freedom for stability — an official Chinese position — as wrong.

Quite the contrary, he said, freedom strengthened stability.

He cautioned China that as the most populous nation, its greatest source of strength resided in the minds and hearts of its citizens.

"It is profoundly in your interest — and the world's — that those minds be free to reach the fullness of their potential.

"That is the message of our times and the mandate of the 21st century," he said.

While admitting such forthright talk might not be effective in converting the Chinese leaders, the Americans were clearly glad that the Chinese allowed Mr Clinton his full airing on two major occasions.

Both speeches were beamed live nationwide, which they thought was the most effective way to spread their beliefs to the Chinese people.

Taiwan's Bad Case of Summit-Phobia

24 June 1998

TAIWAN is extremely nervous on the eve of US President Bill Clinton's visit to China.

Political organisations of all shades have held conferences exploring the likely outcome of the presidential summit and possible responses.

The island's political parties have been able to put aside their differences for the time being to organise a tri-partisan delegation to lobby Washington. Summit-phobia has clearly permeated all levels of society.

According to Foreign Minister Jason Hu, the government has created a task force to handle any developments arising from the summit meeting that may prove detrimental to Taiwan.

At the same time, the authorities will keep a close watch on Mr Clinton's activities in China.

The need for such measures is understandable considering the tremendous, albeit indirect, US pressure piled on Taiwan to negotiate with China following President Jiang Zemin's American visit last year.

A corps of "Track Two Diplomats" — a term first coined by the Atlantic Council of the US to describe former senior officials who try to mediate in cross-strait relations in an unofficial capacity — flocked to Taiwan conveying such messages as:

- American support for Taiwan is not unconditional. Taipei should not hope unrealistically that the US would shed blood to defend the island if it should provoke China.
- What America is concerned about is stability in East Asia. As long as the US is not drawn into a war, it does not care how China is unified.
- It will be in Taiwan's long-term interests to start negotiations with the mainland and work out a way to live with it.

From the American point of view, such a stand was fair, since self-interest dictates a country's foreign policy.

For Taiwan, however, it created a sense of uncertainty about the trustworthiness of official US pledges.

So, is there anything for Taiwan to worry about in the coming summit? The answer is no for the immediate term, but yes in the longer term.

No because the Americans, in fact, have already indicated quite clearly that the summit later this week will not produce any document that will hurt Taiwan.

Ms Susan Shirk, Deputy Assistant Secretary for the East Asian and Pacific Bureau, said in her testimony before the House International Relations Committee last month:

"We will not sacrifice Taiwan's interests...There will be no fourth communique on Taiwan arms sales or Taiwan issues at the summit."

That there will be no fourth communique was again confirmed by the American ambassador to China recently.

In the immediate term, therefore, Taiwan can put its mind at ease.

In the longer term, however, there are worrying signs looming ahead for the Taiwanese.

First, there are indications that some changes to the "Six Assurances" to Taiwan are on the cards.

The "Six Assurances" were made in 1982 by the Reagan administration in tandem with the signing of the third Sino-US communique. To minimise its impact on Taiwan, the US pledged that it:

- Will not alter its position regarding the sovereignty of Taiwan, meaning that the question is one to be decided peacefully by the Chinese themselves;
- Will not force Taiwan to enter into negotiations with China;
- Will not mediate between Taiwan and China;
- Will not alter the terms of the Taiwan Relations Act;
- Will not set a date to end sales of arms to Taiwan;
- Will not consult China before making decisions on US arms sales to Taiwan.

Soon after last October's summit, the second and third pledges showed signs of crumbling. The US showed itself quite ready to assume a mediator role and push Taiwan to negotiate a solution with China.

For example, Ms Shirk told the House hearing that the administration sought to facilitate talks between the two sides. At the same time, "Track Two Diplomacy" was seen as an indirect way of pressuring Taiwan.

The US trend of upgrading relations with Taiwan also seemed to lose steam after the summit.

In 1994, the Clinton administration conducted an extensive inter-agency review of Taiwan policy.

This review produced some results in Taiwan's favour.

Among other things, it recommended that the name of the Taiwan representative office be changed to "Taipei Economic and Cultural Representative Office (Tecro)", and that exchanges in non-political issues be upgraded to Cabinet-level meetings.

It also called for closer and more frequent interaction on economic issues with Taiwan and for the US to support its participation in international organisations where membership is not based on sovereignty.

It was this encouraging development that prompted Taiwan to postulate the theory of "parallel development" — that American interests would be best served by a parallel development of its relations with both Beijing and Taipei.

Hence, any American initiative to improve relations with China would be matched by similar ones to Taiwan.

The result of this policy review led to vastly expanded visits at senior levels, culminating in the US trip by Taiwanese President Lee Teng-hui in 1995.

Then came the Clinton-Jiang summit last October.

According to sources in Beijing, China hailed it as a great success because it reversed the trend towards upgrading of US-Taiwan relations.

At a recent press conference, Mr Hu admitted that once Sino-US relations became warmer, Taiwan's strategy of "parallel development" simply did not work. In this context, the coming summit, which would improve Sino-US relations even more, is likely to restrict further any upgrading of US-Taiwan relations.

The American commitment to continued arms sales to Taiwan, which forms a central feature of the Taiwan Relations Act, has also been called into question.

There were calls in the US to "observe strictly the third joint communique", which limited arms sales to Taiwan in qualitative and quantitative terms to its 1982 level.

Since the signing of that communique, the US has interpreted it in a way which shows that weapons actually delivered to Taiwan exceeded the 1982 level in both quantitative and qualitative terms.

This has been a major complaint by Beijing, which has been urging Washington constantly to keep its word.

The fact that some US officials are now echoing the Chinese calls is indicative of a possible change in American thinking in the future.

These developments are bound to leave Taiwan extremely uneasy about the coming summit.

Strong Ties Allow Airing of Issues

28 June 1998

The Sino-US summit, as well as the display of personal friendship between Chinese President Jiang Zemin and his American counterpart Bill Clinton, will contribute enormously to the security and stability of the world at large, and to East Asia in particular.

Never before had leaders of the world put up a public debate, which lasted more than an hour, right after their summit meeting.

Both leaders had built up a personal friendship that enabled them to address each other's sensitive nerves in a candid manner.

For example, the US President pushed the human-rights issue relentlessly during the last and present summit.

The Tiananmen event, which up to now remained a political taboo in China, was brought up in open debate and broadcast live in China. For the first time, the ordinary Chinese saw their leader defending a tough case.

In return, Mr Jiang pointed an accusing finger at the US media for drumming up all kinds of "news" based on distorted facts, with the intention of discrediting Beijing.

He also questioned the widespread support in the West for the Dalai Lama, Tibet's exiled leader.

All these are extremely sensitive issues but were dealt with in an open manner. It was only possible if both of them have a strong personal friendship.

This high level of transparency regarding the similarities and differences of views, at both philosophical and strategic levels, is certainly conducive to eliminating misunderstanding, misinterpretation and miscalculation — unfortunate hallmarks of past Sino-US relations.

If such a high degree of transparency between two powerful countries can be extended to all fields of interest, it will go a long way to enhance stability and security in the world.

China also did not make things too difficult for Mr Clinton on the Taiwan issue.

Apparently, the Chinese leadership is satisfied with his brief reference to American commitment to the "One China" policy.

The way the US President reiterated American policy towards Taiwan should also make Taipei less worried.

So, for the time being and, indeed, for the foreseeable future, one could reasonably expect a return to stability in what could otherwise be a potentially volatile flashpoint over the complicated Taiwan question.

Clinton to Define China Policy

27 June 1998

The US has expressed confidence that it can evolve a policy which will pacify both China and Taiwan but how can Mr Clinton achieve this?

BEIJING — At his summit talks with Chinese President Jiang Zemin this morning, US President Bill Clinton is expected to try to define America's "one-China policy" in a way which would please both Beijing and Taipei.

He has told reporters before leaving Washington that he would reiterate American commitment to the so-called "three no's" — no to Taiwan independence, no to "two Chinas" or "one China and one Taiwan", and no to United Nations membership for Taiwan.

At the same time, he would also explain to Beijing US attachment and previous commitment to Taiwan under the Taiwan Relations Act.

Although the US has stressed time and again that its China policy is not a zero-sum game and expressed confidence that it could evolve a policy that will pacify both China and Taiwan, it is hard to see, given the belligerent nature of relations across the Taiwan Strait, how Mr Clinton can accomplish his mission.

What is pretty certain is that there will be no fourth communique on Taiwan as China has dropped that request.

In return, the US would be obliged to make a statement reiterating the "three no's".

The Chinese side would like the US to reiterate its commitment preferably in another joint statement following the summit meeting.

However, according to American sources, the occasion and wording to be used to reiterate these commitments have not been decided yet, so much will depend on the progress of the discussion.

Sources close to the Chinese Foreign Ministry say that what China values is a display of goodwill from the American President.

As long as sufficient goodwill is shown, Beijing will not put undue pressure on the US leader.

It is aware that it will be difficult for the US to make any drastic change on the Taiwan issue at this moment.

The sources also say that China values mutual trust above any written document.

If it were to press the US to produce some sort of document, this would not be conducive to the fostering of a relationship based on mutual trust.

After all, a written document could be interpreted at will, as had been the case with the third joint communique.

A formal document, therefore, is no guarantee that one party will not breach promises made to another.

Foreign affairs experts told The Straits Times that Mr Jiang is expected to tell his American guest that both countries should disentangle themselves from the thorny Taiwan issue.

The two powers cannot expect to foster a good and viable relationship which can stand up to the challenges of the 21st century unless they do so.

The Chinese leader is also expected to tell Mr Clinton that as China grows, the scope of mutual cooperation will inevitably expand and assume a more global dimension.

The Taiwan issue will then become increasingly a liability to the US.

Hence the US is faced with two options: drop the Taiwan burden for full fledged cooperation with China, or allow it to backfire on Sino-US relations.

Sources said that as long as Mr Clinton indicated the "right" choice, China would reciprocate by offering full cooperation in a whole range of issues of vital importance to the US.

At the same time, Beijing will wait patiently, giving the US time to gradually adjust its policy towards Taiwan.

Disapproval at Home, But Clinton's Trip Delights China

26 June 1998

While President Bill Clinton left his US home amid calls to postpone or cancel his China trip, he would at least have the consolation of a warm and whole-hearted welcome in the host country.

A refined Tang Dynasty (618–907 AD) welcoming ceremony in Xian — the capital of China for six ancient dynasties — is just an illustration of the way the Chinese lavished their hospitality on a guest they regard with much respect.

Indeed, the visit by an incumbent US president in less than a decade delights most Chinese, regardless of their social status or political beliefs.

To the average man, the visit by the No. 1 man of the world's most powerful country would lift China's pride and status greatly.

To a nation which was once the centre of world attention, communist China is not free from the "Middle Kingdom" mentality that haunted all its emperors.

It demands that countries outside the "Middle Kingdom" should pay annual tributes to it as a gesture of goodwill.

There is no exception for America, although it is far stronger than China now. Thus, the Sino-US thaw began in 1972 with President Richard Nixon's call on then-Chairman Mao Zedong, not vice versa.

To a very large extent, it was the satisfaction of this egoism that accounts for this warm welcome.

To a people battered by imperialist forces for the last 150 years, the Chinese have come a long way towards rebuilding their self-respect and confidence to become a force to be reckoned with.

The American President's visit seemed to acknowledge this status.

The Chinese also learnt the hard way that good relations with the US was more productive than with the former Soviet Union.

Historical circumstances in the immediate post-World War II era dictated that Beijing leaned towards Moscow.

This wrong choice led China into a vicious cycle of poverty and isolation from the mainstream of global development — a plight that lasted for three decades, from 1949 to 1979.

The collapse of the Soviet Union confirmed the tragic nature of the wrong choice.

Fortunately, the normalisation of ties with the US in 1979, a key component in China's reform and open-door policy, changed her beyond recognition.

The Chinese have also come to realise that good Sino-US relations would create a global environment more conducive to their "sacred task" of national unification.

Beijing has found that whenever bilateral ties with the US deteriorate, America would play the Taiwan card while the Taiwanese would play the US card, with both directed against China.

Thus, as long as the US holds the key to Chinese unification, it pays for China to build strong ties with Washington.

Even Chinese dissidents welcome Mr Clinton's visit. While his trip means an endorsement of the regime responsible for the military crackdown at Tiananmen nine years ago, they hope it will lead to a general relaxation in human-rights suppression in China.

"The main reason is that we are the ones to suffer if Clinton cancels his trip. A tense Sino-US relations would lead to a tightening of domestic control," said one.

Asia Hopes Peace and Prosperity Will Get a Fillip

21 June 1998

THE summit between the Chinese and American presidents this week could not have come at a more opportune time for Asia.

The nuclear tests conducted by India and Pakistan last month sparked fears about the possible repercussions for the region.

Then came the sharp depreciation of the yen this month, which again threw the battered economies of the region into disarray and set back any hopes for an early recovery.

To harried Asians, the Sino-US summit will best serve their interests if it can help restore peace and prosperity to the region.

The nuclear proliferation in South Asia jolted the trilateral relations between China, the United States and Russia.

The delicate equilibrium of this "Big Triangle" — upon which the security situation of the rest of world depends — is likely to change.

The Sino-US leg will be strengthened as a result.

In his June 11 speech, US President Bill Clinton had already made it clear that resolving the Indo-Pakistani nuclear race "requires us to co-operate with China".

Faced with the common threat of nuclear proliferation, the two would, perhaps, be more accommodating of each other's demands.

For example, on bilateral security issues, the US has been urging China to reach a "non-targeting" agreement whereby each side refrains from targeting the other in the deployment of nuclear weapons.

China would like the US to reciprocate by agreeing to a "no first use" principle.

On global non-proliferation, the US would like China to make further commitments not to export nuclear and missile technologies.

In return, the US would probably facilitate closer co-operation with China in nuclear and space technologies.

Sino-Russian relations will be somewhat marred by the nuclear race in which their friends are involved. While China openly condemned India, Russia's reaction was rather muted.

According to Mr Igor Khripunov, associate director of the Centre for International Trade and Security at the University of Georgia at Athens, Georgia, Indo-Russian relations are long-standing and complex.

India is the largest purchaser of Russian weapon systems, and current contracts are valued at more than US$8 billion (S$13.2 billion).

More than 60 per cent of the Indian army's hardware, 70 per cent of the navy's equipment, and 80 per cent of that of the air force are from Russia.

Indian defence contracts keep about 800 Russian defence plants in operation. Indo-Russian co-operation is assuming the dimensions of a quasi-alliance.

Given this background, the nuclearisation of India is likely to harm, albeit indirectly, Sino-Russian relations.

The latest nuclear race is likely to stir things up in most of the hot spots in Asia.

It rekindled talk in Taiwan of developing a nuclear capability.

In a talk show aired last week by a television station known to be linked to the pro-independence Democratic Progressive Party, a researcher from the Chung Shan Institute of Science (CSIS) advocated a policy of "strategic ambiguity" regarding the possession of nuclear weapons.

Taiwan started its own nuclear weapons programme soon after China exploded its first atomic bomb in 1964.

The CSIS was set up for this purpose and was on the verge of success when one of its members, Mr Lou Hsien-yi, defected to the US in 1988 and revealed the plan.

Under strong pressure from the US, the programme was abandoned. Yet the government did not disband the entire corps of nuclear scientists or the CSIS.

The nuclear capability is still there. Obviously, the recent nuclear race and the inability of the US to police non-proliferation have tempted the independence-minded sections of Taiwan society to think of acquiring nuclear weapons to back up their demands.

Then there is North Korea. Soon after the race started, its ambassador to Beijing declared openly his country's plan to go ahead with research for the peaceful use of nuclear technology.

People will remember that in 1994, the International Atomic Energy Agency (IAEA) inspected North Korea and reported that it could not confirm whether all of its atomic know-how and materials were for peaceful use. It was a disturbing finding.

One must also not forget Israel. Most Arab countries see the US non-proliferation policy in the Middle East as one of "arming the armed and disarming the disarmed".

Israel, which shares high-level defence technologies and intelligence data with the US, is determined to be the sole nuclear state in the Middle East — by force if necessary.

For example, in 1978, it blew up a French experimental reactor meant for Iran.

In 1981, Israeli warplanes destroyed the nuclear plant in Osirak in Iraq. Now that the "Islamic Bomb" has become a reality, how Israel will react has become an extremely sensitive matter.

All these are burning security issues, the resolution of which require prompt and determined efforts.

Security aside, the region would like to see the Sino-US summit help restore economic order in Asia following the free fall of the yen, which dipped from 136 to 146 against the US dollar in just a month, a drop of 7.4 per cent.

The Japanese government's decision to let the yen fall was viewed negatively in the region.

Japan's foreign exchange reserves amount to an impressive US$224 billion. Its net foreign assets exceed US$920 billion.

The central bank discount rate is at a historical low of 0.5 per cent. These figures suggest that if the Japanese government has the will, it would have the wherewithal to bolster the yen.

Despite repeated lobbying from the US, Japan is unwilling to strengthen the yen.

According to a government econometric model, if the yen is maintained at the present level (145–150 yen to US$1), Japan's gross domestic product would see a gain of 1 per cent growth.

Given the current economic slump in Japan, the government prefers to let the yen fall.

But the outcome of this would be catastrophic for the whole of Asia.

Against this backdrop, the stability of the Chinese yuan has become the last anchor in a turbulent sea. The US government has given up hope on Japan and is turning to China.

Beijing knows that in holding the yuan steady, it would have to sustain great losses. Yet this will also give China a good opportunity to show the world that it is a responsible member of the international community.

To weed out fears that a strong China poses a threat to the world, it is determined to show that this is not the case — even at great economic cost to itself.

If China and the US succeed in taking the Asian economies out of the abyss, it would enhance China's status immensely.

People will see that it is China, and not Japan, which has the goodwill, determination and ability to solve Asia's woes.

In terms of geo-strategic influence, there are potential gains for China.

There are therefore reasons for Asia to expect that the two presidents' meeting might create an environment more conducive to the restoration of economic prosperity in this region.

US & China: Both Share Similar Interests

19 June 1998

THE nuclear arms race in South Asia has added urgency to next week's Sino-US summit.

Nuclear escalation there signified a failure of US policy to prevent proliferation of the deadly weapon.

The US is obsessed with having a nuclear-free sub-continent. This obsession stems from a deep-rooted fear of an "Islamic Bomb".

"Islamic Bomb" was the title of a 1979 BBC television documentary as well as a book by Herbert Krosney and Steven Weismann.

According to Professor Pervez Hoodbhoy of the Department of Physics at Quaid-I-Azam University in Islamabad, the "Islamic Bomb" is construed as "a nuclear weapon acquired for broad ideological reasons — a weapon that supposedly belongs collectively to the Muslim community and as such, is the ultimate expression of Islamic solidarity".

In an article titled "Myth-building: The Islamic Bomb", he said the Western bias against the Muslim world "has created the phantom of their own imagination".

It evokes fearsome images: the power of nuclear annihilation at the hands of Muslim dictators, holy war, and warriors and terrorists. Steve Emerson's film, "Jihad in America", was another expression of this fear.

Now, the American nightmare has become a reality: Pakistan became the first Muslim country to go nuclear. Something has to be done.

There is a role here for China, which enjoys good relations with Pakistan and has been helping it to acquire nuclear capability.

As Mr Bill Clinton stated in his June 11 address, in security matters of concern to the US, "China can choose either to be a part of the problem or a part of the solution".

It is therefore of utmost importance for America that China makes the "right" — by American definition — choice.

What could China do that would harm US interests?

For one, it could resume nuclear testing by suspending temporarily its obligations under the Comprehensive Test Ban Treaty (CTBT).

It could also rescind its May 1996 pledge not to export nuclear technology to Pakistan.

Fortunately, China chose to honour its commitment to both the test ban treaty and the May 1996 pledge.

What made China choose an option that tallied with American interests?

Answer: its own strategic interests.

China has set itself the target of achieving modernisation by 2050.

According to the Institute of Strategic Management, a think-tank closely related to the Chinese military, this endeavour could be affected by three major factors: security, the attitude of major powers towards China's emergence, and China's ability to take up a greater share of the world market.

The policy implications are clear.

First, China will strive to eliminate tensions, especially situations that could draw it into a war. Second, it will try to woo over major powers in order to reduce their resistance to a rising China. Third, it will strive to develop its economy.

These established policies explain its choice.

Security considerations have led Beijing to make a number of peace proposals in the last five years. For example, it advocated complete disarmament (that is, the total elimination of nuclear weapons). It helped ensure the indefinite and unconditional extension of the Nuclear Non-Proliferation Treaty (NPT) and it supported the CTBT.

It also advanced some arms control proposals of its own, such as calls for a treaty committing the five nuclear powers — the US, Russia, China, Britain and France — to the "no first use" principle.

Therefore, even though there is a hot race right next door, China will refrain from taking part in it or siding with any party.

Fostering stronger relations with the US, so that ultimately, the Americans would not stand in its way to modernisation, is another obvious reason.

When Mr Jiang Zemin first met Mr Clinton in 1993, he described China's American policy as one of trying to "increase trust, reduce trouble, develop cooperation and to disengage in confrontation".

Since his state visit to Washington last year, he modified it to one of trying "to increase understanding, expand common grounds, develop cooperation and to jointly work for the future".

From the tone of the wording, it is clear that Beijing treasures stronger ties with Washington.

China also shares, to some extent, the US concern about growing Muslim militancy.

The pan-Islamic movement has caused strong separatist movements in the vast north-western territories of China. It is also producing sporadic bursts of urban terrorism.

Although the movement is unlikely to cause major troubles, it remains a problem plaguing the Chinese. It was partly due to this concern that China suspended its nuclear cooperation plan with Iran in 1996.

It is thus clear that Sino-American interests are almost identical, though for different reasons. Hence, one can expect a fruitful exchange between the two presidents on the nuclear issue next week.

Easing Taiwan Out of American Arms

23 May 1998

SINO-US RELATIONS

China appears to be gaining the upper hand in the upcoming Sino-US summit, and Taiwan is worried its interests may be undermined TAIPEI — United States President Bill Clinton makes a trip to Beijing next month. It would be the first by an American president in a decade.

Not surprisingly, the most anxious party is Taiwan, which is watching with great care, and perhaps trepidation, every signal that is coming out of Washington.

None of the Taiwan analysts had anticipated the tremendous pressure that was brought to bear on the country after Chinese President Jiang Zemin's Washington trip in October.

Initially, Mr Clinton's reiteration of the American position — that the Taiwan issue be resolved by the two rivals on either side of the Taiwan Strait — came somewhat as a relief for Taipei, which had feared that it might be forced into negotiations with Beijing.

Yet, subsequent developments prove that there is no cause for relief.

Since the summit, the US had clearly embarked on a dual-track approach: While official policy or "Track One" remains unchanged, unofficial "Track Two" aimed at applying pressure on Taiwan.

There has been a series of calls from former senior US government officials, since then, prompting Taipei to go to the negotiation table or risk losing American support.

These Track Two messengers, blunt and undiplomatic at times, are deadly effective in puncturing the illusion that the US will come to Taiwan's defence for the sake of democracy.

Beijing is delighted. It considers this development an unexpected bonus from Mr Jiang's summit visit.

A scholar of Chinese diplomacy at the Beijing University told The Straits Times that prior to the summit, Beijing had merely wanted the US to reaffirm its commitment to the three Sino-US communiques (of 1972, 1979 and 1982), which would have forestalled an escalation of Washington-Taipei relations.

Beijing did not anticipate a positive response like the dual-track approach.

According to sources, President Jiang noted with satisfaction that it was possible to bring the US around, even on Taiwan — the toughest issue between Washington and Beijing.

This development greatly increases China's confidence of gaining the upper hand in the coming Clinton-Jiang meeting.

Sources told The Straits Times that China's strategy would be to build on grounds gained in October.

The guiding principle is three-fold:

- On issues over which US commitment is already secured, China wants them implemented;
- On issues about which US position is ambiguous, China wants them clarified;
- On issues to which the US is strongly opposed, China aims to soften its position.

According to sources, the first principle applies to most of the matters pertaining to bilateral trade and technological transfer, in particular, American support for Chinese membership in the World Trade Organisation.

The second refers mainly to the clarification of the new US-Japan defence pact.

The third principle pertains to neutralising, and eventually nullifying, American commitments to Taiwan, as embodied in the Taiwan Relations Act.

China also aims to get America to abide by the third Sino-US Joint Communique, which limits American arms sales to Taiwan in both quantity and vintage to its 1982 level.

Sources told The Straits Times that the US had never observed this important stipulation since it signed the third joint communique 16 years ago. It is by no means a small victory if China succeeds in tying American hands in this regard.

"If we can neutralise the Americans, the prospect for a peaceful unification will look much better because, by then, Taiwan would not harbour any unrealistic hopes of American support for its separatist policy," the diplomatic scholar said.

"We understand that it is not easy for the US to live up to our demands now. Never mind, we can wait.

"We do not expect it to come overnight, but, bit by bit, we shall soften its stance — until we finally remove the biggest stumbling block that stands in the way of unification."

China 'Will Not Rush' Into Reunification

28 May 1998

Chinese commander says that Beijing's long-term strategy is to build up military and economic might and weaken US support for Taiwan before beginning reunification talks.

TAIPEI — The Chinese People's Liberation Army (PLA), generally considered to be hawkish on reunification with Taiwan, is taking a rather long-term view towards this national goal.

"We are in no hurry, we can wait," said a PLA divisional commander, who spoke in depth to The Straits Times but wished to remain anonymous.

"When conditions are ripe, success will come."

While cautioning against generalisation, he claimed this view was very popular in the military.

"This patience stems from our self-confidence," he explained, adding that the 1996 missile tests had bolstered this confidence.

"The more we are confident of our own ability, the more we can afford to be patient.

"The 1996 missile tests made clear to all three sides — Beijing, Taipei and Washington — that China has the military capability to take back Taiwan by force, if there is no intervention from the US."

However, all three parties have chosen to be quiet on this stark fact, he noted.

"Beijing wants to keep quiet because it does not want to appear to be belligerent.

"Taipei wants to keep quiet because acknowledging it will only serve to destabilise its society.

"And Washington wants to keep quiet lest it be drawn into a major international crisis," he said.

But the commander felt each player had one thing it was not too sure about.

"The US wonders whether the military expertise displayed in the 1996 missile tests was all that China has. If not, what else does it possess?

"The question for China is, will the US intervene? If so, in what way and with what intensity?

"For Taiwan, it is the opposite side of the same question: will the US come to its rescue if Beijing applies force?

"Right now, the US is playing the game of strategic ambiguity so that Taiwan will be lured into thinking that it will come to the island's defence," he said.

The US decision to send aircraft carriers to the area during the 1996 missile tests might reinforce such a belief, the commander added.

He said Taiwan should not read too much into this, as Washington's real intention was to monitor the military capability of China and "not to protect Taiwan".

He conceded, however, that this strategic ambiguity also represented a major stumbling block for China.

Since Beijing could not rule out US intervention, it had to be extremely careful in mapping out its long-term strategy for reunification.

"Without American intervention, taking back Taiwan will be just like picking up something from one's own pocket," he said.

"In order to achieve reunification, we have to remove this unknown factor in the equation."

The PLA officer said China's long-term strategy for reunification has three major components.

The most fundamental is to build up China's own economic and military capability. This would form the basis for all other efforts.

The second is to weaken US commitment to Taiwan.

The commander envisaged a step-by-step approach.

China would try to get the US to adhere strictly to the three joint communiques.

The third communique, which limits sales of arms to Taiwan to its 1982 level, was a case in point.

"Ever since it was signed, the US has not honoured it once. So we would like them to abide by their own words," he said.

American commitments to Taiwan were embodied in the Taiwan Relations Act (TRA), he noted.

"We do not envisage the US scrapping the TRA altogether; this is next to impossible.

"But, bit by bit, we expect them to be less serious about it. After all, it is a matter of interpretation.

"If the US can interpret the third communique in such a way as to justify the increased sales of arms, it can also interpret the TRA in such a way that it merely pays lip service to it," he said.

China believed the US would do so eventually.

"One of the guarantees under the TRA is not to force Taipei into negotiation.

"But 19 years after it was enacted, one sees this commitment succumbing to the changes of our times.

"The US government is now sending retired senior officers to Taipei, urging it to talk to us," he said.

Asked how quickly Beijing could get the US to disengage from the Taiwan issue, he said it would depend on Chinese economic and military development.

"Without our rapid economic growth, without our show of force and — more importantly — of determination in 1996, perhaps Bill Clinton would still be talking nonsense about containing us," he said.

Once support for Taiwan had been dislodged, conditions would be ripe for reunification.

By this time, the third component would come into play — peaceful negotiation.

Said the officer: "When there is no more ambiguity in US strategy, the only way out for Taipei is to conduct serious negotiations with us.

"It is only through peaceful negotiation that Taiwan can get most of what it demands, gracefully."

However, if Taiwan still refused to talk, non-peaceful means might be used, which could spell the end of the Republic of China (ROC).

When asked why the German model — in which both parties co-exist in the international arena until they see fit to unify voluntarily — could not be applied, the commander explained:

"As far as we are concerned, the Kuomintang, or the ROC, has already been defeated.

"If they come back as ordinary Chinese citizens, we'll stretch our arms wide to welcome them, and would honour them in whatever way it seems fits.

"However, if they come back demanding a share of power, or to demonstrate their superiority, then, no way."

Reflecting yet again China's confidence, he concluded: "Anyway, we are in no hurry, we can wait, time is on our side.

"When we build up our economy, when American commitments to Taiwan are effectively nullified, reunification will come."